Histories of American Physical Anthropology in the Twentieth Century

Histories of American Physical Anthropology in the Twentieth Century

Edited by
Michael A. Little and
Kenneth A. R. Kennedy

LEXINGTON BOOKS

A division of

ROWMAN & LITTLEFIELD PUBLISHERS, INC.
Lanham • Boulder • New York • Toronto • Plymouth, UK

Published by Lexington Books
A division of Rowman & Littlefield Publishers, Inc.
A wholly owned subsidary of The Rowman & Littlefield Publishing Group, Inc.
4501 Forbes Boulevard, Suite 200, Lanham, Maryland 20706
http://www.lexingtonbooks.com

Estover Road
Plymouth PL6 7PY
United Kingdom

British Library Cataloguing in Publication Information Available

The hardback edition of this book was previously cataloged by the Library of Congress as follows:

Library of Congress Cataloging-in-Publication Data

Histories of American physical anthropology in the twentieth century / edited by
Michael A. Little and Kenneth A. R. Kennedy.
    p. cm.
    Includes bibliographical references and index.
    1. Physical anthropology—United States—History—20th century. I. Little,
Michael A. II. Kennedy, Kenneth A. R.
GN50.45.U6H57 2010
599.90973—dc22   2009033984

ISBN 978-0-7391-3511-2 (cloth : alk. paper)
ISBN 978-0-7391-3512-9 (paper : alk. paper)
ISBN 978-0-7391-3513-6 (electronic)

Printed in the United States of America

™ The paper used in this publication meets the minimum requirements of American National Standard for Information Sciences—Permanence of Paper for Printed Library Materials, ANSI/NISO Z39.48-1992.

Dedicated to Frank Spencer (1941–1999)

This book is dedicated to Frank Spencer,
who devoted most of his professional life to
studying and documenting the history of physical/
biological anthropology. Many of his works serve
as invaluable references in the chapters that follow.

Contents

Preface

Most of the chapters in this volume were originally presented as contributions to a symposium organized by Little and Kennedy at the American Association of Physical Anthropologists (AAPA) annual meeting in Milwaukee, Wisconsin, in 2005. This was an anniversary symposium marking the 75th year of the AAPA, and three of the contributors to this volume (Loring Brace, Matt Cartmill, and Eugene Giles) also contributed to the 50th anniversary volume in 1980 that was edited by Frank Spencer. Two of the chapters here were added to the collection after the symposium: an introduction to the collection by the editors and a biographical overview of the contributions to physical anthropology made by the founder of American anthropology, Franz Boas. The thirteen chapters that constitute the volume do not present a comprehensive *history* of physical anthropology in the United States during the 20th century. Rather, they highlight numerous aspects of *histories* of this science as it developed to maturity during this period. The 20th century began in the United States with only a handful of physical anthropologists continuing antiquated 19th-century practices, and ended with 2,000 professional physical anthropologists throughout the nation participating in modern scientific inquiry. Other major sources of historical and biographical documentation for physical anthropology are reviewed in Chapter 1.

We acknowledge, with our thanks, the assistance of the organizers of the 2005 AAPA meeting and the editors of Lexington Books, particularly Alyc Helms, Jana Wilson, Melissa Wilks, and Patricia Stevenson, who guided this book through the production process. We also thank Adrienne V. Little, who provided valuable assistance with proofreading.

Contributors to the Volume

C. Loring Brace, Museum of Anthropology, University of Michigan, Ann Arbor, Michigan

Kaye Brown, Department of Anthropology, Boston University, Boston, Massachusetts

Matt Cartmill, Department of Anthropology, Boston University, Boston, Massachusetts

Eugene Giles, Department of Anthropology, University of Illinois at Urbana-Champaign, Urbana, Illinois

Bernice A. Kaplan, Department of Anthropology, Wayne State University, Detroit, Michigan

Kenneth A. R. Kennedy, Department of Ecology and Evolutionary Biology, Cornell University, Ithaca, New York

Clark Spencer Larsen, Department of Anthropology, The Ohio State University, Columbus, Ohio

Michael A. Little, Department of Anthropology, Binghamton University, State University of New York, Binghamton, New York

Jonathan Marks, Department of Anthropology, University of North Carolina-Charlotte, Charlotte, North Carolina

Donald J. Ortner, Department of Anthropology, National Museum of Natural History, Smithsonian Institution, Washington, DC

John H. Relethford, Department of Anthropology, State University College at Oneonta, Oneonta, New York

William A. Stini, Department of Anthropology, University of Arizona, Tucson, Arizona

Emőke J. E. Szathmáry, Department of Anthropology, University of Manitoba, Winnipeg, Manitoba, Canada

Chapter 1

Introduction to the History of American Physical Anthropology

by

Michael A. Little and Kenneth A. R. Kennedy

INTRODUCTION

The beginnings of modern physical anthropology (also known as "biological anthropology") date back to the middle of the 19th century, with several areas of exploration developed in Europe and the United States coalescing by the middle of the 20th century. Anatomy, craniology, human origins, race, and evolution were all a part of 19th-century interests that later became known as "anthropology" in Europe and "physical anthropology" in the United States. However, at the transition from the 19th to the 20th century, Darwinian evolution was in decline, races or human populations were viewed as fixed entities, typological approaches were generally applied, studies of human populations did not employ scientific design, and knowledge of environmental influences on humans was very limited. By the early part of the 20th century, key figures in Europe were Arthur Keith (1866–1955), who was at the Medical School of the London Hospital in Whitechapel and was concerned with studies of the evolution of upright posture and ape locomotion; Léonce-Pierre Manouvrier (1850–1927), who began his career under Paul Broca (1824–1880) in France, had contributed to training Aleš Hrdlička (1869–1943) in 1896, and became the director of the Laboratoire d'Anthropologie of the École Practique de Hautes Études in Paris; Rudolph Martin (1864–1925), who was on the faculty at the University of Zurich, and published the *Lehrbuch der Anthropologie* in 1914; and Eugen Fischer (1874–1967), who was chair of anthropology and later rector at the University of Berlin, and who promoted "racial hygiene" and eugenics in Germany. Loring Brace (see his chapter in this volume) describes the influences from Europe on ideas about race and evolution that derive from

1

the mid- to late 1800s and how they, in turn, influenced physical anthropology at the beginning of the 1900s.

In the United States, three individuals dominated physical anthropology during the first half of the 20th century: Franz Boas (1858–1942), Aleš Hrdlička, and Earnest A. Hooton (1887–1954). Franz Boas, as Sherwood L. Washburn (1984a, 395) has noted, was "a major figure in American physical anthropology," but has traditionally been minimized in histories of the profession. Boas had a broad vision of anthropology as a four-field science and contributed to each of these fields. His research in physical anthropology and biometrics alone led to the publication of more than 180 works that ranged from anthropometrics and osteometrics to race and racial origins, to environmental influences, and to human growth and the development of children. He is best known in anthropology for his study of migrants from Europe to the United States (Boas, 1912), but his most significant and lasting research was in child growth. Boas's contributions were an integration of the science of anthropology in the United States and research that was in advance of his times (see Little's chapter on Boas in this volume). Aleš Hrdlička was the driving force to establish physical anthropology as a recognized science among sciences in the United States. He single-handedly founded the *American Journal of Physical Anthropology* in 1918 (see Giles's and Ortner's chapters in this volume) and was the principal organizer and first president of the American Association of Physical Anthropologists in 1930 (see Szathmáry's chapter in this volume). Although he failed in his attempt to establish an institute of physical anthropology in the European style, his energy and enthusiasm were instrumental in "securing the discipline's identity" (Spencer, 1982b, 6). Boas, from his positions at the American Museum of Natural History and Columbia University in New York City, and Hrdlička, from his position at the Smithsonian Institution in Washington, DC, contributed minimally to the training of professional physical anthropologists during their long careers, but they were influential in many other ways. The third individual, Earnest Hooton, began at Harvard University in 1913, having been trained in the classics at Wisconsin (PhD in 1911), and then received the Diploma in Anthropology at Oxford in 1912. During his illustrious career at Harvard he supervised a large number of PhD students beginning in 1926 until his death in 1954. These students of Hooton dominated the profession and played important roles in the American Association of Physical Anthropologists through the 1970s and early 1980s.

Other important figures from the first half of the 20th century were Raymond Pearl (1879–1940) and T. Wingate Todd (1885–1938). Pearl was a Michigan-trained biologist with broad interests in human population biology and strong mathematical training, who worked at Johns Hopkins

University. Todd was a Manchester-trained anatomist, who was influenced by two prominent anthropologists in England and then came to Western Reserve University in the United States to fill a chair in anatomy. He made substantial contributions to skeletal age assessment. Both were president of the American Association of Physical Anthropologists in the 1930s, and both died before the Second World War.

A number of formative areas of physical anthropology were emerging from studies already underway or perspectives just beginning to form: child growth and development from Boas's research and his later migrant design; centers of bone growth and formation and child development from Todd's work; anthropometrics and osteometrics from Manouvrier, Hrdlička, and Martin; primatology and paleoanthropology from Keith and Hooton; and demography, genetics, epidemiology, and statistics from Pearl. Human population biology had not yet arisen as a defined area of study, yet Franz Boas's early studies of growth and of European migrants demonstrated the effects of the environment on individuals in populations. And Raymond Pearl (1939) contributed not only to the development of ideas in human population biology, but he founded two journals that would define the field: *Quarterly Review of Biology* (1926) and *Human Biology* (1929). Within early 20th-century physical anthropology, Boas and Pearl were major figures in the development of scientific approaches to inquiry. Hrdlička played an important role in developing and publicizing the profession through the establishment of the *American Journal of Physical Anthropology* in 1918 and the American Association of Physical Anthropologists in 1930. Hooton's major contributions, despite his traditional approach to living populations that maintained 19th-century biases, was the training of a whole generation of physical anthropologists from the 1920s to the early 1950s (see Giles's contribution to this volume).

A NOTE ON HISTORICAL SOURCES

Any work on the history of a profession must draw on a variety of sources to reconstruct this history. There are different histories to reconstruct. There are the histories of *individuals* who played significant roles in the development of a profession. There are histories of *institutions* that provided an identity for its members and a forum for the dissemination of ideas. Finally, there are the histories of *ideas and traditions* and how they spread through the profession both spatially and temporally. Sources of information include unpublished documents (correspondence, notes, photographs, films, tapes, field notes), both archived by institutions and held by others, published works (histories, biographies, obituaries), and the "gray literature" of unpublished manuscripts and reports. Unpublished materials are the most difficult to access and require considerable exploration from archival and other repositories. What follow are descriptions of published reference materials that are accessible for historical studies of physical anthropology.

Perhaps the most comprehensive source for physical anthropology is the *History of Physical Anthropology: An Encyclopedia,* edited by Frank Spencer (1941–1999; Spencer, 1997a). This two-volume reference work of nearly 1,200 pages has contributions from more than 150 scholars and includes brief biographies, topical items, reference materials, entries on intellectual and institutional development, and areas of scientific inquiry—each entry with a bibliography and archival sources. Spencer also edited two works to celebrate the 50th anniversary of the American Association of Physical Anthropologists (AAPA). The first was a special Jubilee Issue of the *American Journal of Physical Anthropology* (Boaz and Spencer, 1981) based on a historical symposium held in December 1980 in Charlottesville, Virginia, the site of the inaugural meeting in 1930. The second was based on a symposium held in Detroit in April of the following year (Spencer, 1982a) in which the 28 contributors provided historical overviews of topical areas in physical anthropology. Earlier in his career, Spencer (1979) did a biographical dissertation on Aleš Hrdlička, dealing with Hrdlička's life up to the founding of the AAPA in 1930. A comprehensive biographical dissertation was also done for T. Wingate Todd by Kevin Jones-Kern (1997; Kern, 2006).

The only major "history" of the AAPA was done by Juan Comas (1900–1979; Comas, 1969), but it was published in Spanish. However, a recent translation makes it now available in English (Alfonso & Little, 2005). The work has detailed information on annual meetings (up to the 38th) and AAPA activities and is a valuable source of basic information. Comas (1960) published a textbook in English that has substantial early information on the history of physical anthropology. This supplemented the comprehensive historical compilation that Hrdlička (1919) published originally in the first four issues of the *American Journal of Physical Anthropology* in 1918. Other histories of professional associations have been written about the Society for the Study of Human Biology (Tanner, 1999), the Human Biology Association (Little and James, 2005), and the journals *Social Biology* (Osborne & Osborne, 1999) and *Human Biology* (Crawford, 2004). Tanner's (1981) book on human growth describes work done by anthropologists and those closely associated with physical anthropology.

Individual biographical information can be found in a variety of sources, particularly obituaries in major anthropology journals, *Biographical Memoirs of the National Academy of Sciences, Festschriften* or commemorative publications, prefatory autobiographies in the *Annual Review of Anthropology,* and memoirs. Some Festschriften include those for J. Lawrence Angel (Buikstra, 1990), Joseph B. Birdsell (Mai et al., 1981), Paul T. Baker (Little & Haas, 1989), and Sherwood L. Washburn (Strum et al., 1999). Numerous biographical and collected works have been written about Franz Boas (Boas, 2004; Cole, 1999; Stocking, 1974). The *Annual Review of Anthropology* prefatory autobiographical memoirs include those by Paul T. Baker (1996), Joseph B. Birdsell (1987), Carleton S. Coon (1977), William W. Howells (1992), Wilton M. Krogman (1976), and Sherwood L. Washburn (1984b). Memoirs have been written by Carleton S. Coon (1981), Marcus S. Goldstein (1995), and Gabriel W. Lasker (1999).

A historical timeline of events in physical anthropology in the context of other significant world events is presented in an appendix at the end of the book.

THE PERIOD UP TO 1918 (FOUNDING OF THE *AJPA*)

In 1918, Aleš Hrdlička founded the *American Journal of Physical Anthropology,* having persuaded the Wistar Institute of Anatomy and Biology in Philadelphia to publish the new journal. Hrdlička was at that time the curator of physical anthropology in the U.S. National Museum of the Smithsonian Institution. As editor-in-chief, he began the journal with four articles, each in an issue of the inaugural year, which surveyed the history of physical anthropology (collected as Hrdlička, 1919). He was trying to establish an American tradition in physical anthropology, but based on the French model where he identified France (in the preface) as "the mother country of physical anthropology" (Hrdlička, 1919, 5). Hrdlička's history reflects his vision of physical anthropology, which, at that time, was largely medically and anatomically oriented, but also closely tied to human variation in Native American peoples, skeletal biology, and the concept of race. He identified Samuel Morton (1799–1851), a Philadelphia physician and a member of the Academy of Natural Sciences, as a founder of physical anthropology in the United States. Morton was best known for his collection of 968 human crania of Native American and other populations and his measurements and analyses of this substantial collection of skulls. Morton's approaches to craniology were of the times and focused on racial identification and classification according to the theory that five races were believed to exist. Morton also sought ways to measure cranial capacity and general refinement of measurements of the skull. Hrdlička held Morton in high esteem because of Morton's careful measurements, but also because of his studies of Native Americans. Hrdlička's admiration of Morton and his interest in Morton's studies almost certainly led him to conduct his own studies of Native Americans.

Two other important figures from the late 1800s were Frederick Ward Putnam (1839–1915) and Henry P. Bowditch (1840–1911). Both were at Harvard. Putnam, as an archaeologist, promoted physical anthropology, hired Franz Boas to work at the Columbia World's Exposition in Chicago in 1891, and held important offices in the American Association for the Advancement of Science (permanent secretary and president). Bowditch was in the Harvard Medical School and made substantial contributions to the study of the physical growth of children. A third very important figure from this period was, of course, Franz Boas, who participated in substantial research in physical anthropology prior to the turn of the century. Boas's research included the 1888 anthropometric study of natives of British Columbia, the 1891 longitudinal study of Worcester, Massachusetts' schoolchildren, the 1892 massive anthropometric survey of Native Americans conducted as a part of the Chicago World Columbian Exposition, and the compilation of data of nearly 90,000 children (ages 5 to 18 years) from several cities to establish the first growth standards for the United States, also done as part of the Chicago Exposition. Boas's classic migration study was conducted in the early years of the 20th century, and this study brought to a close his work in physical anthropology for nearly two decades.

THE PERIOD BETWEEN 1918 AND 1930

The founding of the *American Journal of Physical Anthropology* is well described by Donald Ortner in a following chapter in this volume. The 12-year period between the establishment of the journal and the founding of the American Association of Physical Anthropologists was marked by new professional physical anthropologists moving into the profession. Hooton had begun training PhD students by the early 1920s, and four students, including Harry L. Shapiro and Carleton S. Coon, got their degrees before 1930. At Columbia University, Franz Boas trained three students during the 1920s, but one very promising student died a few years after being awarded the PhD, and another made only minimal contributions. Prior to the 1920s, Harvard had produced three students (not under Hooton), the University of Pennsylvania had produced one student, and neither Berkeley nor Columbia had produced any PhDs in physical anthropology up until 1922 (Spencer, 1982b).

This period was also marked by a rise in racism, particularly in Germany, and an increased interest in *eugenics*—the belief that the human species can be improved by human agency largely through genetic manipulation (see Marks's contribution to this volume). The American Eugenics Society was founded in 1926 with the support of a number of prominent physical anthropologists and human biologists. In fact, some objection to the founding of the American Association of Physical Anthropologists was based on the argument that there were enough societies, and that the American Anthropological Association, the American Association of Anatomists, and the American Eugenics Society served the interests of physical anthropology quite well (see Szathmáry's contribution to this volume). Marks (1997) described the post–World War I eugenics movement in some detail, which, as "a clearly noble and idealistic goal," was transformed to genetic determinism and then racism. Eugenics beliefs were linked to concerns in the United States about immigration of Eastern Europeans and led to Boas's design and implementation of the migrant study (see Little's contribution on Boas to this volume). Early proponents of eugenics included Raymond Pearl, Aleš Hrdlička, Earnest Hooton, and Harry Shapiro (1902–1990), although Pearl (1927) later rejected these ideas, and most of the others moved away from associations with eugenics ideas in the late 1930s.

An important event in 1929 was the founding of the journal *Human Biology* by Raymond Pearl. This journal published on topics related to physical anthropology, including genetics, osteology, anthropometry, demography, statistics, evolution, and growth. Goldstein (1940), in a survey of the first decade of *Human Biology* (*HB*) and two decades (1920s and 1930s) of the *American Journal of Physical Anthropology* (*AJPA*), suggested that the journal *HB* published articles more in the realm of "biological or group [population] anthropology," whereas the *AJPA* was more prone to publish in "anatomical anthropology." Crawford (2004) noted that both the editorial board during the first year of publication and the content of the articles indicated strong associations with physical anthropology. These patterns of topical publication also implied that the earliest development of a professional human biology and population biology "identity" had begun.

THE YEARS UP TO WWII AND THE WAR YEARS

There were a number of graduate training centers in physical anthropology in the years before the Second World War, including Harvard, Chicago, Pennsylvania, Western Reserve, Berkeley, and a few others. Hooton at Harvard trained the greatest number of PhDs in physical anthropology during this era (fourteen). And even Boas trained three students during the 1930s, including Marcus Goldstein (1906–1997) and a fourth, Ashley Montagu (1905–1999), whose dissertation work was jointly supervised by Ruth Benedict and Boas. The strongest program in growth and development was at Western Reserve University with T. Wingate Todd (1885–1938). Todd, who was a towering figure in skeletal growth studies, trained the first African-American physical anthropologist, W. Montague Cobb (1904–1990). Another important figure in growth studies (and later forensic anthropology) was Wilton M. Krogman (1903–1987), who was trained by Fay-Cooper Cole (1881–1961) at Chicago, but who later joined the faculty with Todd at Western Reserve University in Cleveland.

From 1930, when the American Association of Physical Anthropologists (AAPA) was founded, meetings were held generally once each year, with a few exceptions when meetings were held in conjunction with other associations. During these early years, meetings were always held on the East Coast or Midwest; in fact, the first AAPA meeting west of the Mississippi was only held in 1963 in Boulder, Colorado. At the 1930 inaugural meeting, 30 scientific papers were presented, and the number of presentations fluctuated around this number for the next 20 years. Numbers of presentations began to rise during the 1950s when more professional physical anthropologists moved into the workforce and attendance at the meetings expanded. Despite the increase in the numbers of students trained and new members of the profession, in the words of Geoffrey Harrison (1997, 18), "It is important to appreciate how sterile had become the pursuits of physical anthropology in the inter-war years." Typological pursuits persisted, as did interests in static racial classification and definition during this period.

The rise of imperialism in Germany, Japan, and Italy in the 1930s led to increased racism and ethnocentrism on both sides of the conflict. Caricatures of the Italians as pigs, the Japanese as monkeys, and the Nazis as foxes were common after the United States entered the war in 1941. Prior to this, the United States had attempted to remain neutral (1935 Neutrality Act) in the conflicts in Europe, Asia, and North Africa until the bombing of Pearl Harbor. As early as 1933, Franz Boas tried to marshal support against Nazi anti-Semitism and racism and introduced a resolution at the American Anthropological Association in 1937 condemning Nazi policies. It was passed the next year with the support of two of Boas's colleagues (see Marks's chapter in this volume).

During the World War II years, physical anthropology research, other than that linked to the war effort, was markedly reduced. Also, the 1943 and 1944 meetings of the AAPA were not held because of the war (Comas, 1969). This hiatus in physical anthropology activities during the war was accompanied by considerable military research on climatic, disease, and nutritional stress and the survival of military personnel living under extreme conditions. This led to later interests in how humans were able to adapt to these environmental conditions (Little, in press). In addition, the unfolding knowledge of Nazi atrocities contributed to changes in scientific attitudes about race (Provine,

1973), attitudes that probably reinforced changes in ideas about race in physical anthropology that took place after the war.

One of the most significant positive events for anthropology occurred directly before the United States entered World War II. It was in February 1941 that Paul Fejos (1897–1963), the Hungarian physician, filmmaker, explorer, and ethnographer, persuaded Alex Wenner-Gren, the Swedish industrialist, to contribute $2.5 million of Electrolux Company and Servel Corporation stock to found an anthropological research and educational institution (Dodds, 1973, 80). The Viking Fund (later the Wenner-Gren Foundation) under Fejos's direction was to become the most important private foundation in support of anthropology in the latter half of the 20th century.

POSTWAR YEARS AND THE "NEW PHYSICAL ANTHROPOLOGY"

The years following World War II were marked by recovery of the American academic enterprise, military personnel taking advantage of the GI Bill for college, and a transformation of physical anthropology, moving it into the realm of modern science. Prior to the establishment of U.S. government funding agencies in the 1950s, anthropology had been supported by small, private foundations, universities, museums, and private donors (Baker & Eveleth, 1982). In the years between 1948 and 1950, several new institutes were established within the National Institutes of Health (NIH), and in 1962 the National Institute of Child Health and Human Development (NICHHD) and the National Institute of General Medical Sciences (NIGMS) were established (Baker & Eveleth, 1982). Both of these new institutes benefited physical anthropology. In 1950, the National Science Foundation (NSF) was established with an anthropology program to provide funding for all fields of anthropology. Accordingly, with the expansion of federal funding opportunities, so opportunities for an expanded graduate training of professional anthropologists occurred.

In 1946, two major traditions were established: the Summer Seminars in Physical Anthropology and the *Yearbook of Physical Anthropology* (see Little & Kaplan in this volume). The Summer Seminars, which ran from 1946 to 1955, were originally organized by Sherwood Washburn and designed to bring together senior and junior colleagues and students to meet and exchange new ideas. The *Yearbook*, which was edited by Gabriel Lasker, was planned to report on the Summer Seminars and to review the literature of the previous year. With the AAPA meetings generally held in the springtime, the Summer Seminars doubled the degree of contact that physical anthropologists had during these postwar years.

At the midpoint of the century, Washburn, having built on the new ideas generated by the Summer Seminars and his professional contacts while he taught at Columbia University, co-organized the Cold Spring Harbor Symposium in 1950. His co-organizer was Theodosius Dobzhansky (1900–1975), the distinguished population geneticist, and the conference was sponsored jointly by the Viking Fund/Wenner-Gren Foundation and the Cold Spring Harbor Institute (see Stini in this volume). The nine-day meeting was attended by a host of well-known physical anthropologists and geneticists and was ground-breaking in developing new perspectives for the field. Both the Summer Seminars and the Cold Spring Harbor Symposium transformed the field of physical anthropology and led to Washburn's (1951) classic paper designed to redefine its direction.

Other significant events of the 1950s were the preparation of the UNESCO Statements on Race (see Marks's chapter in this volume), the Civil Rights Movement in the United States beginning in the mid-1950s (also see Marks's contribution), and the beginnings of the transformation of the race concept in physical anthropology (see Relethford in this volume).

THE 1960s AND 1970s

If the late 1940s and 1950s were transformational in physical anthropology, then the 1960s and 1970s saw the profession mature and develop into its modern configuration as a science among sciences. But these years were not without growing pains and controversies, particularly concerning the traditional typological concept of race (see Relethford's chapter). Two undeveloped subfields of physical anthropology in the United States began to grow in the 1960s: primatology, especially field studies of non-human primates, and paleoanthropology or studies of fossil humans. At the same time, human biology of living populations was expanding because of the impetus of the Human Adaptability Component of the International Biological Programme. Each of these three subfields in the United States was stimulated by overseas research and foreign scholars.

Ribnick (1982) described the history of primate field studies from their earliest research in which C. R. Carpenter's (1905–1975) work with howler monkeys (*Aouatta palliata*) in 1934 (Carpenter, 1934) and gibbons (*Hylobates lar*) in 1937, as part of the Asiatic Expedition to Siam (Carpenter, 1940), stands out as a pioneering effort. Another significant event was the establishment by Carpenter of the rhesus monkey (Macaca mulatta) colony on the Puerto Rican Island of Cayo Santiago in 1938. Although primate behavior was being studied in the laboratory, World War II brought a halt to naturalistic primate studies until the 1950s, when the Japanese began provisioning Japanese macaques (*Macaca fuscata*) and studying their behavior. Restudies of howler monkeys on Barro Colorado and rhesus monkeys on Cayo Santiago also were done in the 1950s. One of the most important investigations during that period was of the behavior of the mountain gorilla. It was initiated by Emlen and Schaller (1960) and then continued by George Schaller (1963). Washburn, who had been a participant in the 1937 Asiatic Expedition, initiated a study of the social behavior of baboons with his student Irven DeVore at Amboseli Game Reserve in Kenya (Washburn & DeVore, 1961). As Ribnick (1982) noted, this was the first study of naturalistic primate behavior by a U.S. physical anthropologist. Washburn (1973) vigorously promoted primate studies, and many of his Berkeley students from 1962 to 1974 (beginning with Irven DeVore) did dissertations on a variety of primate species' behavior (Spencer, 1997b). It was also in the 1960s that the now most famous primatologist, Jane Goodall, began her work with Gombe Stream Reserve chimpanzees in Tanzania, where she discovered the remarkable tool-using ability of these African apes (Goodall, 1964).

Up until the 1960s, physical anthropologists from the United States were marginal players in the subfield known today as paleoanthropology. Aleš Hrdlička (1927) was interested in European Neanderthals as antecedents of modern European populations, and other Americans had interests in and opinions on early fossil humans. But most of the field research and study was done by Europeans. A singular exception was Theodore D. McCown (1908–1969), who made remarkable discoveries of skeletal remains beginning in 1931 at the Skhūl Cave at Mount Carmel in Palestine (McCown & Keith, 1939). He collaborated with his mentor, Sir Arthur Keith from the United Kingdom, who contributed to the training of several other American anthropologists (Kennedy, 1997). McCown contributed to changes in the late 1950s and 1960s, when he began training students, such as Kenneth A. R. Kennedy, in paleoanthropology. Early on, Washburn had trained F. Clark Howell at Chicago (PhD in 1953), and then Ralph Holloway, Russell H. Tuttle, and Alan E. Mann in the 1960s after he moved to Berkeley. In 1963, John T. Robinson, who had worked with Robert Broom at several Australopithecine sites, left South Africa to take a faculty position at the University of Wisconsin, where he trained additional American students. As a result of these beginnings, several generations of paleoanthropologists have now been trained to staff several programs throughout the United States to train additional American students.

In 1964, the International Council of Scientific Unions (ICSU; now the International Council for Science) in Paris established the International Biological Programme (IBP). This was to be a decade-long, international program to study the ecology of the planet and the role that humans played in the ecologies of the biosphere. One component of the IBP was "Human Adaptability" (HA), an ambitious research program to be headed by the U.K.'s Joseph S. Weiner (1915–1982) and to deal with the "ecology of mankind." Studies were to focus on human ecology from a variety of perspectives that included population genetics, health and welfare, environmental physiology, child growth, anthropology, and demography. The planning and research that followed resulted in the participation of 40 nations, the completion of more than 230 projects, and several thousand publications under the Human Adaptability banner (Collins & Weiner, 1977). It is quite clear that the professional relations between the British and American human biologists during the IBP were of remarkable value, serving to cross-fertilize ideas and to reinforce the biocultural and environmental perspectives shared by most of the participants (Baker, 1988). One of the major conceptual and lasting contributions of the IBP was in the organization of multidisciplinary research and the recognition of its utility (Little et al., 1997).

THE MOST RECENT TRENDS

Within the past 25 years there have been a number of trends in physical/biological anthropology that are linked both to maturation and expansion of the profession and new scientific discoveries and directions. Numbers of physical anthropologists have increased enormously over the past half century or so, from a postwar group of less than 100 to somewhere between 1,500 and 2,000 academically trained professionals. Professional societies and scientific periodicals have proliferated and subspecializations have become well-defined.

Table 1.1 gives a chronology of societies and journals in physical anthropology in the United States from the earliest to the present. All publications and societies listed are still active. A brief history of the meetings of the American Association of Physical Anthropologists (AAPA), the earliest society in the United States, is given by Brown and Cartmill in this volume. The *American Journal of Physical Anthropology* preceded the founding of the Association by twelve years, whereas the second journal, *Human Biology,* was founded only a year before the AAPA. Over the years, *Human Biology* has been affiliated with several different professional societies. Following World War II, the *Yearbook of Physical Anthropology,* as a reprint and review journal, was founded for a specific task (see Little & Kaplan in this volume). Up until that time, the journals and the AAPA dealt broadly with physical anthropology, incorporating interests in living populations, extinct populations, skeletal biology, and primate studies. Beginning in the early 1970s, specialized journals and societies began to arise, reflecting the increasing specialization in the profession. At present, there are nine periodicals in biological anthropology and nine societies. All of the societies support either professional journals or newsletters, some of which publish papers. Not all of the journals are affiliated with professional societies. It is estimated that the nine journals now (2008) publish more than 600 scientific articles each year.

Table 1.1.   Chronology of Professional Associations and Journals in Physical Anthropology in the United States

Date	Association	Journal
1918		*American Journal of Physical Anthropology*
1929		*Human Biology*
1930	American Association of Physical Anthropologists	
1946		*Yearbook of Physical Anthropology*
1958	Society for the Study of Human Biology (SSHB)	
1963	SSHB affiliated with *Human Biology*	
1972		*Journal of Human Evolution*
1973	Paleopathology Association	
1974	SSHB affiliated with *Annals of Human Biology*	*Annals of Human Biology*
	Human Biology Council (HBC) affiliated with *Human Biology*	
1975	American Dermatoglyphics Association	
1981	American Society of Primatologists	*American Journal of Primatology*
1986	Dental Anthropology Association	
1989	HBC affiliated with *American Journal of Human Biology*	*American Journal of Human Biology*
1992	Paleoanthropology Society	*Evolutionary Anthropology*
1994	HBC becomes Human Biology Association	
	American Association of Anthropological Genetics becomes affiliated with *Human Biology*	
2003	Paleoanthropology Society affiliated with *PaleoAnthropology*	*PaleoAnthropology*

Dramatic changes in the scientific directions of each of the subareas of biological anthropology have resulted from new discoveries, new methods of analysis, and interests in new lines of research.

In human population genetics, the late 1970s and 1980s saw a revolutionary shift from genetic systems being inferred from phenotypes (e.g., blood, tissue, physical appearance) to where the genetics of a system was directly linked to DNA identification (the new molecular genetics). DNA began to be extracted from blood, cheek swabs, hair roots, and other tissue, and various purification and amplification techniques were developed (Crawford, 2000; 2007). New methods of DNA extraction and analysis also led to the Human Genome Project and the controversial Human Genome Diversity Project (Reardon, 2005). Mitochondrial DNA (mtDNA), only transmitted through the maternal line and not recombining, has been very useful in a variety of approaches to human evolution (Cann, 1986), as has the Y chromosome, which is inherited through paternal lineages (Hammer, 1995). Cann, Stoneking, & Wilson (1987, 31) found in a sample of 147 people from around the world that "All these mitochondrial DNAs stem from one woman who is postulated to have lived about 200,000 years ago, probably in Africa" (*Mitochondrial Eve*). This and other DNA work led to the "Out of Africa" hypothesis on modern human origins (Stoneking & Cann, 1989; Vigilant et al., 1991). With these new tools, research was conducted to trace population distributions and migrations in the historic and prehistoric past. Studies of European (Sokol, 1988; Cavalli-Sforza et al., 1994) and New World migrations (O'Rourke, 2000; Merriwether, 2002) have been expanded and informed by direct use of DNA. During the past half century, there has been increasing scientific activity in what Derek Roberts (1965) first referred to as "anthropological genetics." Research in molecular anthropology, genetic epidemiology, forensic anthropology via DNA analysis, human origins, and the history of human migration and dispersal are all areas of exploration that are being pursued by anthropological geneticists today.

In human population biology, an interest in multidisciplinary investigations carried over from the International Biological Programme of the 1960s and early 1970s to the 1980s and 1990s. The high-altitude project of the 1960s in Peru (Baker & Little, 1976) was replicated by another team of investigators in Chile in the 1980s (Schull & Rothhammer, 1990). These large-scale studies were followed by the Samoan Migrant Project (Baker et al., 1986), the Ituri Pygmy Project (Bailey, 1991), the Siberian Evenki Project (Crawford et al., 1992), and the South Turkana Ecosystem Project (Little & Leslie, 1999). Each of these single-population projects, which were based in biological anthropology, drew scientists from a variety of specializations and was international in scope.

There has been a continuing interest in reproduction and child growth that has persisted for more than a century. The first recognition of the central importance of breastfeeding in fertility control was by Konner and Worthman (1980) in studies of !Kung Bushmen. This and other research work stimulated a number of anthropological studies of nursing, energetics, and fecundity in traditional populations (Bentley, 1985; Gray, 1994; Vitzthum, 1994). Rose Frisch's work in the 1970s (Frisch & Revelle, 1970; Frisch & McArthur, 1974) suggested that a given body weight or fat composition triggered menarche and was fundamental in maintaining fecundity. The process turned out to be much more complex than she envisioned, but her early work contributed to the development of a new field of study on the *ecology of reproduction,* which led to research on the evolution and ecology of reproductive function in Western and non-Western peoples (Ellison, 1990; Leslie et al., 1994). At the same time as this new research direction in fertility and reproduction was being taken, so were new discoveries being made in infant, child, and adolescent growth studies. Michelle Lampl (Lampl et al., 1992) conducted new longitudinal research of individual growth patterns in an ingenious study of infant length, where some infants were measured every day for several months. She and her colleagues found that rather than being a continuous process, as believed, growth proceeded in "incremental bursts" (saltatory growth) followed by periods of stasis. Some measurements of infants showed daily increases in length of more than 1 cm in length. This work was extended to adolescents, who also showed saltatory growth (Lampl & Johnson, 1993) and has led to new lines of research in bone and soft tissue growth and in the endocrine control of growth.

In forensic anthropology, there has been an explosion of interest since the last decade of the 20th century, such that there are probably more students today who are interested in forensic science than in any other subarea of biological anthropology. From its earliest beginnings with work by T. Dale Stewart (1901–1997) and Wilton M. Krogman, forensic studies have focused on skeletal remains, including pathology, trauma, and conditions of death. More recent studies in forensic anthropology have expanded to incorporate (1) DNA analysis and experimental studies of postmortem events (Bond & Hammond, 2008), (2) trauma analysis (Kimmerle & Baraybar, 2008), (3) taphonomy and variables associated with decomposition (Haglund & Sorg, 2002), (4) human rights (Cox et al., 2008), and (5) massive disaster events (Sledzic et al., 2009). Prior to the Second World War, work in forensic anthropology was conducted by persons with medical backgrounds and by anatomists. In 1972, a new section of the American Academy of Forensic Sciences (AAFS founded in 1948) was named *Physical Anthropology.* It was organized by a few eminent biological anthropologists and is the principal organization along with other forensic specializations within the academy: for example, toxicology, odentology, pathology, engineering, and jurisprudence. The official organ of the AAFS is the *Journal of Forensic Sciences*. Present membership in the association includes over 300 members in the Physical Anthropology Section as of 2008. Within the Physical Anthropology Section, there are nearly 80 members who are certified with the Diplomate from the American Board of Forensic Anthropology (ABFA). This is an indication of the increasing professionalization of forensic anthropology. Finally, the Disaster Mortuary Operational Response Team (DMORT) is a U.S. federal team of forensic scientists (including anthropologists) that can be assembled rapidly for disasters, such as the World Trade Center disaster on September 11, 2001.

In primatology, there was an equivalent upsurge of interest in the latter years of the 20th century. With Sherwood Washburn's promotion of the field in the 1950s and 1960s and his graduate program at Berkeley, there were a number of young scientists who began training a new generation of biological anthropologists with interests in primatology (Washburn, 1973; Haraway, 1988). These interests were combined with increased research in non-human primate paleontology and the biology of living primates. As concerns grew about loss of living primate numbers and threatened and endangered species, primate conservation became increasingly important, with funds made available to study the ecology of primate species in the context of declining land resources, particularly resources of the tropical forests of Africa, Madagascar, Southeast Asia, and South America, but also in other areas where human population expansion has infringed on non-human primate habitats (Wolfheim, 1983). Another major trend in primatology has been the reclassification of many primate species based on DNA. This new information base has increased the number of recorded species, while at the same time providing misleading information on the status of primate species worldwide. Primate biology has also flourished, as has study of the behavior and biology of the Bonobo chimpanzee, now generally agreed to be our closest relative.

In paleoanthropology, discovery, interpretation, and reinterpretation have accelerated in the past quarter century. This has resulted from the trends of increased exploration of new and old sites, the enhanced training of paleoanthropologists in the United States, and the greater involvement of overseas paleoanthropologists in their own national heritage. Some discoveries (*Sahelanthropus* [Chad], *Orrorin* [Kenya], *Ardipithecus* [Ethiopia]) made in the transition between apes and upright hominids have pushed back our ancestry to between 6 and 7 million years ago. At the same time, the species diversity of the Australopithecines has expanded, as has the geographic and temporal distribution of this hominid genus. The Awash River Valley of northeast Ethiopia has proved to be a rich source of hominid fossil remains from pre-Australopithecines through early and modern *Homo* (Clark et al., 1984). The Middle Awash Project was initiated in 1981 jointly between Addis Ababa and Berkeley. Dmanisi, in the Republic of Georgia, was identified as an important site in the mid-1980s with the discovery of stone tools and has produced abundant hominid remains dating back to 1.8 million years ago (Rightmire et al., 2008). These are identified as the earliest hominids in Europe. Also in Europe, Atapuerca in northern Spain, rediscovered in the early 1970s, has been a rich source of remains of *Homo* in the period between 800,000 and 400,000 years ago that are identified as early archaic *Homo sapiens* (Falguères et al., 1999). Still controversial is the *Homo floresiensis* specimen with *Homo erectus* attributes, dating back to only 18,000 years ago (Morwood et al., 2004). This pygmoid specimen was found on a remote Indonesian Island in 2003. As noted above, the "Out of Africa" hypothesis revolutionized our understanding of the evolution of modern humans. In addition to DNA analysis contributing to a better understanding of modern *Homo sapiens,* ancient DNA has demonstrated also the substantial genetic distance between Neanderthals and modern humans.

SPECIALIZATION IN BIOLOGICAL ANTHROPOLOGY

Another inevitable trend in biological anthropology—probably characteristic of all sciences in these times—is that of increasing specialization. At the mid-point of the 20th century following the Second World War, biological (physical) anthropologists were few in number and broadly educated in the principles of the profession. Fifty years later, at the beginning of the 21st century, biological anthropologists identify their interests as either the human skeleton (skeletal biology, forensic anthropology, paleoanthropology), living human populations (growth, reproduction, nutrition, disease, environmental stress), population genetics (molecular anthropology, evolutionary models, migration, DNA analyses), or primatology (primate ecology, naturalistic behavior, paleontology, biology). These specializations are integrated conceptually in the introductory course in biological anthropology, and classroom arguments are presented on the value of integration and holism in the profession. However, the differences in professional identity are clear during national meetings when segregation of the subfields occurs during specialized sessions reporting on research. In some ways, this is a healthy trend reflecting the development of a mature science with increasing sophistication of methods, theory, and content. On the other hand, there is a loss of anthropological fundamentals and commitment to integrated studies that led to the expansion of biological anthropology during the second half of the 20th century.

* * * * *

The chapters that follow provide a background to the growth of biological (physical) anthropology during the past 100 years and provide a framework for the future development of the profession.

REFERENCES

Alfonso, M. P., & Little, M. A. (transl. & ed.). (2005). Juan Comas's Summary History of the American Association of Physical Anthropologists (1928–1968). *Yearbook of Physical Anthropology, 48,* 163–195.

Bailey, Robert C. (1991). *The Behavioral Ecology of Efe Pygmy Men in the Ituri Forest, Zaïre.* Anthropological Papers of the Museum of Anthropology No. 86. Ann Arbor: University of Michigan.

Baker, P.T. (1988). Human Population Biology: A Developing Paradigm for Biological Anthropology. *International Social Science Journal,* 116, 255–263.

Baker, Paul T. (1996). Adventures in Human Population Biology. *Annual Review of Anthropology, 25,* 1–18.

Baker, Paul T., & Little, Michael A. (eds.). (1976). *Man in the Andes: A Multidisciplinary Study of High-Altitude Quechua.* Stroudsburg, PA: Dowden, Hutchinson & Ross.

Baker, Paul T., Hanna, Joel M. & Baker, Thelma S. (eds). (1986). *The Changing Samoans: Health and Behavior in Transition.* New York: Oxford University Press.

Baker, Thelma S., & Eveleth, Phyllis B. (1982). The Effects of Funding Patterns on the Development of Physical Anthropology. In *A History of American Physical Anthropology: 1930–1980,* ed. by Frank Spencer, pp. 31–48. New York: Academic Press.

Bentley, Gillian R. (1985). Hunter-Gatherer Energetics and Fertility: A Reassessment of the !Kung San. *Human Ecology, 13,* 79–109.

Birdsell, Joseph B. (1987). Some Reflections on Fifty Years in Biological Anthropology. *Annual Review of Anthropology, 16,* 1–12.

Boas, Franz. (1912). *Changes in the Bodily Form of Descendants of Immigrants.* New York: Columbia University Press.

Boas, Norman F. 2004. *Franz Boas, 1858-1942: An Illustrated Biography.* Mystic, Connecticut: Seaport Autographs Press.

Boaz, Noel T., & Spencer, Frank (eds.). (1981). 1930–1980: Jubilee Issue. *American Journal of Physical Anthropology,* 56(4), 327–535.

Bond, John W., & Hammond, Christine. (2008). The Value of DNA Material Recovered from Crime Scenes. *Journal of Forensic Sciences, 53,* 797–801.

Buikstra, Jane E. (ed.). (1990). *A Life in Science: Papers in Honor of J. Lawrence Angel.* Kampsville, IL: Center for American Archaeology Scientific Papers 6.

Cann, Rebecca L. (1986). Nucleotide Sequences, Restriction Maps, and Human Mitochondrial DNA Diversity. In *Genetic Variation and Its Maintenance: With Particular Reference to Tropical Populations,* ed. D. F. Roberts and G. F. De Stefano, pp. 77–86. Society for the Study of Human Biology Symposium Series No. 27. Cambridge: Cambridge University Press.

Cann, Rebecca L., Stoneking, Mark, & Wilson, Alan C. (1987). Mitochondrial DNA and Human Evolution. *Nature, 325,* 31–36.

Carpenter, C. Ray. (1934). A Field Study of the Behavior and Social Relations of Howling Monkeys (*Alouatta palliata*). *Comparative Psychology Monographs, 10*(2), 1–168.

———. (1940). A Field Study in Siam of the Behavior and Social Relations of the Gibbon (*Hylobates lar*). *Comparative Psychology Monographs, 16*(5), 1–212.

Cavalli-Sforza, L.L., Menozzi, P., & Piazza, A. (1994). *The History and Geography of Human Genes.* Princeton, NJ: Princeton University Press.

Clark, J. Desmond, Asfaw, Berhane, Assefa, Getaneh, Harris, J. W. K., Kurashina, H., Walter, R. C., White, Tim D., & Williams, M. A. J. (1984). Paleoanthropological Discoveries in the Middle Awash Valley, Ethiopia. *Nature, 307,* 423–428.

Cole, Douglas. (1999). *Franz Boas, The Early Years: 1858–1906.* Seattle: University of Washington Press.

Collins, K. J., & Weiner, J. S. (1977). *Human Adaptability: A History and Compendium of Research.* London: Taylor and Francis.

Comas, Juan. (1960). *Manual of Physical Anthropology.* Springfield, IL: Charles C. Thomas.

———. (1969). *Historia Sumaria de la Asociación Americana de Antropólogos Físicos (1928–1968).* Mexico: Instituto Nacional de Antropologia e Historia.

Coon, Carleton S. (1977). Overview. *Annual Review of Anthropology* 6:1–10.

———. (1981). *Adventures and Discoveries: The Autobiography of Carleton S. Coon.* Englewood Cliffs, NJ: Prentice-Hall.

Cox, Margaret, Flavel, Ambika, Hanson, Ian, Laver, Joanna, & Wessling, Roland. (2008). *The Scientific Investigation of Mass Graves: Towards Protocols and Standard Operating Procedures.* Cambridge: Cambridge University Press.

Crawford, Michael H. (2000). Anthropological Genetics in the 21st Century: Introduction. *Human Biology, 72,* 3–13.

———. (2004). History of Human Biology (1929–2004). *Human Biology, 76,* 805–815.

———. (2007). Foundations of Anthropological Genetics. In *Anthropological Genetics: Theory, Methods and Applications,* ed. M. H. Crawford, pp. 1–16. Cambridge: Cambridge University Press.

Crawford, Michael H., Leonard, William R., & Sukernik, Rem I. (1992). Biological Diversity and Ecology in the Evenkis of Siberia. *Man and the Biosphere Northern Sciences Network Newsletter, 1* (April), 13–14.

Dodds, John W. (1973). *The Several Lives of Paul Fejos: A Hungarian-American Odyssey.* New York: The Wenner-Gren Foundation.

Ellison, Peter T. (1990). Human Ovarian Function and Reproductive Ecology: New Hypotheses. *American Anthropologist, 92,* 933–952.

Emlen, John T., & Schaller, George B. (1960). Distribution and Status of the Mountain Gorilla (*Gorilla gorilla beringei*). *Zoologica, 45,* 41–52.

Falguères, C., Hahain, J. J., Yokohama, Y., Arsuaga, J. L., Bermudez de Castro, J. M., Carbonell, E., Bischoff, J. L., & Dolo, J. M. (1999). Earliest Humans in Europe: The Age of TD6 Gran Dolina, Atapuerca, Spain. *Journal of Human Evolution, 37,* 343–352.

Frisch, Rose E., & Revelle, Roger. (1970). Height and Weight at Menarche and a Hypothesis of Critical Body Weights and Adolescent Events. *Science, 169,* 397–399.

Frisch, Rose E., & McArthur, J. W. (1974). Menstrual Cycles: Fatness as a Determinant of Minimum Weight for Height Necessary for Their Maintenance or Onset. *Science, 185,* 949–951.

Goldstein, Marcus S. (1940). Recent Trends in Physical Anthropology. *American Journal of Physical Anthropology, 26,* 191–209.

———. (1995). *An Odyssey in Anthropology and Public Health.* Department of Anatomy and Anthropology. Tel Aviv, Israel: Tel Aviv University.

Goodall, Jane. (1964). Tool-Using and Aimed Throwing in a Community of Free-Living Chimpanzees. *Nature, 201,* 1264–1266.

Gray, Sandra J. (1994). Comparison of Effects of Breast-Feeding Practices on Birth-Spacing in Three Societies: Nomadic Turkana, Gainj, and Quechua. *Journal of Biosocial Science, 26,* 69–90.

Haglund, William D., & Sorg, Marcella H. (2002). *Advances in Forensic Taphonomy: Method, Theory, and Archaeological Perspectives.* Boca Raton, FL: CRC Press.

Hammer, Michael F. (1995). A Recent Common Ancestry for Human Y-Chromosomes. *Nature, 378,* 376–378.

Haraway, Donna J. (1988). Remodelling the Human Way of Life: Sherwood Washburn and the New Physical Anthropology, 1950–1980. In *Bones, Bodies, Behavior: Essays on Biological Anthropology,* ed. by G. W. Stocking, pp. 206–259. Madison: University of Wisconsin Press.

Harrison, Geoffrey A. (1997). The Role of the Human Adaptability International Biological Programme in the Development of Human Population Biology. In *Human Adaptability: Past, Present, and Future,* ed. by S. J. Ulijaszek and R. Huss-Ashmore, pp. 17–25. Oxford: Oxford University Press.

Hrdlička, Aleš. (1919). *Physical Anthropology: Its Scope and Aims; Its History and Present Status in the United States.* Philadelphia: The Wistar Institute of Anatomy and Biology.

———. (1927). The Neanderthal Phase of Man. *Journal of the Royal Anthropological Institute, 47,* 249–274.

Howells, William W. (1992). Yesterday, Today and Tomorrow. *Annual Review of Anthropology, 21,* 1–17.

Jones-Kern, Kevin F. (1997). T. Wingate Todd and the Development of Modern American Physical Anthropology, 1900-1940. PhD Dissertation in History. Bowling Green, Ohio: Bowling Green State University.

Kennedy, Kenneth A.R. (1997). McCown, Theodore D(Oney) (1908–1969). In *History of Physical Anthropology: An Encyclopedia, Volume 2*, ed. by F. Spencer, pp. 627–629. New York: Garland.

Kern, Kevin F. (2006). T. Wingate Todd: Pioneer of Modern American Physical Anthropology. *Kirtlandia* (Cleveland), *55*, 1–42.

Kimmerle, Erin H., & Baraybar, José Pablo. (2008). *Skeletal Trauma: Identification of Injuries Resulting from Human Rights Abuse and Armed Conflict*. Boca Raton, FL: CRC Press.

Konner, M., & Worthman, C. (1980). Nursing Frequency, Gonadal Function, and Birth Spacing Among !Kung Hunter-Gatherers. *Science, 207*, 788–791.

Krogman, Wilton M. (1976). Fifty Years of Anthropology: The Men, the Material, the Concepts, the Methods. *Annual Review of Anthropology, 5*, 114.

Lampl, Michelle, & Johnson, M. L. (1993). A Case Study of Daily Growth During Adolescence: A Single Spurt or Changes in the Dynamics of Saltatory Growth? *Annals of Human Biology, 20*, 595–603.

Lampl, Michelle, Veldhuis, J. D., & Johnson, M. L. (1992). Saltation and Status: A Model of Human Growth. *Science, 258*, 801–803.

Lasker, Gabriel W. (1999). *Happenings and Hearsay: Experiences of a Biological Anthropologist*. Detroit: Savoyard.

Leslie, Paul W., Campbell, Kenneth L., & Little, Michael A. (1994). Reproductive Function in Nomadic and Settled Women of Turkana, Kenya. In *Human Reproductive Ecology: Interactions of Environment, Fertility, and Behavior*, ed. K. L. Campbell and J. W. Wood. *Annals of the New York Academy of Sciences, 709*, 218–220.

Little, Michael A. (In press). History of the Study of Human Biology. In *Human Evolutionary Biology*, ed. by M.P. Muehlenbein. Cambridge: Cambridge University Press.

Little, Michael A., & Haas, Jere D. (eds.). (1989). *Human Population Biology: A Transdisciplinary Science*. New York: Oxford University Press.

Little, Michael A., & James, Gary D. (2005). A Brief History of the Human Biology Association: 1974–2004. *American Journal of Human Biology, 17*, 41–154.

Little, Michael A., & Leslie, Paul W. (eds.). (1999). *Turkana Herders of the Dry Savanna: Ecology and Biobehavioral Response of Nomads to an Uncertain Environment*. Oxford: Oxford University Press.

Little, M. A., Leslie, P. W., & Baker, P. T. (1997). Multidisciplinary Research of Human Biology and Behavior. In *History of Physical Anthropology: An Encyclopedia*, ed. F. Spencer, pp. 695–701. New York: Garland Publishing.

Mai, Larry L., Shanklin, Eugenia, & Sussman, Robert W. (eds.). (1981). *The Perception of Evolution: Essays Honoring Joseph B. Birdsell*. Anthropology UCLA, 7(1 & 2), Department of Anthropology. Los Angeles: University of California.

Marks, Jonathan. (1997). Eugenics. In *History of Physical Anthropology: An Encyclopedia, 2 Volumes*, ed. by F. Spencer, pp. 362–366. New York: Garland.

McCown, Theodore D., & Keith, Arthur. (1939). The Relationship of the Fossil People of Mount Carmel to Prehistoric and Modern Types. *The Fossil Human Remains from the Levallois-Mousterian*. Oxford: Clarendon Press.

Merriwether, D. Andrew. (2002). A Mitochondrial Perspective on the Peopling of the New World. In *The First Americans: The Pleistocene Colonization of the New World*, ed. by N. G. Jablonski, pp. 295–310. San Francisco: *Memoirs of the California Academy of Sciences*, No. 27, pp. 295–310.

Morwood, M. J., Soejono, R. P., Roberts, R. G., Sutikna, T., Turney, C. S. M., Westaway, K. E., Rink, W. J., Zhao, J-X., van den Bergh, G. D., Due, Rokus Awe, Hobbs, D. R., Moore, M. W., Bird, M. I., & Fifield, L. K. (2004). Archaeology and Age of a New Hominin from Flores in Eastern Indonesia. *Nature, 431*, 1087–1091.

Osborne, Richard H., & Osborne, Barbara T. (1999). The History of the Journal *Social Biology*, 1954–1999. *Social Biology, 46*, 164–178.

O'Rourke, Dennis H. (2000). Genetics, Geography, and Human Variation. In *Human Biology: An Evolutionary and Biocultural Perspective*, ed. S. Stinson, B. Bogin, R. Huss-Ashmore, & D. O'Rourke, pp. 87–133. New York: Wiley-Liss.

Pearl, Raymond. (1927). The Biology of Superiority. *American Mercury, 12*, 257–266.

———. (1939). *The Natural History of Population*. London: Oxford University Press.

Provine, William B. (1973). Geneticists and the Biology of Race Crossing. *Science, 182*, 790–796.

Reardon, J. (2005). *Race to the Finish: Identity and Governance in an Age of Genomics*. Princeton, NJ: Princeton University Press.

Ribnick, Rosalind. (1982). A Short History of Primate Field Studies: Old World Monkeys and Apes. In *A History of American Physical Anthropology: 1930–1980*, ed. by F. Spencer, pp. 49–73. New York: Academic Press.

Rightmire, G. Philip, Van Arsdale, A. P., & Lordkipanidze, David. (2008). Variations in the Mandibles from Dmanisi, Georgia. *Journal of Human Evolution, 54*, 904–908.

Roberts, Derek F. (1965). Assumption and Fact in Anthropological Genetics. *Journal of the Royal Anthropological Institute, 95*, 87–103.

Schaller, George B. (1963). *The Mountain Gorilla: Ecology and Behavior*. Chicago: University of Chicago Press.

Schull, William J. & Rothhammer, F. (eds.). (1990). *The Aymara: Strategies in Human Adaptation to a Rigorous Environment*. Dordrecht: Klewer.

Sledzik, Paul S., Dirkmaat, Dennis, Mann, Robert W., Holland, Thomas D., Mundorff, Amy Zelson, Adams, Bradley J., Crowder, Christian M., & DePaolo, Frank. (2009). Disaster Victim Recovery and Identification: Forensic Anthropology in the Aftermath of September 11. In *Hard Evidence: Case Studies in Forensic Anthropology*, 2nd Ed., ed. by D. W. Steadman, pp. 289–301. Upper Saddle River, NJ: Prentice Hall.

Sokal, Robert R. (1988). Genetic, Geographic, and Linguistic Distances in Europe. *Proceedings of the National Academy of Sciences, 85*, 1722–1726.

Spencer, Frank. (1979). Aleš Hrdlička, M.D., 1869–1943: A Chronicle of the Life and Work of an American Physical Anthropologist (Volumes I and II). Dissertation in Anthropology. Ann Arbor, MI: University of Michigan.

———. (1982a). *A History of American Physical Anthropology: 1930–1980*. New York: Academic Press.

———. (1982b). Introduction. In *A History of American Physical Anthropology: 1930–1980*, ed. by F. Spencer, pp. 1–10. New York: Academic Press.

———. (ed.). (1997a). *History of Physical Anthropology: An Encyclopedia*, 2 Volumes. New York: Garland.

———. (1997b). Washburn, Sherwood L. (1911–). In *History of Physical Anthropology: An Encyclopedia*, Vol. 2, ed. by F. Spencer, pp. 1104–1106. New York: Garland.

Stocking, George W., Jr. (1974). *The Shaping of American Anthropology, 1883–1911: A Franz Boas Reader*. New York: Basic Books.

Stoneking, Mark, & Cann, Rebecca L. (1989). African Origin of Human Mitochondrial DNA. In *The Human Revolution: Behavioral and Biological Perspectives on the Origin of Modern Humans*, ed. P. A. Mellars and C. B. Stringer, pp. 1730. Princeton, NJ: Princeton University Press.

Strum, Shirley C., Lindberg, Donald G., & Hamburg, David (eds.). (1999). *The New Physical Anthropology: Science, Humanism, and Critical Reflection*. Upper Saddle River, NJ: Prentice Hall.

Tanner, James M. (1981). *A History of the Study of Human Growth*. Cambridge: Cambridge University Press.

———. (1999). The Growth and Development of the *Annals of Human Biology:* A 25-year retrospective. *Annals of Human Biology, 26*, 3–18.

Vigilant, L., Stoneking, M., Harpending, H., Hawkes, K., & Wilson, A. C. (1991). African Populations and the Evolution of Human Mitochondrial DNA. *Science, 253*, 1503–1507.

Vitzthum, Virginia J. (1994). Comparative Study of Breastfeeding Structure and its Relation to Human Reproductive Ecology. *Yearbook of Physical Anthropology, 37*, 307–349.

Washburn, Sherwood L. (1951). The New Physical Anthropology. *Transactions of the New York Academy of Science, 13*, 298–304.

———. (1973). The Promise of Primatology. *American Journal of Physical Anthropology, 38*, 177–182.

———. (1984a). Book review of *A History of American Physical Anthropology, 1930–1980*, edited by Frank Spencer. *Human Biology, 56*, 393–410.

———. (1984b). Evolution of a Teacher. *Annual Review of Anthropology, 12*, 1–24.

Washburn, Sherwood L., & DeVore, Irven. (1961). The Social Life of Baboons. *Scientific American, 204*(6), 63–71.

Wolfheim, Jaclyn H. (1983). *Primates of the World: Distribution, Abundance, and Conservation*. Seattle: University of Washington Press.

Chapter 2

"Physical" Anthropology at the Turn of the Last Century

by

C. Loring Brace

INTRODUCTION

There were two aspects of concern in the nascent field of biological—
"physical"—anthropology at the end of the 19th and the beginning of the
20th centuries. One of these was the assessment of human biological variation
represented by the study of "race," and the other was a consideration of the
course of human evolution. What is virtually never considered is how politi-
cal/cultural factors heavily influenced the outlook of both of those aspects.
The lingering effects of those factors, particularly where they bear on the
consideration of human "evolution," have continued to have their influence
right on into the 21st century. It seems appropriate, then, to look at what those
factors were and how they exerted their influence.

What happened in Europe during the first two decades of the 20th century was a complete realignment of national sympathies from what they
had been for the previous 850 years. For the first time since the Norman
invasion of England in 1066, the English and the French found themselves
allied against a common enemy, an expansion-minded Germany (Keegan,
1999; Eisenhower, 2001). Spoken English, after all, is a Germanic language, and it is a lot easier for a native English speaker to learn simple
street German than the equivalent level of spoken French. The English
monarchy—the House of Hanover—was of German origin, and the English did not have the derogatory stereotypes for Germans that were common in France. English speakers then picked up some of these from the
French during World War I. Prominent among them was the denigration
of Germans collectively as "the *Boche*," derived from the word "*caboche*,"
which means "cabbage head." It is pronounced "bosh," but does not have

the implications conveyed by that word in colloquial English (Brace, 2000, 16–17).

The military alliance between the French and English-speaking communities during World War I had all kinds of consequences. This was partially prefigured by the *"Entente Cordiale"* (1904–1914) promoted by Queen Victoria's son, Albert Edward ("Bertie," later King Edward VII; St. Aubyn, 1979). After the war was over, a number of the English-speaking troops stayed on as "the lost generation" in Paris, the "epicenter of Modernism" (Stein, 1937, 52; Everdell, 1997, 142). The realm denoted in that usage of the term "modernism" was largely restricted to literature and the arts, one of the "two cultures" identified by C. P. Snow in his Rede Lecture at Cambridge University in 1959, *The Two Cultures and the Scientific Revolution* (Snow, 1959). Lord Snow clearly showed the extent to which the literary and scientific worlds had each lost touch with what was happening in the other (Brace, 2005a, 62–63). Both realms had undergone quantum changes. If Pablo Picasso and James Joyce embodied "modernism" in art and literature, surely Albert Einstein had to embody an equally important representation in science (Holton, 1982). Unfortunately, the major developments that influenced biological anthropology were to have much less positive results for much of the 20th century and on into the new millennium.

THE FRENCH CONNECTION: RACE

What launched the approach to "race" that was to characterize the American anthropological outlook for more than the first half of the 20th century were the Lowell Institute Lectures given by William Z. Ripley (1867–1941) in Boston in 1896 (Ripley, 1897–1898). At the time, Ripley was giving lectures in physical geography and anthropology in the School of Political Science at Columbia University in New York City, as well as serving as assistant professor of economics at the Massachusetts Institute of Technology in Cambridge, Massachusetts (Ripley, 1899, v; Hrdlička, 1918, 274). These lectures then were the basis for his book, *The Races of Europe: A Sociological Study* (Ripley, 1899). In this, he promoted the idea that there were three "races" in Europe—Nordic, Alpine, and Mediterranean—a view he attributed to the librarian at the Muséum National d'Histoire Naturelle in Paris, Joseph Deniker (1852–1918; Ripley actually preferred Shaler's term "Teutonic" over Deniker's "Nordic" [Ripley, 1899, 128; Livingstone, 1987, 186–187]). In actual fact, Ripley's depiction was almost a caricature of simplification over the more sophisticated scheme of Deniker (Deniker, 1892; 1897a; 1897b; 1898; 1900; Brace, 2005a, 169–172).

According to Ripley, credit for the full articulation of the concept of "race" was assigned to Paul Topinard (1830–1911). Purporting to quote Topinard, Ripley declared that

> race in the present state of things is an abstract conception, a notion of continuity in discontinuity, of unity in diversity. It is the rehabilitation of a real but directly unattainable thing. (Ripley, 1899, 111–112)

Ripley attributed this statement to a paper that Topinard wrote in 1879, although those words do not appear there nor are they to be found in the book he wrote dedicated to Paul Broca in 1876. Nor have I been able to find them in anything else Topinard wrote. The "continuity in discontinuity" and "unity in diversity" verbiage represents the stance of Romanticism as opposed to the outlook of faith in the scientific method of the Enlightenment (Lovejoy, 1936; Brace, 2005a, Chapter 5). Topinard did exemplify some of the stance of Romanticism, although not to the extreme degree represented by Ripley. Topinard in fact declared that "race, like type, is an abstraction" (Topinard, 1879, 567). As a good polygenist, Topinard declared,

> Races are fixed realities with permanent characteristics, not varying under the influence of their milieu and perpetuating themselves across the centuries, in spite of mixtures, migrations and changes of habitation. They die, but they do not vary. (Topinard, 1879, 627 [my translation])

Based upon the "unity in diversity" wording attributed to Topinard by Ripley, the latter added his own conclusions:

> In this sense alone do we maintain that there are three ideal racial types in Europe to be distinguished from one another. They have often dissolved in the common population; each particular trait has gone its own way; so that at the present time rarely, if indeed ever, do we discover a single individual corresponding to our racial type in every detail. It exists for us nevertheless. (Ripley, 1899, 112)

Needless to say, this is not science but a peculiarly American form of Romantic faith bolstered by an admiration for what was perceived as continental sophistication. But then, Ripley was trained in economics and not science. In fact, Ripley came very close to saying "there are only clines," but in his faith in the existence of "races," he exemplifies "the pathos of the esoteric":

> [T]he "insight [is] . . . reached, not through a consecutive progress of thought guided by the ordinary logic available to every man, but through a sudden leap

whereby one rises to a plane of insight wholly different from the level of mere understanding." "How exciting and how welcome is the sense of initiation into hidden mysteries." (Lovejoy, 1936,11)

This in turn is a close relative of the "Metaphysical pathos":

[T]he pathos of sheer obscurity, the loveliness of the incomprehensible. (idem)

Ripley's book was the stimulus for the writing of *The Passing of the Great Race* by Madison Grant (1916) and the even more bigoted *The Rising Tide of Color Against White World Supremacy* by Lothrop Stoddard (1920). These significantly contributed to the Congressional passage of the Johnson-Lodge Immigration Restriction Act of 1924, which established "racially" based quotas for annual immigrants to the USA (Brace, 2005a, 172ff). Subsequently, the Macmillan publishing company commissioned Carleton Stevens Coon (1904–1981), then on the anthropology faculty at Harvard, to rewrite Ripley's book. He did a complete rewrite, removing the blatant anti-Semitism and some of the other obvious manifestations of racism that had permeated Ripley's original, although he dedicated the ensuing volume to Ripley himself (Coon, 1939). If it was clearly less bigoted than Ripley's version, it accepted the categorical reality and different capabilities of "races" just as Ripley had done 40 years earlier. In essence, this was the outlook of American biological anthropology, and it is clear that not a great deal had changed since the end of the 19th century. The public accepted it as indicative of just how things were.

Subsequently, Coon produced *The Origin of Races* (Coon, 1962) and, with the assistance of Edward E. Hunt, Jr., *The Living Races of Man* (Coon & Hunt, 1965) among a number of other works. Coon had been a student and, prior to World War II, a colleague of Earnest Albert Hooton (1887–1954) at Harvard. Hooton had practically created American biological anthropology single-handedly, which, as will be treated subsequently, is why there is so little of the outlook of evolutionary biology in the field to this day. Certainly, Darwinian expectations are largely missing from the work of Carleton Coon.

If the prestige that Ripley's presentation enjoyed had benefited from reflecting the manifestation of French scholarship late in the previous century, it was completely forgotten that the French treatment of the subject had been heavily influenced by a still earlier version of American views. The French ethos of Topinard and Deniker that had such an effect on Ripley was the outlook of the Société d'Anthropologie de Paris of Paul Broca (1824–1880). Broca had created the Société in 1859 and gone on to found a

Laboratoire and an École (School) d'Anthropologie as well (Schiller, 1979). Topinard had been his pupil and successor in the École, although he had run into philosophical/political troubles, and the edifice that Broca had built had in effect collapsed by the time Ripley was picking up on the French enterprise (Harvey, 1983, 305). What has been almost universally missed, however, is that Broca's whole approach was shaped by the earlier views of the American anatomist, Samuel George Morton (1799–1851).

THE AMERICAN SCHOOL OF ANTHROPOLOGY

It has been completely forgotten that, at the mid-point of the 19th century, Samuel George Morton was internationally recognized as one of the very most distinguished scientists in America (Patterson, 1853). As a result of Morton's study and description of the Cretaceous fossils brought back by the Lewis and Clark expedition earlier in the century, he effectively founded invertebrate paleontology in America (Stanton, 1960, 29). Further, he worked at analyzing the fossils discovered during the excavation of the Chesapeake & Delaware canal, and it could be said that he founded American vertebrate paleontology as well (Abrahams, 1966, 49). He became aware of the similarities and the simultaneous changes in the vertebrate fossils in the Cretaceous strata of the western edge of Europe and the eastern United States, and he dedicated his 1834 monograph to his "dear friend," the discoverer of Iguanodon, Gideon Mantell of Brighton, England (Morton, 1834; Meigs, 1851, 84). It was further work of this sort that led to the documentation of continental drift nearly a century later (Wegener, 1920; Wilson, 1963). Morton was president of the Academy of Natural Sciences in Philadelphia, the most active organization for the pursuit of scientific endeavors in America in the first half of the 19th century (Phillips, 1953). He was also a prominent author, a physician, and a professor of anatomy at the Pennsylvania Medical College.

He was best known, however, for having founded what was called "the American School of Anthropology" (sometimes called the American School of "Ethnology," where the words anthropology and ethnology were effectively regarded as synonyms; Brace, 2005a, Chapter 7). In his most widely cited work, *Crania Americana* (1839), Morton compared the cranial form of Native Americans to that of the other varieties of humans described in the previous century by the eminent German anatomist Johann Friedrich Blumenbach of Göttingen. Morton subsequently did the same thing for Egyptian material in his *Crania Ægyptiaca* (Morton, 1844). Blumenbach had originally presented his treatment of human craniofacial form in his doctoral dissertation of 1775, *De Generis Humani Varietate Nativa,* better known from the third edition of 1795, itself translated into English by Thomas Bendyshe as *On the Natural Varieties of Mankind* (Bendyshe, 1865). Blumenbach had expanded the four varieties of the human species recognized by Linnaeus into five, although he regarded them all as having diverged from a single original form, and he considered the drawing of lines between them as a more or less arbitrary activity. Morton, however, changed the name from "varieties" to "races," and, to Broca and anthropological orthodoxy, they have been "races" ever since.

Just after World War I, the founder of the *American Journal of Physical Anthropology*, Aleš Hrdlička (1869–1943), recognized Morton as being the founder of biological anthropology in America (Hrdlička, 1918; 1919). As he put it,

> Morton may justly and with pride be termed the father of American Anthropology; yet it must be noted with regret that, like others later on, he was a father who left many friends and even followers, but no real progeny, no disciples who would continue his work as their special or life vocation. (Hrdlička, 1919, 41)

Despite his own familiarity with and enthusiasm for French biological anthropology, Hrdlička completely missed the fact that it was Paul Broca himself who was the "disciple" who would continue Morton's work as his own "special or life vocation" (Brace, 2005a, 148ff). It has been said that Paul Broca regarded Morton as "his hero and model" and that he analyzed "Morton's techniques in the most minute detail" (Gould, 1981, 84; and see Pouchet, 1865, 203–204). Specifically, Broca derived much of the perspective that led him to create the field of biological anthropology in France from the pre–Civil War views of Samuel George Morton (Morton, 1839; 1847; Broca, 1859; 1873; Dally, 1862a; 1862b; Pouchet, 1865; Brace, 2005a, Chapter 7).

The views of the "American School" survived Morton's death in 1851 to be offered to the South by a Morton admirer, the Alabama physician Josiah Clark Nott (1804–1873), in collaboration with a somewhat frenetic English opportunist, George Robins Gliddon (1809–1857; Horsman, 1987). They put together two books—*Types of Mankind* (1854) and *Indigenous Races of the Earth* (1857)—honoring the work of Samuel George Morton and offering his views to the South as a justification for slavery. Gliddon did much of the writing of those two volumes in a style that was almost flatulently verbose, and I have not included the whole outpouring of each title here, but, if interested, the reader can check them elsewhere (Brace, 2005a, 128–129).

When Ripley transmitted the French outlook on "race" to an American readership to start off the 20th century, it fit American preconceptions so well that it was adopted as self-evident, but there was no realization that, in effect, "it was essentially an American turkey come home to roost" (Brace, 2005a, 175). Morton's role had been completely forgotten and, although Gould subsequently pointed to his influence on Broca, he denigrated Morton as having engaged in

> a patchwork of fudging and finagling in the clear interest of controlling a priori convictions. (Gould, 1978, 504; 1981, 54; 1996, 86)

The irony of that accusation is that it fits the assessment of Gould's treatment of Morton, but not of Morton's treatment of the data. Morton's measurements were recalculated and his specimens remeasured as part of an undergraduate honors thesis in geology, and, aside from some minor slips, partially because Morton did not have calculating equipment available, his work was shown to be objective and reliable (Michael, 1988).

Gould, however, paid no attention to his own error in treating Morton's data as demonstrated by an undergraduate until it was subsequently pointed out by a professional colleague. As he noted, he had worked from a Xerox copy of Morton's data and reported a mean capacity of African-American skulls as 80 cubic inches, when the bottom of the range was actually 84 and the mean should have been 89. As Gould said,

> The reason for this error is embarrassing. . . . I never saw the inconsistency pre-sumably because a low value of 80 fit my hopes. (Gould, 1993, 109)

Interestingly enough, after initially concluding that Morton's conclusions were "a patchwork of finagling and fudging," he had said,

> Yet—and this is the most intriguing aspect of the case—I find no evidence of conscious fraud. (Gould, 1981, 54)

One could use exactly the same words to characterize the work of Stephen Jay Gould, even if they do not apply to Morton. Gould continued to accuse Morton of fraud in the subsequent revised edition of his *Mismeasure of Man*, with no mention of the fact that he had previously admitted that it was his own work and not that of Morton that was an unconscious example of "fudging and finagling." (Gould, 1996, 86, 101)

By the turn of the century, Morton's contribution to the reification of the "race" concept had been completely forgotten, yet the American public accepted the findings of the French manifestation as the obvious conclusions of "science." As a result of Nott and Gliddon's use of Morton's work, it was identified as being part of the Southern outlook that had led to the Civil War. Views that are associated with the losing side of a war are themselves often consigned to oblivion. Actually, the South may have lost the actual military conflict, but with the collapse of Reconstruction in the 1870s, and the legal endorsement of segregation by the "separate but equal" decision in the *Plessy v. Ferguson* case of 1896, the institution of slavery continued to survive in everything but the name until well after the midpoint of the 20th century (Brown, 1896 [2000]; Ayers, 2005; Brace, 2005a, 133ff, 190). In this case, Morton's name was what was consigned to oblivion, while the views with which he was associated continued to flourish in France without mention of his role in their promotion. They also were perpetuated in America particularly because of the influence of the Louis Agassiz protégé and successor, Nathaniel Southgate Shaler (1841–1906). Shaler himself was a Southerner who hailed from a slave-owning family in Kentucky, although, during the Civil War, he actually fought briefly on the Northern side (Shaler, 1909, 219ff; Livingstone, 1987, 30). Leaving the military long before the end of the war, he returned to Harvard where he spent the next four decades as a professor in, and later dean of, an organization of Agassiz's creation, the Lawrence Scientific School.

Referred to in the Harvard community as the "Confederate General," he was a "popular and flamboyant" teacher of a "notorious gut course ('all the geology necessary to a gentleman')" (Livingstone, 1987, 249–250; Pauly, 2001, 108). Over the years he taught more than 6,000 students, including such subsequently influential figures as Theodore Roosevelt and Henry Cabot Lodge. His Lowell Lectures of 1888–1889 were influential in shaping the outlook of William Z. Ripley (Shaler, 1891; Livingstone, 1987, 172). Throughout his writings, he practically quotes Josiah Clark Nott word for word, but never makes any reference to him. In fact, he includes few if any references to support his obvious role as the continuity of the Southern manifestation of the American School of Anthropology.

Shaler's defense of "lynch law" in the South showed the extreme to which New England casuistry went in attempting to renounce the politics of Reconstruction and to leave the race problem in the hands of the southerners. (Haller, 1971, 184)

This, then, was the ethos surrounding the nascent field of anthropology at the beginning of the 20th century, and it was to remain so for more than 50 years. Only with Ashley Montagu's *Man's Most Dangerous Myth: The Fallacy of Race* (1942) and Frank Livingstone's "There are no races, there are only clines" (1962, 279; 1964, 47) did the ethos of the American School prior to the Civil War finally begin to change.

HUMAN "EVOLUTION"?

At the turn of the century, samples of previous manifestations of human forms were available, even if the means of calculating their actual antiquity were still a long way in the future. Starting in the early 1890s, the Dutch anatomist, Eugène Dubois, working in Java, found and published on pieces of jaw, teeth, skull cap, and leg bones of an ancient hominid with a brain that was literally halfway between chimpanzee and human in sheer size (Dubois, 1894; Theunissen, 1989). In 1893, Dubois had telegraphed to Holland that he had discovered "the long-expected Missing Link of Darwin" (Corbey, 1995, 4). He christened his discovery *"Pithecanthropus" erectus.* His specific designation is widely accepted, although most specialists now regard the generic designation as unwarranted and relegate his material to our own genus, *Homo,* making it properly *Homo erectus* (Asfaw et al., 2002).

Almost 40 years earlier, workmen in the Kleine feldhofer Grotte in 'Newman's Valley' (Neanderthal) had discovered robust human bones as they were cleaning out the cave in the summer of 1856 (Mowbray & Gannont, 2001). The bones themselves were studied by Hermann Schaaffhausen, a professor of anatomy at Bonn, and sympathetic to the idea of evolution even before becoming a Darwinian (Montgomery, 1974, 82). Schaaffhausen's work constituted the first full study of an ancient human skeleton, and it established Neanderthal form as something to be expected prior to the emergence of modern humans as the inhabitants of Europe (Schaaffhausen, 1857; 1858; 1861). That valley has given its name to human fossils found in excess of 40,000 years in age (Schmitz et al., 2002) and characterized by a degree of robustness and brow-ridge thickening not found on more recent human remains.

Actually, fossils of the same kind of hominid had been found earlier. A less than seven-year-old representative had been found in the Province of Liège in Belgium in 1829, at a site, Engis, that was subsequently visited by Sir Charles Lyell who confirmed the antiquity of the fauna (Lyell, 1873, 72). In 1848, an adult female of obvious Neanderthal affinities was found in a quarry on the north face of the Rock of Gibraltar. This, of course, was over a decade prior to Darwin's *Origin of Species* (1859) and over two decades before his *Descent of Man* (1871). It was discussed by George Busk and Hugh Falconer at the 34th annual meeting of the British Association for the

Advancement of Science held at Bath in 1864 and its "primitive" aspects duly noted (Busk, 1864; 1865; Falconer, 1865). Busk and Falconer duly visited Gibraltar on behalf of the British Association, and Busk brought the Gibraltar skull back to England. They praised the contribution of Captain Broome, the head of the military prison on Gibraltar, whose efforts had led to the recovery of that remarkable skull. In an illustration of why the designation "military intelligence" is often considered an oxymoron, Captain Broome "was cashiered for allowing military prisoners to be employed in private excavations," the actual efforts that had led to the uncovering of the Gibraltar skull (Millar, 1972, 59). It was not until the next century that Engis and Gibraltar received the kind of comparative treatment that they properly deserved (Schwalbe, 1906; Sollas, 1908; Fraipont, 1936).

In 1886, Marcel de Puydt, an archaeologist from Liège, and Max Lohest, a geologist at the Belgian University of Liège, found two Neanderthal-like skeletons in a cave at Spy (pronounced the way Spee would be rendered in English) in the Belgian Province of Namur. The skeletons were in a Mousterian archaeological layer. Since archaeological work at the sites of Le Moustier (Mousterian), Aurignac (Aurignacian), and La Madeleine (Magdalenian) in the Vézère region of southwestern France had shown the existence of an archaeological sequence, this allowed Neanderthal form to be reliably placed in a relative archaeological context for the first time (Clark & Lindly, 1989; Straus, 1995). Lohest and de Puydt enlisted the help of the professor of paleontology at Liège, Julien Fraipont, and their reports confirmed the anatomical characteristics of the Neanderthals and placed them in the correct archaeological context (Fraipont & Lohest, 1886; de Puydt & Lohest, 1886).

In addition to the increasing number of Neanderthal specimens, a series of sites had been yielding Upper Palaeolithic skeletons late in the 19th century. The most famous of these was the Cro-Magnon rock shelter excavated in 1868 at the town of Les Eyzies on the banks of the Vézère River in the Dordogne Departement of southwestern France (Lartet, 1868; Broca, 1868). More extensive and even better preserved material came from sites in what is now the Czech Republic, but was then the Austrian Province of Moravia, especially starting in 1879 from the site called Předmostí (Maška, 1885). It was more than half a century before a full descriptive treatment was published (Matiegka, 1934), but there was enough information available so that an assessment should have been possible (Maška, 1901; Szombathy, 1901). Somewhat later, this assessment in fact was made (Hrdlička, 1914), but, for reasons treated subsequently, it has been ignored from that day to this. Early in the 20th century, the addition of a quantity of Neanderthal remains from the site of Krapina in Croatia (Gorjanović-Kramberger, 1901; 1906), now shown to be 130±10 thousand years old (Rink et al., 1995), should have set the stage for a general interpretive treatment of the known hominid fossil record. This indeed took place.

The most carefully worked-out scheme was the one offered by the Strassburg anatomist, Gustav Schwalbe (1844–1916; Schwalbe, 1906). He cited the outlook of Charles Darwin, Thomas Henry Huxley, and Ernst Haeckel and applied it to dealing with the known human fossil record. Previously he had published the most exhaustive quantitative studies of Dubois's *"Pithecanthropus"* (Schwalbe, 1896; 1899) and of the original Neanderthal skeleton (Schwalbe, 1901). In his summary treatment, he produced the most extensive quantitative analysis of the Neanderthal status of the Gibraltar skull (Schwalbe, 1906, 154–160). A Neanderthal affinity had been previously suggested (Busk, 1865; Broca, 1869, 146; Quatrefages & Hamy, 1882, 21), but Schwalbe's was the first full metric documentation of the matter.

Schwalbe was the first to treat the Neanderthal and *erectus* samples as representing the course of human evolution. In his words,

> In my view, Neandertal man would always stand exactly intermediate between Pithecanthropus and Homo sapiens. (Schwalbe, 1906, 13 [my translation])

Schwalbe presented a possible picture of the line of descent of the groups involved which is reproduced here as Figure 2.1 (Schwalbe, 1906, 14). In the upper part of his diagram, the sequence *erectus* — Neanderthal — *Homo sapiens,* represents a linear evolutionary trajectory, while, in the lower half, the two prehistoric samples represent side branches. In Schwalbe's view, there is no way to decide which interpretation is correct, but he added that in essence it does not matter since the relationships are genetic in either case.

> In a purely zoological sense in both cases Homo primigenius [his designation for Neanderthal] is an intermediate between Homo sapiens and Pithecanthropus erectus. (Schwalbe, 1906, 14 [my translation])

Three years later, Schwalbe repeated his stance in an essay translated into English as a celebration of the centennial of Darwin's birth and the 50th anniversary of the publication of *The Origin of Species* (Schwalbe, 1909). In this he presents the same view and once again, although it is clear that he grasps Darwin's outlook, he makes no attempt to deal with the actual causes of human evolution.

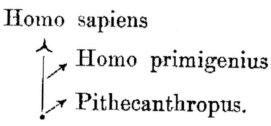

1. Auffassung:

Homo sapiens

Homo primigenius

Pithecanthropus.

2. Auffassung:

Homo sapiens

Homo primigenius

Pithecanthropus.

Figure 2.1. Schwalbe's depiction of two possible ways in which the *erectus* and Neanderthal samples could fit in the course of human evolution (Schwalbe, 1906, 14).

Directly influenced by Schwalbe's synthesis of 1906, the Oxford geologist William J. Sollas discussed Neanderthal facial characteristics based on a study of the most complete, known Neanderthal facial skeleton, that of the Gibraltar skull (Sollas, 1908, 321–339). Accepting Schwalbe's general outlook, Sollas aptly generalized:

> Looked at from this point of view, the Neandertal and Pithecanthropus skulls stand like the piers of a ruined bridge which once continuously connected the kingdom of man with the rest of the animal world. (Sollas, 1908, 337)

This view was so generally accepted during the first decade of the 20th century that it was initially echoed by the person who effectively founded biological anthropology in the English-speaking world, Arthur (later, Sir Arthur) Keith (1866–1955). As he declared,

> The supposition we proceed on at the present time is that the Neanderthal type is the precursor and ancestor of the modern type. The Neanderthal type represents an extinct stage in the evolution of man. (Keith, 1911, 78–79)

That view vanished just one year later, however, and Keith presented a radically different interpretation:

[T]he evidence points to an extermination of the ancient or Neanderthal type early in the Aurignacian period. (Keith, 1912, 155)

As he subsequently said, "A more virile form extinguished him" (Keith, 1915, 136). This was the first articulation in English of the view that "modern" *Homo sapiens* had invaded Europe and killed off the resident Neanderthals.

THE FRENCH CONNECTION (AGAIN)

Since there is no archaeological or skeletal support for such a view, one might well ask, "what happened to produce such a complete change of mind?" While some have been "puzzled" by his flip-flop (Trinkaus & Shipman, 1992, 196), Keith himself has provided us with the reason in his autobiography (Keith, 1950, 319–320). Keith and his wife visited France in September of 1911, spent a few days in Paris, and then took the train down to the village of Les Eyzies in the Dordogne region of southwestern France, from which they went on a walking tour of the Vézère River valley. They visited the Aurignacian site of Cro-Magnon, the Mousterian site of Le Moustier, the Magdalenian site of La Madeleine, and a whole series of other sites that had yielded the tools and bones of the Late Pleistocene inhabitants of the region. It amounted to a conversion experience. Keith was dazzled and left completely open to the French interpretation of the lives and times of the former inhabitants of that romantically gorgeous landscape.

There was another key occurrence that took place in 1911. This was the publication of the first installment of the study of one of the most complete Neanderthal skeletons found to date, namely, the "Old Man" of La Chapelle-aux-Saints that had been excavated in 1908 from beneath the floor of a cave in the Département of Corrèze, just east of Les Eyzies (Boule, 1911). The author, Marcellin Boule (1861–1942), was professor and chair of paleontology at the Muséum National d'Histoire Naturelle in Paris and controlling editor, 1893–1942, of *L'Anthropologie* which has remained the voice of French biological anthropology for well over a century now.

Boule was the student and successor of Albert Gaudry (1827–1908; Glangeaud, 1910; Heberer, 1955; Hammond, 1988), and it was abundantly clear that he shared Gaudry's outlook on "evolution" (Boule, 1908). In Gaudry's own words,

> If I have attempted . . . to accumulate several proofs in favor of the idea of evolution, I have had to leave aside the question of the processes that the Author of the world must have employed to produce the changes of which paleontology shows us the tableau. This study of processes is what is called Darwinism after the name of the illustrious scholar who has been its principal promoter. Assuredly the subject which examines the causes of modifications of beings is well worthy of the attention of naturalists. But on this subject I avow my ignorance. (Gaudry, 1878, 257 [my translation])

Ignorance has continued to characterize the French treatment of process in the fossil record and particularly that part of it that bears on understanding the course of human development through time.

Marcellin Boule exemplified another aspect of the French treatment of such matters:

> Whatever sources may be utilized to illustrate the French reception of Darwin in a positive way, none can be as impressive as the countless books and articles where silence alone stands testimony to the French intellectual developments. Silence may be harder to document than the trumpet fanfare, but in its own way it is equally impressive. (Stebbins, 1974, 167)

Boule was essentially silent about Darwin and his ideas, and his only treatment of the possibility of the evolution of one kind of fossil hominid from another was to deny it. He articulated the human succession in France by noting,

> The first of the Aurignacians who brusquely succeeded the Mousterians in our country were humans of the Cro-Magnon type, that is to say humans extremely close to certain living human races and different from the Mousterians as much by the superiority of their culture as by the superiority or the diversity of their physical characteristics. (Boule, 1913, 34–35)

He wrote in glowing terms about the Cro-Magnon form and accomplishments, contrasting them with the crude and benighted Neanderthals. He declared that Cro-Magnons possessed

> a more elegant body, a finer head, an upright and expansive forehead, who left such witness of their manual skills in the caves where they lived, the

resources of their inventive spirit, their artistic and religious preoccupation, their faculties of abstraction, who were the first to merit the glorious title of *Homo sapiens*. (Boule, 1913, 19)

The Neanderthals, on the other hand, were denigrated in every possible way, starting with reference to their "bestial or simiesque character" (Boule, 1909, 266). For example,

platycephaly, the absence of a forehead, the flattening of the occiput, the supra-orbital brow ridge, the absence or fleeting nature of the chin, the muzzle-like configuration of the face as a result of the special conformation of the maxillae, the reduction of the frontal lobes of the brain. (Boule, 1913, 31)

No one can doubt that this type represents a degree of morphological inferiority compared to any step in the scale of living humans and that it shows a cranium clearly separated from the superior cranium. The study of the La Chapelle-aux-Saints remains has revealed to us a long series of primitive or pithecoid traits that are inscribed on each element of the skeleton which can only be interpreted as marks of a less advanced stage of evolution than what we can see in living humans, and the difference is such that it plainly justifies . . . a distinction at the species level. (Boule, 1913, 32)

Further,

we can conclude, if not the probable absence of an articulate language, at least the existence of a rudimentarily articulated language. (Boule, 1913, 1)

Boule assumed, erroneously, that Neanderthals and "modern" humans lived at the same time in the Late Pleistocene (Boule, 1913, 34–35), but he declared that

there never was an infusion of neanderthaloid blood by way of hybridization with other human groups belonging to the branch or one of the branches of *Homo sapiens*. But what appears certain to me is that such an infusion was only accidental because no living human type could be considered as a direct even if modified descendant of the Neanderthal type. (Boule, 1913, 40)

Homo Neanderthalensis was a species with archaic characteristics a little less removed from the apes than present humans. Many pithecoid traits are preserved which are singularly attenuated in or effaced in diverse forms of *H. sapiens,* especially in the white races. (Boule, 1913, 34)

In addition, Boule was equally scornful of the Mousterian tools of the Neanderthals:

> There is hardly a more rudimentary or more miserable industry than that of our Mousterian man. The use of a single basic material, stone, (outside of wood and perhaps bone), the uniformity, the simplicity and crudity of his lithic tools. The probable absence of all traces of concerns of an esthetic order or of a moral order are well in agreement with the brutal aspect of the heavy, vigorous body, of that bony head with its robust jaws, and which further affirms the predominance of the purely vegetative or bestial over cerebral functions. (Boule, 1913, 19)

Needless to say, all of this is a long way from the stance of Gustav Schwalbe and William J. Sollas—and even Arthur Keith—before the end of the first decade of the 20th century. Even though much of it is based on assertions unsupported by any demonstrable evidence, it is eerily like the orthodox views of human evolution at the end of the 20th and the beginning of the 21st centuries (Stringer & McKie, 1997; Tattersall & Schwartz, 2000; Klein, 2000; 2001; 2003). While the similarity to Boule's stance has been denied,

> the Neanderthals *were* a separate species from modern humans, but for entirely different reasons than Boule's. Our theory is based on the special nature of the Neanderthal fossils rather than the features they supposedly shared with apes. (Stringer & Gamble, 1993, 26)

Yet they had already noted that the Neanderthals were

> too primitive or specialized to be closely related to living humans, particularly the supposedly highly advanced white European race. (Ibid., 14)

That, of course, is vintage Boule.

Finally, Boule felt that once "modern" humans appeared on the scene, evolution was over:

> We have arrived at a moment beyond which the physical evolution of humans can be considered as terminated; the problem of human origins loses its zoological character to become purely anthropological or ethnographic. (Boule, 1921, 40)

A version of this patently anti-evolutionary and anti-Darwinian stance was alive and well as the 20th century drew to a close:

> *Homo sapiens* today is in a mode of intermixing rather than of differentiation, and the conditions for significant evolutionary change simply don't exist. (Tattersall, 1995, 247)

And further,

> Before 50-40 ky ago, anatomy and behavior evolved relatively slowly and in parallel. Afterwards gross anatomical change all but ceased, while behavioral (cultural) change accelerated dramatically. (Klein, 2000, 18)

These statements are made in the complete absence of any treatment of the available skeletal data, and it is obvious that the intellectual tradition of Marcellin Boule is alive and well at the dawn of the 21st century.

In reaction to Boule's manifestly anti-evolutionary treatment of the whole Neanderthal question in his monograph of 1911–1912–1913, Schwalbe delivered an 80+ page review in which he did not reject Boule's conclusions, although he did note that Boule had botched the assessment of the heel and ankle morphology of his La Chapelle skeleton (Schwalbe, 1914, 585, 589). Boule had presented his Neanderthal skeleton as a not completely erect-walking biped (Boule, 1913, 19, 24), and Schwalbe's critique was on solid anatomical grounds. His caution about the larger evolutionary issues has to be seen in the context of the times. World War I had broken out in 1914, and one of the sticky issues between France and Germany was who should get control of Elsass-Lothingen or Alsace-Lorraine as it had been known before the German conquest in the Franco-Prussian War of 1870–1871. Schwalbe of course was a resident of its capital, Strassburg, when it was under German control, and Strasbourg, when it was under French control, and which later became the case after the end of World War I, although Schwalbe had died two years before that happened (Hoche, 1939; Brunschwig, 1966).

Boule repeatedly claimed that the Neanderthal frontal lobes of the brain were reduced in size and "primitive" (Boule, 1913, 19; 1921, 235–236) which was not true.

> From the point of view of relative development of his frontal lobe, depressed and constricted, the fossil man is located between the anthropoid apes and people of today, and even closer to the former than the latter. (Boule, 1921, 235)

More than 75 years later it was shown that Boule (1912, 1913) had also botched the reconstruction of the La Chapelle-aux-Saints brain case (Heim, 1989). Curiously enough, Boule made no comparisons with the extensive Neanderthal material from La Ferrassie in the Dordogne of southwestern France, whose discovery began only a year after La Chapelle-aux-Saints was excavated and which was under Boule's care in the Museum in Paris. His only mention of La Ferrassie was in a brief footnote near the beginning of his report on La Chapelle. A full description of the La Ferrassie material was only accomplished four decades after Boule's death (Heim, 1976, 1982).

Again, almost precisely corresponding with the publication of Boule's treatment of La Chapelle and the outbreak of World War I, the biological anthropologist at the Smithsonian Institution in Washington, DC, Aleš Hrdlička, presented the case that the Early Upper Paleolithic Czech fossil remains from Předmostí provided support for a Neanderthal ancestry of modern human form:

> The writer has seen this collection on two occasions and he regards it as by far the most important assemblage of material from the transitional period between earlier and the latest paleolithic forms. It represents in a measure the much searched-for bridge between the Neanderthal and recent man. (Hrdlička, 1914, 551)

A decade and a half later this would be the theme of Hrdlička's Huxley Memorial Lecture (Hrdlička, 1927), and it would be at the core of his volume dealing with the fossil evidence for human evolution (Hrdlička, 1930), a work that was rarely cited and was basically never used in the biological anthropology curriculum. In his treatment of the matter, Hrdlička posed a series of well-thought-out questions for those who supported the idea of Neanderthal extinction, but these were basically ignored from that day to this (Brace, 1964, 13–14). Curiously enough, Hrdlička was assessed as not being a theoretician (Schultz, 1945, 312; Barkan, 1992, 97), and said to be conservative scientifically and more outdated over time (Barkan, 1992, 99–100). Even one of those who often supported him declared that his mind was not original (Montagu, 1944, 115). As time goes on, however, it may become apparent that his critics will be seen to be the ones who did not have original minds, who were scientifically conservative, and became more outdated as time went on (Brace, 2000, esp. Chapter 12).

When the cranial outlines of a "classic" Neanderthal, an early Upper Paleolithic "modern," and a recently living European are superimposed on each other as in Figure 2.2, it can be seen that the cranial outlines are almost identical—all based on material readily available in the first decade of the 20th century. What clearly differs is the size of the tooth-bearing portion of the face, and that is completely consistent with the evidence for the gradual change in tooth size through time (Brace, 1979; 1995; 2002; 2005b; Brace et al., 1987; 1991). The documented change of 1% every 2,000 years over the last 130,000 years was quite sufficient to transform a Neanderthal face into a modern one. Since the use of pottery in food preparation reduced the selection for tooth size even more during the last 10,000 years, tooth size reduction has gone up to 1% per 1,000 years (Brace et al., 1991, 47–48).

> Using just this evidence alone, one could argue that we are living in the midst of a "speciation event" although it is proceeding so slowly that we are unaware of it. (Brace, 2005b, 23)

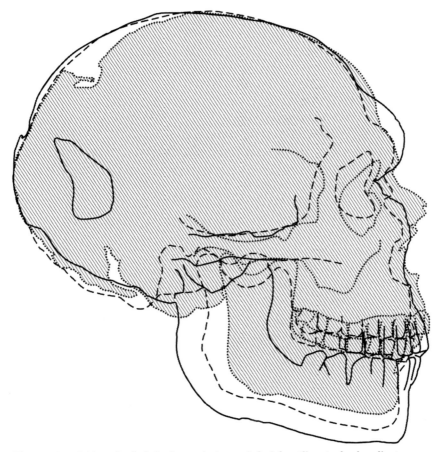

Figure 2.2. A Neanderthal, La Ferrassie I, craniofacial outline (unbroken line) super-imposed on the outline of Předmostí 3 (dashed line) and a modern northwest European male from the Faeroe Islands (dotted line). All three representatives have approximately the same nasion-opisthocranion length, and this was used to align them for purposes of comparison (see Brace, 2005b, 54).

Almost simultaneously with the publication of Hrdlička's Huxley Memorial Lecture, Franz Weidenreich published a nearly identical gambit, something that he explicitly realized at the time (Weidenreich, 1928, 59). Weidenreich had been a student and subsequently a colleague of Gustav Schwalbe in the anatomy department at Strassburg, and it is hardly surprising that he should have supported similar views. After World War I was over, he was fired by the French along with the rest of the German faculty in 1918 (Gregory, 1950, 252). Subsequently, he fled from a position at Heidelberg because his partial Jewish ancestry made him at risk from Nazi persecution in the 1930s. After a peripatetic career including his productive time with the "*Sinanthropus*" material in Beijing, China, he settled in New York under the friendly sponsorship of the American Museum of Natural History from 1941 until his death in 1948. It was during this period that he finished publishing the Chinese *erectus* material for which he is best known, but he also continued to produce a number of papers where the Neanderthals are portrayed as a stage between an *erectus* and a modern form of human (Weidenreich, 1940; 1943; 1947).

The evolutionary outlook of both Hrdlička and Weidenreich has been treated in caricature by a biological anthropology community that is marching to the beat of a different drummer. The field is clearly out of step with the outlook of evolutionary biology, and the reason evidently is the unacknowledged dominance of the non-evolutionary outlook of French biological anthropology, and especially Marcellin Boule, dating from the beginning of the 20th century (Brace, 1974, 205–206). Keith's conversion experience came during the time when Earnest Albert Hooton was a Rhodes Scholar at Oxford. He had earned his doctorate in classics from the University of Wisconsin in 1911. It was during his Oxford stint of 1910 to 1912 that he gained his anthropological orientation. He earned a "diploma" in anthropology in 1912, and a B. Litt. in 1913 (Giles, 1997, 499). While Keith had no actual connection with the Oxford program, Hooton came to Keith's laboratory in the Museum of the Royal College of Surgeons in London to learn how to deal with the human skeletal remains of prehistoric populations. "I became, in some sense, a disciple of Arthur Keith" (Hooton, 1946, v). This was the ethos that Hooton took away from England and used to establish the program at Harvard, which he began in 1913 and promoted for the next four decades. In essence, "Hooton was attempting to build American physical anthropology in the image of Sir Arthur Keith" (Brace, 1964, 16).

Among the consequences of this was that there was effectively no thread of a Darwinian evolutionary outlook in the ensuing edifice. At first this may appear counter-intuitive since Keith spent the last two-plus decades of his long life in a house on the Darwin property at Down and explicitly referred to himself as a Darwinian:

> For I believe in Darwin and Darwinism. I have lived now almost a quarter of a century in the place he made world-famous as a centre of biological research, and I have a hope that his spirit will continue to influence the work done. (Keith, 1955, 289)

Yet, Keith uttered some of the most un-Darwinian sentiments such as this:

> I could as easily believe the theory of the Trinity as one which maintains that living, developing protoplasm, by mere throws of chance, brought the human eye into existence. The essence of living protoplasm is its purposiveness. (Keith, 1946, 217)

Evidently, Keith was completely unfamiliar with Darwin's detailed and thoughtful treatment of the evolution of the eye by means of natural selection in *On the Origin of Species* (Darwin, 1859 [1964], 186ff, 204). In this and many other ways, it is clear that he had no idea what Darwinian evolution was really all about.

Both the study of living humans and the treatment of the evidence for humans over the stretch of evolutionary time were heavily influenced by adopting the ideas of the newly allied French early in the 20th century. The realization has yet to sink in that the outlook on living human variation was heavily influenced by American assumptions early in the 19th century that had been adopted by the French. Where the treatment of the evidence for human evolution is concerned, as yet there is no realization that the French synthesis adopted early in the 20th century was in fact profoundly at odds with the outlook of modern evolutionary biology. The same can be said for the outlook of many of those in the English-speaking world who have devoted their professional efforts to what has been purported to be the story of human "evolution."

REFERENCES

Abrahams, Harold J. (1966). *Extinct Medical Schools of Nineteenth-Century Philaldelphia.* Philadelphia: University of Pennsylvania Press.

Asfaw, B., Gilbert, W. H., Beyene, Y., Hart, W. K., Renne, P. R., Wolde-Gabriel, G.,Vrba, Elizabeth S., & White, Tim D. (2002). Remains of *Homo erectus* from Bouri, Middle Awash, Ethiopia. *Nature, 416,* 317–320.

Ayers, E. L. (2005). The First Occupation. *New York Times Magazine*, May 29, p. 20.

Barkan, Elazar. (1992). *Retreat of Scientific Racism: Changing Concepts of Race in Great Britain and the United States Between World Wars*. New York: Cambridge University Press.

Bendyshe, T. (1865). *The Anthropological Treatises of Johann Friedrich Blumenbach*. London: Longman, Green, Longman, Roberts, & Green.

Blumenbach, Johann F. (1795). *De Generis Humani Varietate Nativa*. Göttingen: JC Dietrich.

Boule, Marcellin. (1908). Albert Gaudry. Notice Nécrologique. *L'Anthropologie, 19*, 604–611.

———. (1909). L'homme Fossile de La Chapelle-aux-Saints (Corrèze). *L'Anthropologie, 20*, 257–271.

———. (1911). L'homme Fossile de La Chapelle-aux-Saints. *Annales de Paléontologie, 6*(3–4),109–172.

———. (1912). L'homme Fossile de La Chapelle-aux-Saints. *Annales de Paléontologie, 7*(1), 21–56; 7(2), 85–104; 7(3–4), 105–192.

———. (1913). L'homme Fossile de La Chapelle-aux-Saints. *Annales de Paléontologie, 8*(1), 1–70.

———. (1921). *Les Hommes Fossils: Éléments de Paléontologie Humaine*. Paris: Masson & Cie.

Brace, C. Loring. (1964). The Fate of the "Classic" Neanderthals: A Consideration of Hominid Catastrophism. *Current Anthropology, 5*(1), 1–41.

———. (1974). Problems in Early Hominid Interpretations. *Yearbook of Physical Anthropology, 17*, 202–207.

———. (1979). Krapina, "Classic" Neanderthals, and the Evolution of the European Face. *Journal of Human Evolution, 8*(5), 527–550.

———. (1995). Bio-Cultural Interaction and the Mechanism of Mosaic Evolution in the Emergence of "Modern" Morphology. *American Anthropologist, 97*(4), 711–721.

———. (2000). *Evolution in an Anthropological View*. Walnut Creek CA: AltaMira Press.

———. (2002). Background for the Peopling of the New World: Old World Roots for New World Branches. *Athena Review, 3*(2), 50–59.

———. (2005a). *"Race" Is a Four-Letter Word: The Genesis of the Concept*. New York: Oxford University Press.

———. (2005b). "Neutral Theory" and the Dynamics of the Evolution of "Modern" Human Morphology. *Human Evolution, 20*(1), 19–38.

Brace, C. Loring, Rosenberg, K., & Hunt, K. D. (1987). Gradual Change in Human Tooth Size in the Late Pleistocene and Post-Pleistocene. *Evolution, 41*(4), 705–720.

Brace, C. Loring, Smith, S. L., & Hunt, K. D. (1991). What Big Teeth You Had, Grandma! Human Tooth Size, Past and Present. In *Advances in Dental Anthropology*, ed. by M. A. Kelley and Clark S. Larsen, pp. 33–57. New York: Wiley-Liss.

Broca, Paul. (1859). Des Phénomènes d'Hybridité dans le Genre Humain. *Journal de la Physiologie de l'Homme et des Animaux*, 2(8), 601–625.

———. (1868). Sur les Crânes et Ossements des Eyzies. *Bulletin de la Societe d'Anthropologie de Paris*, 2e Série, *3*, 350–392, 432–446, 454–510, 554–574, 571–573.

———. (1869). Crânes et Ossements Humains des Cavernes de Gibraltar. *Bulletin de la Societe d'Anthropologie de Paris*, 2e Série, *6*, 146–158.

———. (1873). Sur la Mensuration de la Capacité du Crâne. *Mémoirs de la Societe d'Anthropologie de Paris*, 2 Série, *1*, 63–152.

Brown, H.B. (1896/2000). *Plessy v. Ferguson*, the Decision of the Court. In *Civil Rights Since 1787: A Reader on the Black Struggle*, ed. by J. Birnbaum and C. Taylor, pp. 165–167. New York: New York University Press. .

Brunschwig, H. (1966). *French Colonialism 1871–1914: Myths and Realities*. London: Pall Mall Press.

Busk, George. (1864). Pithecoid Priscan Man from Gibraltar. *The Reader*, 82(4), 109–110.

———. (1865). On a Very Ancient Human Cranium from Gibraltar. Report of the Thirty-Fourth Meeting of the British Association for the Advancement of Science, pp. 91–92. London: John Murray.

Clark, Graham A., & Lindly, J. M. (1989). The Case for Continuity: Observations of the Biocultural Transition in Europe and Western Asia. In *The Human Revolution: Behavioural and Biological Perspectives on the Origins of Modern Humans*, ed. by Paul Mellars and Chris Stringer, pp. 626–676. Edinburgh: Edinburgh University Press.

Coon, Carleton S. (1939). *The Races of Europe*. New York: The Macmillan Company.

———. (1962). *The Origin of Races*. New York: Alfred A Knopf.

Coon, Carleton S, & Hunt Jr., Edward E. (1965). *The Living Races of Man*. New York: Knopf.

Corbey, R. (1995). Introduction: Missing Links or the Ape's Place in Nature. In *Ape, Man, Apeman: Changing Views Since 1600*, ed by R. Corbey and B. Theunissen, pp. 1–10. Leiden: Department of Prehistory, Leiden University.

Dally, Eugène. (1862a). Rapport sur les Races Indigènes et sur l'Archéologie du Nouveau-Monde. *Bulletin de la Societe d'Anthropologie de Paris*, *3*, 374–408.

———. (1862b). Note en Réponse à M. Pruner-Bey sur les Travaux Anthropolgiques de l'École Américaine. *Bulletin de la Societe d'Anthropologie de Paris*, *3*, 450–455.

Darwin, Charles. (1859/1964). *On the Origin of Species. A Facsimile of the First Edition with an Introduction by Ernst Mayr*. Cambridge, MA: Harvard University Press.

———. (1871). *The Descent of Man, and Selection in Relation to Sex*. London: J. Murray.

Deniker, Joseph. (1892). Anthropologie et Ethnologie. *La Grande Encyclopédie*, *16*, 807–813.

———. (1897a). Les Races Européens. *Bulletin de la Societe d'Anthropologie de Paris*, IVe Série, *8*, 189–208.

———. (1897b). Les Races de l'Europe. *Bulletin de la Societe d'Anthropologie de Paris*, IVe Série, *8*, 291–302.

———. (1898). Les Races de l'Europe. *L'Anthropologie, 9*, 113–133.

———. (1900). *Les Races et les Peoples de la Terre.* Paris: Schleicher Frères.

De Puydt, M, & Lohest, M. (1886). L'Homme Contemporain du Mammouth à Spy (Namur). *Annales Fédération Archéologie Historique de Belgique, 2*, 207–235.

Dubois, Eugene. (1894). *Pithecanthropus erectus, eine Menschenänliche Uebergangsform aus Java.* Batavia: Landesdruckerei.

Eisenhower, John S. D. (2001). *Yanks: The Epic Story of the American Army in World War I.* New York: The Free Press.

Everdell, William R. (1997). *The First Moderns: Profiles in the Origin of Twentieth-Century Thought.* Chicago: University of Chicago Press.

Falconer, Hugh. (1865). *On Fossil and Human Remains of the Gibraltar cave.* Report of the Thirty-Fourth Meeting of the British Assoc. for the Advancement of Science. London: John Murray.

Fraipont, Charles. (1936). Les Hommes Fossils d'Engis. *Archives de l'Inststite de Paléontologie Humaine Mémoire, 16*, 1–52.

Fraipont, H, & Lohest, M. (1886). La Race Humaine de Néanderthal ou de Canstadt en Belgique. *Bulletin de l'Academie Royale Belgique, 12*, 741–784.

Gaudry, Albert. (1878). *Les Enchainements du Monde Animal dans les Temps Géologiques: Mammifères Tertiaires.* Paris: G. Masson.

Giles, Eugene. (1997). Hooton E(arnest) A(lbert). In *History of Physical Anthropology: An Encyclopedia. Volume I*, ed. by Frank Spencer, pp. 499–501. New York: Garland Publishers.

Glangeaud, P. (1910). *Albert Gaudry and the Evolution of the Animal Kingdom. Annual Report of the Board of Regents of the Smithsonian Institution, 1909*, pp. 417–429. Washington, DC: Government Printing Office.

Gorjanović-Kramberger, K. (1901). Der Paläolitische Mensch und seine Zeitgenossen aus dem Diluvium von Krapina in Kroatien. *Mitteil Anthropology Gesell in Wien* 31: 164–197.

———. (1906). *Der diluviale Mensch von Krapina in Kroatien.* Wiesbaden: C.W. Kriedel.

Gould, Stephen J. (1978). Morton's Ranking of Races by Cranial Capacity: Unconscious Manipulation of Data May Be a Scientific Norm. *Science, 200*, 503–509.

———. (1981). *The Mismeasure of Man.* New York: WW Norton.

———. (1993). American Polygeny and Craniometry before Darwin: Blacks and Indians as Separate, Inferior Species. In *The "Racial" Economy of Science: Toward a Democratic Future*, ed by S. Harding, pp. 84–115. Bloomington: Indiana University Press.

———. (1996). *The Mismeasure of Man, Revised Edition.* New York: Norton.

Grant, Madison. (1916). *The Passing of the Great Race.* New York: C. Scribner's Sons.

Gregory, William K. (1950). Franz Weidenreich, 1873–1948. In *The Shorter Anthropological Papers of Franz Weidenreich Published in the Period 1939–1948*, ed. by Sherwood L. Washburn and D. Wolfson, pp. 256–267. New York: The Viking Fund.

Haller, J. S. (1971). *Outcasts from Evolution: Attitudes of Racial Inferiority, 1859–1900*. Urbana: University of Illinois Press

Hammond, Michael. (1988). The Shadow Man Paradigm in Paleoanthropology. In *Bones, Bodies, Behavior: Essays on Biological Anthropology*, ed. by George W. Stocking, Jr., pp. 117–137. *History of Anthropology*, Vol. 5. Madison: University of Wisconsin Press.

Harvey, J. (1983). Evolutionism Transformed: Positivists and Materialists in the Société d'Anthropologie de Paris from the Second Empire to the Third Republic. In *The Wider Domain of Evolutionary Thought*, ed. by D. Oldroyd and I. Langham, pp. 289–310. Dordrecht: D. Reidel.

Heberer, G. (1955). Pierre Marcellin Boule. In *Forscher und Wissenschaftler in Heutigen Europa*, ed. by H. Schwerte and W. Spengler. *Gestalter Unserer Zeit* 4: 288–295.

Heim, Jean-Louis. (1976). Les Hommes Fossiles de La Ferrassie. Tome I: Le Gisement. Les Squelettes Adultes (Crâne et Squelette du Tronc). *Archives de la Institute de Paléontologie Humaine, 35*, 1–331

———. (1982). Les Hommes Fossiles de La Ferrassie. Tome II: Les Squelettes Adultes (Squelettes des Members). *Archives de la Institute de Paléontologie Humaine, 38*, 1–272.

———. (1989). La Nouvelle Reconstitution de Crâne de la Chapelle-aux-Saints: Méthode et Resultants. *Bulletin et Mémoires de la Societe d'Anthropologie de Paris, 1*(1–2), 95–118.

Hoche, AE. (1939). Strassburg und seine Universität. Ein Buch der Erinnerung. München: I.F. Lehmann's Verlag.

Holton, G. (1982). Introduction: Einstein and the Shaping of Our Imagination. In *Albert Einstein: Historical and Cultural Perspectives*, ed. by G. Holton and Y. Elkana, pp. vii–xxxi. Princeton: Princeton University Press.

Hooton, Earnest A. (1946). *Up From the Ape, 2nd Ed*. New York: The Macmillan Co.

Horsman, Reginald. (1987). *Josiah Nott of Mobile: A Southerner, Physician and Racial Theorist*. Baton Rouge: LSU Press.

Hrdlička, Aleš. (1914). The Most Ancient Skeletal Remains of Man. Annual Report of the Board of Regents of the Smithsonian Institution for the Year Ending 1913, pp. 491–552. Washington, DC: Smithsonian Institution.

———. (1918). Physical Anthropology: Its Scope and Aims, Its History and Present Status in America. C. Recent History and Present Status of the Science in North America. *American Journal of Physical Anthropology, 1*(4), 377–402.

———. (1919). *Physical Anthropology, Its Scope and Aims; Its history and Present Status in the United States*. Philadelphia: Wistar Institute of Anatomy and Biology.

———. (1927). The Neanderthal Phase of Man. Huxley Memorial Lecture. *Journal of the Royal Anthropological Institute, 57*, 249–291.

———. (1930). *The Skeletal Remains of Early Man.* Washington, DC: Smithsonian Institution .

Keegan, John. (1999). *The First World War.* New York: Alfred A Knopf.

Keith, Arthur. (1911). *Ancient Types of Man.* London: Harper & Brothers.

———. (1912). The Relationship of Neanderthal Man and Pithecanthropus to Modern Man. *Nature, 89,* 155–156.

———. (1915). *The Antiquity of Man.* London: Williams & Norgate.

———. (1946). *Essays of Human Evolution.* London: Watts & Co.

———. (1950). *An Autobiography.* London: Watts & Co.

———. (1955). *Darwin Revalued.* London: Watts.

Klein, Richard G. (2000). Archeology and the Evolution of Human Behavior. *Evolutionary Anthropology, 9*(1), 17–36.

———. (2001). Southern Africa and Modern Human Origins. *Journal of Anthropological Research, 57*(1), 1–16.

———. (2003). Whither the Neanderthals? *Science, 299,* 1525–1527.

Lartet, Louis. (1868). Une Sépulture des Troglodytes du Périgord (Crânes des Eyzies). *Bulletin de la Societe d'Anthropologie de Paris,* 2e Série, *3,* 335–349.

Livingstone, David N. (1987). *Nathaniel Southgate Shaler and the Culture of American Science.* Tuscaloosa, AL: University of Alabama Press.

Livingstone, Frank B. (1962). On the Non-Existence of Human Races. *Current Anthropology, 3*(3), 279.

———. (1964). On the Non-Existence of Human Races. In *The Concept of Race,* ed. by Ashley Montagu, pp. 46–60. New York: The Free Press of Glencoe.

Lovejoy, Arthur O. (1936). *The Great Chain of Being: A Study in the History of an Idea.* Cambridge, MA: Harvard University Press.

Lyell, Charles. (1873). *The Geological Evidences of the Antiquity of Man: With an Outline of* Glacial and Post-Tertiary Geology and Remarks on the Origin of Species With *Special Reference to Man's First Appearance on the Earth, 4th Ed. Revised.* London: John Murray.

Maška, C. (1901). La Station Paléolithique de Predmost en Moravie (Autriche). *L'Anthropologie, 12,* 147–149.

———. (1885). *Der Diluviale Mensch in Mähren.* Neutitschein: R. Horsch.

Matiegka, J. (1934). *Homo Předmostensis. Fosilní člověk z Předmostí na Moravě.* I. Lebky. L'homme Fossile de Předmostí en Moravie (Tchécoslovaquie). V. Praze— Prague: Nákladem České Akademié Věd a Uměni.

Meigs, C.D. (1851). *A Memoir of S. G. Morton.* Philadelphia: T.K. & P.G. Collins.

Michael, John S. (1988). A New Look at Morton's Craniological Research. *Current Anthropology, 29*(2), 349–354.

Millar, R. (1972). *The Piltdown Man.* New York: Ballantine Books.

Montagu, Ashley. (1942). *Man's Most Dangerous Myth: The Fallacy of Race.* New York: Columbia University Press.

———. (1944). Aleš Hrdlička, 1869–1943. *American Anthropologist, 46*(1), 113–117.

Montgomery, W. M. (1974). Germany. In *The Comparative Reception of Darwinism,* ed. by T.F.Glick, pp. 81–116. Austin: University of Texas Press.

Morton, Samuel G. (1834). *Synopsis of the Organic Remains of the Cretaceous Group of the United States.* Philadelphia: Key & Biddle.

———. (1839). *Crania Americana: Or, a Comparative View of the Skulls of Various Aboriginal Nations of North and South America; to Which Is Prefixed an Essay on the Varieties of the Human Species.* Philadelphia: J. Dobson.

———. (1844). *Crania Ægyptiaca; Or Observations on Egyptian Ethnography Derived from Anatomy, History and the Monuments.* Philadelphia: John Pennington.

———. (1847). Hybridity in Animals, Considered in Reference to the Unity of the Human Species. *American Journal of Science,* 2nd Series, *3*(7), 39–50; *3*(8), 203–212.

Mowbray, K, & Gannont, P. J. (2001). Unique Anatomy of the Neanderthal skull. *Athena Review, 2*(4), 59–64.

Nott, Josia C., & Gliddon, George R. (1854). *Types of Mankind.* Philadelphia: Lippincott & Grambo.

———. (1857). *Indigenous Races of the Earth.* Philadelphia: JB Lippincott.

Patterson, Henry S. (1853). Memoir of the Life and Scientific Labors of Samuel George Morton. In *Types of Mankind: or Ethnological Researches Based Upon Ancient Monuments, Paintings, Sculptures, and Crania of Races, and Upon their Natural, Geographical, Philological, and Biblical History: Illustrated by Selections from the Unedited Papers of Samuel George Morton, M.D., and by Additional Contributions from Prof. L. Agassiz, LL.D.; W.Usher, M.D.; and Prof. H. S. Patterson, M.D. 7th ed.,* ed. by Josia C. Nott and George R. Gliddon, pp. xvii–lvii. Philadelphia: Lippincott, Grambo & Co.

Pauly, Philip J. (2001). *Biologists and the Promise of American Life: From Merriwether Lewis to Alfred Kinsey.* Princeton: Princeton University Press.

Phillips, M.E. (1953). The Academy of Natural Sciences of Philadelphia. *Transactions of the American Philosophical Society, 43*(1), 266–271.

Pouchet, G. (1865). *De la Pluralité des Races Humaines: Essai Anthropologique.* Paris: V. Masson et Fils.

Quatrefages, A., & Hamy, E.-T. (1882). *Crania Ethnica.* Paris: JB Baillière & Fils.

Rink, W. J., Shwarcz, H. P., Smith, Fred H., & Radovčić, J. (1995). ESR Dating of Tooth Enamel from the Neanderthal Site of Krapina, Croatia. *Nature, 378,* 24.

Ripley, William Z. (1897–1898). The Racial Geography of Europe: A sociological Study. *Appleton's Popular Science Monthly, 50,* 454–468, 577–594, 757–780; *51,* 17–34, 192–209, 289–307, 423–453, 433–453, 613–634,721–739; *52,* 49–68, 145–170, 304, 469–486, 591–608.

———. (1899). *The Races of Europe: A Sociological Study.* New York: D. Appleton and Co.

Schaaffhausen, Hermann. (1857). Theilen des Menschlichen Skelettes im Neanderthal bei Hochdal. *Verhand Naturhistor Verein Preuss Rheinlande Westfalens, 14,* 50–52.

———. (1858). Zur Kentniss der älteren Rassenschädel. *Archives fur Anatomie und Physiologie Wissensch Medizin,* 453–477.

———. (1861). On the Crania of the Most Ancient Races of Men. *Natural History Review, 1*(2), 155–175.

Schiller, F. (1979). *Paul Broca: Founder of French Anthropology; Explorer of the Brain.* Berkeley, CA: University of California Press.

Schmitz, R., Serre, D., Bonani, G., Feine, S., Hillgruber, F., Krainitzki, H., Pääbo, S., & Smith, F. H. (2002). The Neandertal Type Site Revisited: Interdisciplinary Investigations of Skeletal Remains in the Neander Valley, Germany. *Proceedings of the National Academy of Sciences, 99*(20), 13342–13347.

Schultz, Adolph H. (1945). Biographical Memoir of Aleš Hrdlička. National Academy of Sciences. *Biographical Memoirs, 23,* 305–338.

Schwalbe, Gustav. (1896). *Pithecanthropus erectus,* eine Stammform des Menschen. *Anatomie Anziger, 12,* 1–22.

———. (1899). Studien über *Pithecanthropus erectus* Dubois. *Zeitschrift Morphologie Anthropologie, 1,* 1–240.

———. (1901). Der Neandertal Schädel. *Jahrbüch des Vereins der Altertums im Rheinlande, 106,* 1–72.

———. (1906). *Studien zur Vorgeschichte des Menschen.* Stuttgart: E. Schweizerbartsche Verlagsbuchhandlung (E. Nägele).

———. (1909). The Descent of Man. In *Darwin and Modern Science. Essays in Commemoration of the Centenary of the Birth of Charles Darwin and the Fiftieth Anniversary of the Publication of the Origin of Species,* ed. by A.C. Seward, pp. 112–136. Cambridge: Cambridge University Press.

———. (1914). Kritische Besprechung von Boules Werk: L'Homme Fossil de la Chapelle aux Saints mit Eigenen Untersuchungen. *Zeitschrift für Morphologie und Anthropologie, 16,* 527–610.

Shaler, Nathaniel S. (1891). *Nature and Man in America.* New York: C. Scribner's Sons.

———. (1909). *The Autobiography of Nathaniel Southgate Shaler with a Supplementary Memoir by His Wife.* Boston: Houghton Mifflin.

Snow, Clyde P. (1959). *The Two Cultures and the Scientific Revolution.* New York: Cambridge University Press.

Sollas, William J. (1908). On the Cranial and Facial Characters of the Neanderthal race. *Philosophical Transactions of the Royal Society of London, 199,* 281–339.

Stanton, William R. (1960). *The Leopard's Spots: Scientific Attitudes Toward Race in America, 1815–1859.* Chicago: University of Chicago Press.

St. Aubyn, G. (1979). *Edward VII: Prince and King.* London: Collins.

Stebbins, Robert E. (1974). France. In *The Comparative Reception of Darwinism,* ed. by T. F. Glick, pp. 117–163. Austin: University of Texas Press.

Stein, G. (1937). *Everybody's Autobiography.* New York: Random House.

Stoddard, Lothrop. (1920). *The Rising Tide of Color: Against White World Supremacy.* New York: Scribner.

Straus, Lawrence G. (1995). The Upper Paleolithic of Europe: An Overview. *Evolutionary Anthropology, 4*(1), 4–16.

Stringer, Chris, & Gamble, C. (1993). *In Search of the Neanderthals: Solving the Puzzle of Human Origins.* London: Thames & Hudson.

Stringer, Chris, & McKie, R. (1997). *African Exodus: The Origins of Modern Humanity.* New York: Henry Holt & Co.

Szombathy, Josef. (1901). Un Crâne de la Race de Cro-Magnon Trouvé en Moravie. *L'Anthropologie, 12,* 150–157.

Tattersall, Ian. (1995). *The Fossil Trail: How We Know What We Think We Know About Human Evolution.* New York: Oxford University Press.

Tattersall, Ian, and Jeffrey H. Schwartz. (2000). *Extinct Humans.* New York: Westview Press.

Theunissen, B. (1989). *Eugène Dubois and the Ape-Man from Java: The History of the First "Missing Link" and Its Discoverer.* Dordrecht: Kluwer Academic Publishers.

Topinard, Paul. (1876). *L'anthropologie.* Paris: C. Reinwald.

———. (1879). De la Notion de Race en Anthropologie. *Revue d'Anthropologie,* Série 2, *8*(4), 589–660.

Trinkaus, Erik, & Shipman, Pat. (1992). *The Neandertals: Changing the Image of Mankind.* New York: Alfred A Knopf.

Wegener, Alfred. (1920). *Die Entstehung der Kontinente und Oceane, 2nd Ed.* Braunschweig: F. Vieweg & Sohn.

Weidenreich, Franz. (1928). Entwicklungs-und Rassentypen des *Homo primigenius. Naturund Volk, 58*(1), 1–13; *58*(2), 51–62.

———. (1940). Some Problems Dealing with Ancient Man. *American Anthropologist, 42*(3), 375–383.

———. (1943). The "Neanderthal Man" and the Ancestors of "Homo Sapiens." *American Anthropologist, 45*(1), 39–48.

———. (1947). The Trend of Human Evolution. *Evolution, 1*(4), 221–236.

Wilson, J. Tuzo. (1963). Continental Drift. *Scientific American, 208*(4), 86–100.

Chapter 3

Franz Boas's Place in American Physical Anthropology and Its Institutions

by

Michael A. Little

INTRODUCTION

Sherwood Washburn (1911–2000; 1984, personal communication) observed that there is a tradition of ignoring Franz Boas (1858–1942) in representing the history of physical anthropology. Why this is so is not clear. It may be that Boas's contributions to sociocultural anthropology, anthropological linguistics, and folklore overwhelmed his contributions to physical anthropology; but this is unlikely since he produced more than 180 works that were in the subfield of physical anthropology. Another reason might be that Boas only trained six students in physical anthropology at Columbia University, one of whom made major contributions to the field, whereas he trained many others in branches of sociocultural anthropology—former students who dominated the profession up until the end of World War II (Darnell, 2001, 33). On the other hand, his research designs in physical anthropology influenced a number of physical anthropologists who were trained at Harvard University and elsewhere, so he clearly had influences on younger students. Since Boas founded and promoted the four-field approach to an integrated anthropology, one would expect him to have had loyalties to each subfield. But was that the case and were they equivalent loyalties? Boas had many identities and many loyalties in science and in his profession of anthropology over time, and he was extraordinarily active during his long life. He also played important political roles in numerous professional associations including the National Academy of Sciences (NAS, in which he was an elected member), the National Research Council (NRC) of the NAS, the American Association for the Advancement of Science (AAAS), the American Anthropological Association (AAA), the American Association of Physical Anthropologists

(AAPA), and many others. Despite his incredible physical and intellectual energies up until his early 80s, he must have had priorities in devoting his time and energy to each of these endeavors, as well as to promoting specific areas in anthropology.

Boas was a very powerful figure and certainly the most influential anthropologist in the United States during the first four decades of the 20th century (see Figure 3.1). Most importantly, this was the period in which anthropology became defined as a profession in the United States, and more than any other anthropologist, Boas and his students defined this professional identity. The purpose of this chapter is to provide a review in the broad sense of Boas's contributions to physical anthropology—that is, to provide an overview not only of his research and scholarly activities, but also his contributions to defining the field of physical anthropology as it exists today: its research ideas, its institutions, and its directions. In addition to Boas, there were several other scientists who were central figures in the subfield of physical anthropology: Aleš Hrdlička (1869–1943) at the Smithsonian Institution, Earnest A. Hooton (1887–1954) at Harvard University, Raymond Pearl (1879–1940) at Johns Hopkins University, and T. Wingate Todd (1885–1938) at Western Reserve University (now Case Western Reserve University). Franz Boas's relations with these figures will be explored, as well.

BOAS'S PHYSICAL ANTHROPOLOGY RESEARCH

Biographical material on Franz Boas is extensive (Kroeber, 1943; Herskovits, 1953; Cole, 1999; N. Boas, 2004), so his early life will not be discussed here, except to say that he grew up in Minden (Westphalia), Germany, and received his doctorate in physical sciences at Kiel University. Because of his creative drive, genius, and adventurousness, he was capable of exploring and generating interest in a variety of topics and fields. In addition, a combination of almost obsessive hard work and rapid learning ability enabled him to master large amounts of material very quickly. Another quality that he had was a truly superior logical sense that was reinforced by his strong scientific training in the German tradition. His broad schooling in Germany in the "hard sciences" and mathematics, biology, geography, and later, ethnology, anatomy, anthropometry, and Native American languages gave him the unique background to synthesize what later became "American Anthropology." It was the two major field experiences of Baffin Island Eskimos (1883–1884) and Northwest Coast Indians (1886–1887) that bracketed his further training in Berlin (1884–1886) with Adolf Bastian (1826–1905) and Rudolf Virchow (1821–1902) that defined his later professional life. Although he had some

Figure 3.1. Franz Boas in the early 1900s (courtesy of the American Philosophical Society).

training in anatomy, skeletal biology, and anthropometry in Germany, his interests in physical anthropology research did not begin in earnest until 1888. At this time, he traveled to British Columbia for two months under the support of the British Association for the Advancement of Science (BAAS) and, among other activities, conducted anthropometric measurements and collected skeletal material of Native Americans. The following year (1889) he took his first full academic position at Clark University in Worcester, Massachusetts, and developed further interests in physical anthropology, particularly in child growth (Cole, 1999,142ff).

Anthropometrics of Native North Americans

Boas was well trained in anthropometric measurement technique by Virchow in Germany (Boas, 2004, 27; Cole, 1999, 67), but had little opportunity to apply these skills until the late 1880s. Between 1888 and 1902, Boas supervised the anthropometric measurements of about 16,000 living Native North Americans (U.S. and Canadian), with an additional 2,000 Siberian natives who were measured. These surveys were conducted as a part of the BAAS work in British Columbia and later in Southern California, the Chicago World's Columbian Exposition, the Jessup North Pacific Expedition, and the Huntington California Expedition. By far, the largest number of Native Americans were measured for the World's Columbian Exposition in 1892. Some of these data were analyzed by Boas (1894a), but the vast amount of data remained unanalyzed until recovered by Jantz (Jantz et al., 1992; see below). A part of this vast program of Native American anthropometry was commissioned, but the question arose about why Boas would collect such substantial amounts of data, yet with a limited ability to thoroughly analyze the data (by hand, using mathematical calculations).

Clearly, Boas was interested in Native American origins (Stocking, 1974, 190), and in the case of the World's Columbia Exposition, some of the data were used for exhibits. Jantz (1995) cited an early German paper by Boas (1895) in which he suggested that the need for large samples was justified by the very slight differences among *human varieties* of Native American peoples. The question of admixture and "racial crossing" effects also were important to Boas, in the context of the prevailing view that admixed offspring of Native American and European parents were somehow inferior and had reduced fertility. This issue arose because of Boas's interests in "deviation from type" or variation outside the fixed racial model. Based on stature, craniofacial measurements, and fertility, Boas (1884) demonstrated that the stature of hybrids was greater than for either parent, that facial measurements were intermediate, but tended toward one parent or the other, and that fertility of Native American–European unions was equivalent to full Native American unions. Jantz (2006) believed that Boas's careful accumulation of all of the data on Native Americans reflected his awareness that these peoples were in decline and that there was a need to preserve as much of their biological characteristics and life ways as possible.

Biometrics

Before discussing the growth studies, a brief comment on Boas's skills in statistics (biometrics) is required. Much of the early, but limited, analysis that was done on anthropometry of Native North Americans required only basic descriptive statistics. Later work on the growth of children, on attempts to sort out hereditary from environmental causes, and on the migrant data required more sophisticated statistics. It was these new statistical procedures that Boas explored and developed and began to apply during the late 1880s and early 1890s. Tanner (1959) reported that Boas (1894b) wrote a paper on correlation only six years after Francis Galton (1822–1911) introduced the correlation coefficient. And Boas corresponded with Karl Pearson (1857–1936), Galton's student, who refined the correlation method. Boas met Pearson on a later trip to England. In the 1894 paper, Boas discussed the cephalic index and differences in predictions of length from breadth and breadth from length, suggesting that because the two measures were not well correlated, then other factors were influencing the cephalic index. Early on in the paper, he stated the fundamental problem in which he was interested: "Any anatomical or physiological measurement of an organism may be considered a function of the general conditions of heredity and environment affecting the measured individual as a whole and in those parts which have been subjected to measurement" (Boas, 1894b, 313–314). He continued pursuing correlations with cephalic index in a later paper (Boas, 1899) where he found that there was much more variation in head length than in head breadth. In both papers he attempted to get at the sources of hereditary and environmental variation that were expressed in this index that so many anthropologists held to be inviolate.

Tanner (1959), Herskovits (1943), and Howells (1959) have all emphasized Boas's sophistication and brilliance in attempting to solve conceptual problems by systematic use of mathematics and statistics. It is quite clear that few anthropologists understood the bases of Boas's arguments from his mathematics, and it was only in the second half of the 20th century that the scope of his discoveries was appreciated. Gabriel Lasker (1999, 65) as a student at Harvard visited Boas shortly before Boas's death in 1942 to seek advice on his dissertation that dealt with a "Boas model" of Chinese migration in America. While Lasker sat before him, Boas, with pencil and paper, did a statistical power analysis and informed Lasker that his sample size was too small to demonstrate a change in cephalic index! Lasker noted that despite flaws in the design that Boas pointed out, he was still able to demonstrate differences for other measures.

Growth Studies

James M. Tanner (1959, 1981), a British human biologist, rediscovered Boas's growth research and has described, in some detail, the magnitude of his contributions. Boas was drawn into human growth research by G. Stanley

Hall (1844–1924), who invited Boas to join the faculty at the newly founded Clark University in Worcester, Massachusetts. He arrived at Clark in the fall of 1889. His earliest research was to initiate a longitudinal anthropometric study (repeated measures of the same individuals) of Worcester schoolchildren in 1891—the first survey ever conducted in the United States. Boas realized that longitudinal data give much greater precision and information than cross-sectional growth data (measures of groups of individuals of different ages, all at about the same time). Using these longitudinal data studies, he was able to explore statistical correlation of the Worcester schoolchildren from one age to the next (i.e., height at age five years vs. height at age six years). As noted above, this work was done only very shortly after Karl Pearson had developed the statistical procedure in the United Kingdom. Although Boas left Clark University after only a year of the study, these longitudinal data (collected in May 1891 and May 1892) gave him important insights into variations in growth rates (Boas, 1897). This was also probably the first experimental evidence that he accumulated to give him information on human plasticity.

The next major contribution was under the auspices of the World's Columbian Exposition in Chicago. In addition to the anthropometric survey of Native North Americans, Boas organized the compilation of child growth data (ages 5 to 19 years) from his own Worcester study, and existing data from Oakland, Toronto, Boston, Milwaukee, and St. Louis. There were nearly 90,000 children in this sample from cities across the United States which served as the first reference values for comparison of child growth in the United States (Boas, 1898). Boas also was strongly interested in the relationship between physical growth and mental growth and their relationships to social class (Tanner, 1959, 82ff), and he was interested in debunking the belief that mental development depended wholly on physical development. He also argued that the biased words "bright" and "dull" were a reflection of mental *development* and should be replaced with the more descriptive words, "advanced" and "retarded." In conjunction with some of these ideas, he developed a concept of "physiological age" (later called "biological age") that reflected the developmental age of given children. This developmental age was related to but not perfectly correlated with chronological age and showed considerable individual variation. Several years later, he observed from tooth eruption sequences that boys were substantially behind girls in their development by as early as five years of age.

Whereas many of Boas's contributions to our knowledge of child growth were substantial and innovative, his most lasting contribution was in characterizing the complexity of adolescent growth. This was built on his work before 1912, but between this date and 1930 he published nothing about his research on human growth. This later work, however, was substantial, despite the fact that Boas was 72 years old when he began publishing again in this area (Boas, 1930; 1932; 1933; 1935). What he did in this later work was to identify the basic characteristics of adolescent growth velocity by grouping boys and girls separately according to peak velocity. He found that those who were taller at age 11 years were not necessarily taller as adults, and the earlier the growth acceleration, the higher the peak velocity (Tanner, 1981).

In a later study, Boas (1936; 1940a) reported that age cohorts of children from the Horace Mann School of Columbia University had become larger between 1909 and 1935. He attributed this to positive changes in social and economic conditions, leading to modification of the "tempo of development" of children. This phenomenon has been documented repeatedly since that time and is referred to as the "secular trend" in growth (Tanner, 1962, 143–155).

All of this later, detailed analytical work was done at the same time that he served as editor of the *Handbook of American Indian Languages, Columbia University Contributions to Anthropology,* and the *International Journal of American Linguistics.* As Tanner (1981, 235) observed, "Boas' first paper on growth appeared in 1892, his last in 1941." During the course of those 50 years his original discoveries about the processes of child growth alone would have established him as a great scientist and a founder of a major area of research.

The Migration Study

The study for which Boas (1911a; 1912a; 1912b) is best known is that of eastern and southern European immigrants to New York City. It was one of the earliest research designs applied to investigate the influence of the environment on human biological characteristics, and the design has been used frequently since then. An important smaller-scale study by a close younger colleague of Boas in New York City preceded his study by several years. Maurice Fishberg (1979–1934) (1905; 1905–1907), a physician, was Boas's colleague who measured immigrant Jews in New York City and compared them with published data on Jews from Eastern Europe (Mascie-Taylor & Little, 2004). Fishberg (1905–1907) found that first-generation migrant adults (born in Europe) were taller than their European counterparts, and that second-generation migrants (born in the U.S.) were taller than first-generation migrants. Here Fishberg observed the process of *selective migration* as well as *plasticity* in a new environment. This work stimulated Boas's interest in testing the effects of environmental change on immigrants. In 1908, at the suggestion of Fishberg, Boas applied for funds to the U.S. Immigration Commission, which had the task of assessing the effects of eastern and southern European migration to the United States (Stocking, 1968, 175; 1974, 190). Later that year, Boas conducted a pilot study of 14-year-old Jewish boys in New York high schools, comparing those whose parents arrived before 1880, between 1880 and 1890, and after 1890. The boys whose parents arrived earlier were taller and performed better in school than those arriving most recently. He also observed that head shape was less brachycephalic (round-headed) in those boys whose parents had migrated to the United States earlier (letter from Boas, September 3, 1908, in Stocking, 1974, 206–210).

Between 1908 and 1910, Boas's team of anthropometrists measured nearly 18,000 immigrants. Differences between Boas's and Fishberg's earlier results were that Boas measured head dimensions and the stature of large numbers of children, as well as adults, by age of immigration. Boas's results supported Fishberg's observations on stature and these results have withstood the test of time. However, their conclusions on cephalic measurements were not in agreement. According to Fishberg (1905–1907, 137), "While the effects of environment are to be considered in speaking of stature, this is a negligible quantity in the case of the head form. Extensive craniological research has conclusively shown that the shape of the head depends only on race and heredity." Boas (1911a; 1912a), on the other hand, found changes in cephalic indices among first- and second-generation Eastern European, Sicilian, and Neapolitan migrants, which led him to argue against the fixity of racial characteristic for the skull. Typology, racial purity, the predominance of heredity, and the inferiority of some races were concepts against which Boas was fighting, and these results led him to conclude that a changing cephalic index was evidence against these traditional beliefs. A finding that was independent of the cephalic index results was that working-class and poor children from large sibships tended to be smaller on average than those from small sibships, demonstrating the combined effects of poverty and family size on developmental plasticity. Since there was considerable criticism leveled against the migrant study, Boas (1912b) published a long paper in the *American Anthropologist*, which was largely a summary of the work and a defense against critics of the larger work (Boas, 1911a, 1912a).

Several years later, Fishberg's and Boas's data on Jews was re-examined by Morant and Samson (1936) who found that the American-born children were only barely significantly different from their parents in some head dimensions after approximate age and sex corrections were made. The next year, Fisher and Gray (1937) reanalyzed Boas's data on Sicilians and were concerned about non-paternity and reliability. They also suggested that the published head measurements seemed open to serious suspicion. Much of the criticism of this classic study seems to focus on interpretation of the results and the magnitudes of the differences or patterns of change. Some of these same issues were raised in modern restudies of Boas's data described below.

Race, Heredity, and Environment

The late 19th and early 20th centuries were characterized by beliefs in fixed racial types, accompanied by beliefs in the superiority of some racial groups over others (racism or racialism). There was a contrary opinion in the form of Franz Boas. Boas made remarkable contributions to dispelling the myth of fixed or pure races and the importance of the environment in structuring the character of human populations. He was not, however, a disbeliever in the importance of inheritance or even "race" (as a population of genetically related individuals) in characterizing and understanding humans. Rather, he was interested in the superimposition of environmental influences on these hereditary characteristics, particularly during growth or development from conception to adulthood. These interests in human plasticity in the context of race were almost certainly stimulated, perhaps initiated, by his research on child and adolescent growth and development at Clark University in 1891 (Stocking, 1968, 165,; Tanner, 1959; 1981). Prior to this, his ideas were probably somewhat more traditional and based on his training with Rudolf Virchow in Berlin (Stocking, 1968, 166). Another experience contributing to Boas's maturation as a population scientist came from his exposure to the work of Galton and his younger associate, Pearson (both pioneers in biometrics), during a visit to England in 1889. Stocking (1968, 167–168) suggested "that Boas' point of view was developed in a Galtonian context." Galton, who is now pejoratively identified as the "Father of Eugenics," was, in fact, a distinguished population biologist who made many positive contributions to human sciences. It was after this visit to England that Boas corresponded with Pearson and published his first statistical paper on correlation (Boas, 1894b).

Throughout Boas's professional career as an anthropologist, he used the term "type" which was synonymous with "race," "population," or any group that had some sort of hereditary relationship (Goldstein, 1948). Boas had a sophisticated and modern view of a population that matured as he grew older, and he knew very well the difference between his use of the term "type" and a *typological* use of the term. His use of the term "type" was not in the traditional context of physical anthropologists in the early 1900s (Darnell, 1982). In one of Boas's (1943, 312) last papers, published posthumously in *Science* (from a talk for the American Ethnological Society on May 13, 1942), he gave a good example of the dangers of typological thinking. With reference to "ideal type," he stated in a study conducted of all 1,024 Harvard students measured (with averages determined) that only one might conform to the ideal type. "In other words, the type is a subjective construct. Whether it has an objective reality must be determined by special investigations" (Boas, 1943, 312). Later, Boas (1943, 313) stated with reference to evolution, demography, and plasticity, "It has been recognized that differential birthrate, mortality and migration may modify the frequency of various types, but insufficient stress has been laid on the question in how far the children of parents of a given form may differ for physiological reasons from their parents, in other words in how far external conditions may modify the type."

Following World War II, during the resurgence of cultural evolutionism, Boas's form of historicism, "particularism," and opposition to late-19th-century cultural evolutionism was criticized by Leslie White (1963) and by Marvin Harris (1968; Lewis, 2001). It has sometimes been suggested, therefore, that Boas was anti-evolutionist or anti-Darwinian in a general sense. This is not true. Like Charles Darwin, Boas did not think well of Herbert Spencer (1820–1903) with his broad generalizations about social evolution. As already noted, Boas was interested in heredity, process and change, and population. As Lewis (2001, 393) stated, "Boas . . . was aware of the usefulness of the idea of 'variation and selective retention' for a model of human history." Moreover, *population variation* and *selection* were the backbone of Darwinian evolution, and Boas incorporated these ideas into his thinking. Boas's "particularism" was consistent with his scientific outlook and rigor, and is, in fact, similar to the approach to science that many physical anthropologists take today. Contemporary theory in physical anthropology incorporates evolutionary theory, historical process (within evolution), and theory about relationships between human behavior, human biology, and the influences of the social and physical environment.

* * * * *

To summarize: by the age of 42 years at the turn of the century, Boas had organized programs of anthropometric measurements of about 3% of living Native North Americans, had conducted pioneering work on fundamental statistics and applied them to problems of human biology, and had established human growth as an appropriate area of investigation in physical anthropology. Within human growth studies, he had conducted the first longitudinal study, had established the earliest national reference standards for child growth, and had discovered principles of growth (growth tempos, correlations, environmental influences) that were major scientific discoveries. By the age of 72 years in 1930, he had designed and conducted a large-scale study of migration in which the findings ran counter to basic outdated 19th-century beliefs about race, he continued to write on race and human rights (a lifelong commitment), and, after a hiatus of 18 years, returned to studies of human growth to make additional pioneering discoveries. Hence, in addition to his identity as the founder of American anthropology, he can be acknowledged as one of the founders of human biology or the physical anthropology of living populations in the United States, because he (1) debunked the idea of fixed races and understood population concepts, (2) established a migration research design that continues to be used up to the present in studies of human adaptation to the environment, (3) incorporated the social and material environment as influencing human biology (plasticity), (4) made numerous discoveries about the patterns of growth in children and adolescents and established a new field of study within biological anthropology, and (5) advocated an understanding of humans as products of their biology and their behavior that is followed today. Marcus Goldstein (1948) listed all of Boas's publications in physical anthropology, which amounted to more than 180 works. The numbers of publications by category are given in Table 3.1.

Table 3.1.   Franz Boas's Works in Physical Anthropology (after Goldstein 1948).

No. of Papers/Works	Topics
73	Anthropometrics and Osteometrics—particularly of Eskimos and Northwest Coast Indians and other Native Americans.
56	Race and Racial Origins—including critical reviews on prevailing views of races as static units, racial inequality, racism, race prejudice, etc.
26	Human Growth and Development—including the statistics of growth, growth standards, tempo of growth, growth at adolescence, secular changes, etc.
11	Heredity and the Environment—family inheritance, intelligence, eugenics, etc.
9	Migration and Changes in Bodily Form—immigrant study, instability of human types
8	Biometrics (statistics)—including correlation among measurements, anthropology and statistics, etc.
183	Total Papers/Works

BOAS'S TRAINING OF AND INFLUENCES ON STUDENTS

Despite the remarkable amount of research that Boas conducted and the number of graduate students employed as anthropometrists, Boas trained only a handful of students through the PhD degree in physical anthropology. His first student (also the first anthropology doctorate in the U.S.), Alexander F. Chamberlain, was trained at Clark University and assisted with the longitudinal growth study of Worcester schoolchildren initiated in May 1891. But Chamberlain worked with the Algonkian Mississauga Indian language and continued to work in areas of language and folklore. When Boas left Clark University in 1892, after a dispute with G. Stanley Hall, the Clark University president, Chamberlain replaced Boas on the Clark faculty (Cole, 1999, 146).

Boas's first student in physical anthropology at Columbia was Louis R. Sullivan, whose degree from Columbia was conferred in 1922. He did work in craniometry and anthropometry, worked in Hawai'i on Polynesian populations at the Bishop Museum, and had a permanent position at the American Museum of Natural History. According to Hooton (1925), Sullivan had remarkable promise, but died at age 33 years. Isabel Gordon Carter completed her PhD degree on inbreeding in 1928. She published two papers in the *American Journal of Physical Anthropology* (Carter, 1928; 1932), but did little or no work in physical anthropology after this. Ruth Otis Sawtell (Wallis) did an MA degree in 1923 at Radcliffe with Hooton. She worked in France on Azilian skeletal remains while on a Radcliffe fellowship in 1923–1925, but later transferred to Columbia University to work with Boas because of her interests in growth (Collins, 1979). She completed her dissertation on growth and ossification in children at Columbia in 1929 and had a productive career in growth studies and anthropology (Sawtell, 1928; 1929; Wallis, 1931). In later life, she was a successful mystery writer. Eleanor M. Phelps finished the PhD degree in 1932 on the horizontal plane of the skull, and Carolyn Adler Lewis completed her dissertation in 1936 on basal metabolism and human growth. Marcus S. Goldstein also finished his degree at Columbia University in 1936 just a few months before Boas retired from his academic position to become emeritus professor. Goldstein, who had worked both for Aleš Hrdlička at the U.S. National Museum and Harry L. Shapiro, went to New York City as a research associate with F. L. Stanton at the New York University Dental School (Goldstein, 1995). He enrolled at Columbia in 1933 and finished the PhD degree on growth and development of the head and face from infancy to old age in 1936, a topic that Boas had suggested. Goldstein had a long and highly productive career in physical anthropology in the United States and was well respected by his colleagues (Lasker, 1999, 172). After he retired in 1971, he continued his work when he moved to the University of Tel Aviv in Israel.

Another student, Ashley Montagu, who finished the PhD at Columbia in cultural anthropology in 1937, pursued physical anthropology and became quite distinguished after leaving Columbia. Montagu, an Englishman who migrated to the United States in 1927, finished his dissertation under the direction of Ruth Benedict and Franz Boas on procreative beliefs in Australian Aborigines (Marks, 2000). He had studied physical anthropology in London and, following his Columbia PhD, taught anatomy at Hahnemann Medical College in Philadelphia. He became the popularly known physical anthropologist during the latter half of the 20th century in the United States. Montagu conducted studies of adolescent reproduction, was a severe critic of racism and the traditional concept of race, and he was known for popular books on a variety of topics with anthropological perspectives (Montagu, 1942; 1971; 1975). He was also known by his frequent appearances on national televised talk shows. Although Ashley Montagu came to Columbia already having liberal views against racism in the early 1930s, Boas's ideas on race and plasticity must have strengthened Montagu's own outlook on the topic.

Why Boas did not train more students in physical anthropology is not clear. One factor may have been the unpopularity of Boas's brand of physical anthropology. Few individuals in this small profession during the first half of the 20th century were conducting creative, problem-oriented research, and Boas probably realized that it would have been difficult to secure academic positions for his students. Another reason could have been that Boas's major research in physical anthropology was done before the turn of the 20th century, with the migrant study about 10 years later, and then with the revival of the growth studies nearly 20 years later. Hence, Boas's commitment to physical anthropology research was probably subordinated to his other commitments in folklore, language, and cultural studies, particularly since his activities in physical anthropology seemed to punctuate his other professional work. His extended involvement with training of cultural anthropology and linguistic anthropology students while at Columbia University probably gave him less time for other training. Finally, his research into the growth of children and adolescents was personal and both intellectually and quantitatively complex, and graduate students with a background to work in this area were probably rare. Ruth Wallis was one of the rare exceptions.

Despite Boas's limited record of formal student training of physical anthropologists at Columbia University, his influence on students outside of Columbia was substantial, especially on Hooton's students at Harvard. But this influence was felt toward the end of Boas's career during the late 1930s. The earliest study of migrants that was stimulated by Fishberg's and Boas's original work on immigrants was by a cultural anthropologist trained by Boas, Leslie Spier (1929), who measured Japanese-American schoolchildren in Seattle, Washington. His results were consistent with those of Boas. Less than a decade later, Harry S. Shapiro (a former Hooton student), who, along with Frederick S. Hulse (also Hooton's student), studied Japanese who had migrated to Hawai'i and their Hawai'ian-born children (Shapiro, 1939). Other Japanese migrant studies included those of Ito (1942) and Greulich (1957). Goldstein (1943) and Lasker worked with Mexican migrants (1954), Lasker (1946) studied Cantonese Chinese in the United States, and Thieme (1957) worked with Puerto Rican migrants. Frederick Hulse (1981) reviewed these and other of his own studies of migrants (1957; 1968; 1979) in the context of plasticity as a tribute to Boas's initiation of this research design. More recently, there were several migration research designs formulated during the 1960s and 1970s that were proposed to investigate adaptation to the environment or environmental stress (Little & Baker, 1988; Little & Leslie, 1993). Harrison (1966), and later Baker (1976), suggested several research designs for high altitude research, all of them built on Boas's original model. Consequently, Boas's influence on research directions in physical anthropology and on younger students in the field continues to the present.

BOAS'S LEGACY AND RESTUDIES OF BOAS'S DATA

Within the past two decades there have been two major kinds of restudy of Boas's rich databases and his research results: (1) a detailed reanalysis and restudy of the anthropometry of Native North Americans and Siberians initiated by Richard Jantz (1995; 2003; 2006; Jantz et al., 1992; Szathmáry, 1995), and (2) a critical reanalysis of the data from the migration study (Sparks & Jantz, 2002; 2003; Gravlee et al., 2003a; 2003b; Relethford, 2004). Both of these re-inspections of Boas's data reflect the lasting value of his research efforts and his meticulous care in measurement and preservation of basic or raw data.

The Anthropometric Data Collected on Native North Americans

In the 1980s, Richard L. Jantz read a comment by T. Dale Stewart (1973, 107) about the anthropometric measurements of Native North Americans collected or supervised by Franz Boas. After inquiries by Jantz (Jantz et al.,1992), many of the data sheets were found in the basement of the American Museum of Natural History in New York City. This was a veritable treasure trove of information that included data sheets on more than 15,000 individuals, much of the data never fully published. This collection was further augmented by the discovery of 3,000 more data sheets that were held at the American Philosophical Society along with Boas's other papers. As noted above, the bulk of the measurements were gathered as a part of the World's Columbian

Exposition in 1892 and 1893. It was at this time that Frederic Ward Putnam (1839–1915) hired Boas and Boas hired more than 50 anthropometrists who measured nearly 15,000 Native Americans from the United States and Canada (12 measurements were taken, 6 of the head and 6 of the body; Jantz & Spencer, 1997). This work extended over three years. In addition, measurements were done in the Northwest and southern California from 1888 to 1897 (British Association for the Advancement of Science supported), as a part of the Jessup North Pacific Expedition from 1897 to 1902 (Northwest Coast and Siberian populations), and of central California native populations as a component of the Huntington California Expedition from 1899 to 1902 (American Association for the Advancement of Science supported). Jantz (2006) noted that at the time that Boas was active in collecting anthropometric data on Native North Americans, their total population size was estimated at 530,000 and was at its nadir (turn of the 19th century). It is remarkable that based on the 16,000 or so subjects measured, this sample constituted more than 3% of the total population of Native North Americans alive at that time! Szathmáry (1995, 338) observed that "The sheer size of the collection and the diversity of peoples it represents are staggering." And as Jantz (2003, 282) has underlined, "Boas's data, collected between 1891 and 1911, provide a resource with many as yet unexplored research possibilities."

Jantz (1995) identified several questions about the measurements from an unpublished manuscript of Boas that was linked to the Chicago Exhibits: (1) What are the principal characteristics of Native Americans? (2) Can a number of types be distinguished among them? (3) Does the distribution of types give a clue to the ancient migration in North America? (4) Does intermixture result in any negative effects? (5) Does the mixed population differ from the unmixed? Jantz (1995) further noted that although Boas used the term "type," his aim was to understand the variation in a population, and because of this, adequate sample sizes were absolutely necessary. Boas's interests in intermixture were based on the common belief at that time that miscegenation was harmful and produced weakened and reproductively deficient offspring. Concerning the effort that Boas expended on these measurements and his strong commitment to physical anthropology, Jantz (1995) calculated that Boas, himself, measured nearly 2,100 subjects between 1890 and 1897, which would have taken about four months of full-time work, not including statistical analyses conducted with pencil and paper and publication.

In addition to Jantz's (1995; 2003; 2006; Jantz et al., 1992) analyses of Boas's data based on his extensive computer database, he has encouraged others to work on these data. As a result, a considerable literature has accumulated with both validation of some of Boas's observations and new findings, as well. Studies of secular changes are possible because of 50- to

60-year variations in dates of birth in Boas's data. This has been studied by Prince (1995) in Plains equestrian populations, especially the Sioux. Circumstances surrounding the very tall stature of Plains natives were explored, as well (Steckel & Prince, 2001). High degrees of relationship in body and head/ face variables were found with geographic patterning in the whole Native American series (Jantz et al., 1992) and with climatic variables including rainfall, mean-July and mean-January temperatures in Natives of California, Oregon, Washington, British Columbia, and Alaska (Hall & Hall, 1995). Boas's inclusion of pedigree and family data allows genetic relationships to be studied, which was done by Konisberg and Ousley (1995). They found a close fit between phenotypic variation (anthropometric measurements) and genetic variation, and this makes the Boas data particularly valuable for reconstructing the biological relationships and origins of these turn-of-the-century Native Americans. Jantz (2006) has done some work with Boas's data on sexual dimorphism in height, trunk, and limb proportions, but there has been virtually no research done with the Native American data on growth of children.

The Migration Study

The completed immigration study, published by Boas (1911a; 1912a), was accompanied by the publication several years later of the raw data of many of the thousands of subjects who were measured in the migration study (Boas, 1928). For some reason, not all of the migration raw data were published: the original study included 17,821 subjects, whereas the 1928 publication included only 13,836 subjects (Gravlee et al., 2003a). Nonetheless, this remarkable published source of the raw data forms from this classic study allowed transcription of the data and reanalysis. The independent reanalyses of these data by two sets of collaborators, however, stimulated a new controversy (Sparks & Jantz, 2002; Gravlee et al., 2003a) over Boas's analyses and interpretations. Sparks and Jantz (2002) established a computer file of the original data and, after a modern reanalysis, argued that Boas's immigrant data did *not* demonstrate cranial plasticity. Gravlee, Bernard, & Leonard (2003a), on the other hand, argued that "Boas got it right" and *did* demonstrate cranial plasticity. The arguments are both statistical and interpretive. Both research groups used slightly different statistical analyses and discussed the *relative* importance of *developmental plasticity* vs. the *relative* importance of *genetic structuring* of cranial characteristics. Discussions of these issues were published in the *American Anthropologist,* where the authors were unable to reach any agreement on their interpretations (Gravlee et al., 2003b; Sparks & Jantz, 2003). In a further inspection of the evidence, John Relethford (2004) was able to explain more clearly the bases for the disagreement about cranial plasticity by comparing both the statistics and their interpretation.

Relethford (2004) identified three ways that craniometric variation can change over time: (1) developmental plasticity through environmental change, (2) long-term changes through natural selection, and (3) within-group and among-groups variation by gene flow. Each of these has been shown to operate, but what Relethford (2004) noted was that the debate about Boas's study centered on the relative importance of these three causes of craniometric change. Based on the two major studies, the question that Relethford raises "is whether developmental plasticity has a significant effect on craniometric variation" (p. 380). Relethford approached this question by using a figure based on data from Gravlee, Bernard, & Leonard (2003a; see Figure 3.2). Three of the seven

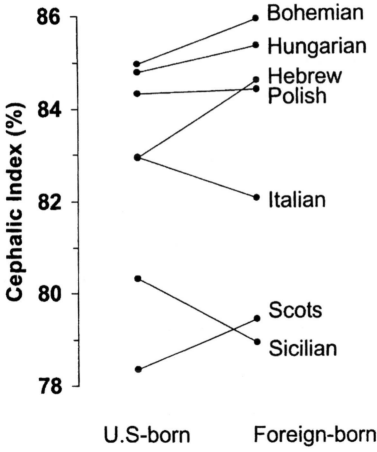

Figure 3.2. Comparison of U.S.-Born and Foreign-Born immigrants to New York City from Boas's (1911a; 1912a) study. (Redrawn from Relethford, 2004.)

European ethnic groups showed no statistical difference between U.S.-born and European-born migrants (Hungarians, Polish, and Scots). The remaining four groups do show statistically significant differences, but these are relatively slight differences. Based on this, Relethford (2004) suggested that these data do demonstrate developmental plasticity, but this plasticity does not obscure the underlying genetic differences that separate the ethnic groups. In other words, both genetic and developmental plasticity contribute to the variation, but the genetic contribution to the total variation, in this case, is the stronger of the two. Relethford's (2004) conclusion was anticipated by Boas (1936, 523) in a later paper referring to the plasticity of the immigration study in which he stated, "These changes do not obliterate the differences between genetic types but they show that the type as we see it contains elements that are not genetic but an expression of the influence of the environment."

BOAS'S ROLE IN THE *AMERICAN JOURNAL OF PHYSICAL ANTHROPOLOGY* AND THE AMERICAN ASSOCIATION OF PHYSICAL ANTHROPOLOGISTS AND HIS RELATIONS WITH ALEŠ HRDLIČKA

The two major anthropologists conducting research in physical anthropology in the United States at the turn of the last century were Aleš Hrdlička and Franz Boas. Hrdlička, who was Boas's junior by 11 years, had an intense commitment and dedication to physical anthropology, whereas Boas's dedication was to anthropology in its broader sense encompassing all four subfields. By 1900, Hrdlička had published 37 works, all in physical anthropology and anatomy (Spencer, 1979), and was modestly known, while Boas had 260 anthropology publications, 49 of which were in physical anthropology (Goldstein, 1948), and was very well known in the profession. Both individuals were European immigrants to the United States: Hrdlička was Bohemian (Czech) and Boas was German. Both individuals were also ambitious, competitive, hard working, politically astute, and leaders in anthropology. However, their backgrounds were quite different: Hrdlička was trained in medicine and anatomy, was strongly opposed to statistical treatment of skeletal and anthropometric data, and identified with French anthropology (physical anthropology; Spencer, 1979). Boas was trained in physics and geography, was a highly sophisticated biometrician, and was identified with German pragmatism (Cole, 1999; Lewis, 2001). Boas and Hrdlička were never close friends or close colleagues, but they shared a mutual respect. Hrdlička included Boas as a member of the Editorial Board of the *American Journal of Physical Anthropology* from its beginning in 1918, and Boas was a charter member of the American Association of Physical Anthropologists, serving on its Executive Committee from 1935–1938 (Goldstein, 1948). Both men had influential supporters. In Boas's case, Frederick Ward Putnam, an archaeologist at Harvard, hired Boas for the ethnographic work at the Chicago World's Columbian Exposition in 1892 and was almost certainly his sponsor for his election to the National Academy of Sciences (NAS) in 1900. Hrdlička also had a powerful supporter and mentor in William Henry Holmes, also an archaeologist (and geologist) at the U.S. National Museum, who, as with Putnam, was also a strong advocate for physical anthropology (Spencer, 1979, 626ff). It is likely that Holmes sponsored Hrdlička's election to the NAS in 1921. Active membership of both Boas and Hrdlička in the NAS, the American Association for the Advancement of Science (AAAS), and the American Anthropological Association (AAA) gave them considerable influence in the profession. However, Boas's influence and power was substantially greater than Hrdlička's because he was older and better known, but also because Boas had trained a large group of students in anthropology (18 students between 1900 and 1918), most of whom were in key university positions in the United States, were members of the governing council of the AAA, and were members of Section H (anthropology) of the AAAS (Spencer, 1979, 634). Since these former students were very loyal to Boas, their roles in maintaining and promoting Boas's ideas and programs were central in the development of American anthropology during the first half of the 20th century. As noted above, Boas's first student in physical anthropology finished only in 1922, Hrdlička trained no students at the U.S. National Museum, and Hooton had no PhDs until 1926 (Harry L. Shapiro). Hrdlička *did* offer instruction in physical anthropology at the U.S. National Museum between 1914 and 1920 to Hooton, some of Boas's students, and others (Spencer, 1981), but his only genuine student was T. Dale Stewart (1981). Hence, by the end of the first quarter of the 20th century, physical anthropology was growing at a snail's pace, while the other subfields were moving ahead (Spencer, 1982).

Boas participated actively in physical anthropology institutions such as the *American Journal of Physical Anthropology* (*AJPA*), which was founded in 1918 by Hrdlička. Although Boas was a charter member of the American Association of Physical Anthropologists (AAPA) when it was formed in 1930, he was reluctant to encourage the formation of the AAPA earlier because he saw this as a new association that would draw members away from the AAA (history has shown this to be true). Twelve years earlier, when Boas saw that Hrdlička was struggling financially to launch the *AJPA* in 1918, he encouraged Hrdlička to affiliate with the newly established Galton Society for the Study of the Origin and Evolution of Man in order to give the journal an institutional base (Spencer, 1979, 680–681). Hrdlička declined largely because he wished the journal to remain under his control, but also probably because he was not in favor of eugenic approaches. Although the Galton Society was heavily "eugenic" in its perspectives, many of its members were respected scientists with a variety of views, and it is the case that eugenics ideas were judged less negatively at that time than they are today. Hence, Boas's tolerance of the Galton Society, although he was opposed to eugenics, was probably linked to his positive view of Galton's and colleagues' contributions to quantitative research and biometrics.

The late Frank Spencer's dissertation dealt quite sympathetically with Aleš Hrdlička. In it, he described the circumstances surrounding the establishment of the National Research Council (NRC) of the NAS and the early role of anthropology in the NRC (Spencer, 1979, 625ff). An oversimplification of the political and ideological conditions in anthropology during this period between 1916 and 1920 is presented here. Basically, there were two main groups who were rivals: a Smithsonian Institution group from Washington, DC, and a northeastern group, largely from New York City. The NRC was proposed in April 1916 by President Woodrow Wilson during World War I to offer "the services of the scientific community to the President of the United States in the interest of national preparedness" (Spencer, 1979, 625). Anthropologists, including Hrdlička, Boas, and others saw this as an opportunity to become involved and to promote their own research agendas.

Spencer's (1979) careful research from correspondence during this period described the complex political maneuvering that took place between 1916 and 1919 to control the anthropology committee of the NRC. The struggles appeared to be between, on the one hand, the Smithsonian group and the New York City/American Museum group, and Hrdlička versus Boas and Hrdlička versus Charles B. Davenport (1866–1944) (and the eugenicists). All of these rivalries appear to have been played out within the context of the NAS/NRC, in which Hrdlička was connected with William Henry Holmes (1846–1933) as his mentor. At that time Boas was a member of the NAS and Hrdlička was not. Hrdlička was pushing for his own research agenda and a prominent place for physical anthropology; Boas wanted a more broadly represented anthropology on the NRC Anthropology Committee; Davenport had strong interests in his eugenics program as represented by the Cold Spring Harbor Institute, which he headed. The impression is that both Hrdlička and Boas were attempting to exert influence on the composition of the NRC anthropology committee, and that Boas and some of his former students were attempting to keep Hrdlička and his supporter, William Henry Holmes, off of the NRC committee (Spencer, 1979, 703ff). Spencer (1979, 710) contended that Boas actively blocked Hrdlička's election to the NAS "because he knew if Hrdlička was elected to the NAS it would be exceedingly difficult, if not impossible, to justify his further exclusion from the Research Council" (Spencer, 1979, 710). At this time in late 1919, relations between Boas and Hrdlička were at a low point. These political struggles between them continued through 1920, after which Hrdlička was elected to the NAS in 1921 (not blocked by Boas) and later appointed to the NRC anthropology committee in 1923. Despite conflicts between the two anthropologists, they remained collegial and Boas participated in many professional physical anthropology activities that Hrdlička initiated (Spencer, 1979, 686ff).

BOAS'S RELATIONS WITH OTHER PROMINENT PHYSICAL ANTHROPOLOGISTS

Boas had close professional contacts and corresponded with numerous other physical anthropologists whom he knew personally from meetings and other activities. Three important figures were Raymond Pearl, Earnest A. Hooton, and T. Wingate Todd.

Raymond Pearl was a brilliant population biologist who began his career with a dissertation on flatworms, but finished it at a relatively young age in areas of human biology and physical anthropology. He even was memorialized in literature by appearing briefly in Sinclair Lewis's (1925) *Arrowsmith* (Kingsland, 1984) and was a close friend of H. L. Mencken, journalist and social critic. He studied biometry in England with Karl Pearson in 1905–1906, which was a formative experience for him, and much later he founded two important journals that are still being published: *The Quarterly Review of Biology* in 1926 and *Human Biology* in 1929. The former is strongly evolutionary and populational, whereas the latter focuses on human population biology (Goldstein, 1940) and has been edited by biological anthropologists since 1953. He was elected to the NAS in 1916 at the precocious age of 37 years. Nearly 20 years later, he was elected president of the American Association of Physical Anthropologists from 1934–1936. Raymond Pearl's association with Boas was based on several commonalities: they were both acquainted with Karl Pearson and were enthusiastic practitioners of biometrics; they were both oriented toward population studies; they were both interested in integrated science; and they met at meetings of the NAS after Pearl's election in 1916. Also, in the early 1930s when Boas returned to his growth research, he published several papers in Pearl's newly founded journal, *Human Biology* (Boas, 1932; 1933; 1935). In the early 1900s, Pearl was a "mainline" eugenicist, as were many biological scientists and physical anthropologists of the time (Barkan, 1992, 211–212; Jones-Kern, 1997,

144–145; Hendricks, 2006). However, he repudiated these eugenic views in an article that he published in H. L. Mencken's magazine, *American Mercury* (Pearl, 1927). Following his death, letters that he wrote in the 1920s revealed a "private" anti-Semite, in which he supported limiting admission to Jews at universities and quotas on election of Jews to the NAS (Barkan, 1992, 215–217). Since these opinions were not public, it is unlikely that Boas would have known about Pearl's anti-Semitism, but he might have suspected.

Earnest A. Hooton was the primary physical anthropologist at Harvard from 1913 until his death in 1954. Although trained in the classics at the PhD level, his anthropology was acquired in England with R. R. Marett (1866–1943), Arthur Keith (1866–1955), and others, and through other experiences in the United States (Garn & Giles, 1995). He was a charismatic and inspiring teacher who trained more than 25 students in physical anthropology who, in turn, became the academic leaders of the next generation in this subfield of anthropology (Giles, 1997). Hooton's research in criminology and somatology has not withstood the test of time, but he was instrumental in stimulating primate field studies in anthropology (Hooton, 1942; 1954). As Keeley and Sussman (2007, 407) noted, "It is he who provided the fertile ground from which the academic genealogy of American field primatology is most firmly based." His training of graduate students from a Harvard base was done with generosity and openness to students' interests. All indications are that he was a sensitive and likeable individual. As with Hrdlička, he served to promote physical anthropology, but largely by virtue of his personality, his mentorship, and his very popular writing of magazine articles and books (Hooton, 1937; 1942). Hooton was also sufficiently distinguished to be elected to the NAS in 1935. The views that he held on race, heredity, criminality, and body constitution were really incompatible with Boas's and more in the realm of traditional typological ideas in physical anthropology. His views were much closer to those of Hrdlička's and there is every indication that Hooton and Hrdlička had a much more cordial relationship than did Hooton and Boas. Nevertheless, as is noted below, Hooton was one of the few physical anthropologists who supported Boas after 1933 when Boas spoke out against Nazi racialism.

T. Wingate Todd was trained in anatomy in England but he developed interests in anthropology through contacts with Grafton Elliot Smith while he was at the University of Manchester and later Arthur Keith (Jones-Kern, 1997, 155ff). At the recommendation of Arthur Keith, Todd was offered a position to fill the Howard Wilson Payne Chair of Anatomy at Western Reserve University, and he moved to Cleveland in the late fall of 1912 (Jones-Kern, 1997, 172). His interests in anatomy were broadly based—including evolution and human origins—but he is best known in physical anthropology for studies of growth of the skeleton (Todd, 1930; 1937). Todd was also quite liberal for the times, with egalitarian views on race, and he was the only physical anthropologist who trained an African-American physical anthropologist through the PhD degree—W. Montague Cobb. Cobb, who later went on to be the first and only African-American president of the American Association of Physical Anthropologists (1957–1959) and a president of the National Association for the Advancement of Colored People (NAACP, 1976–1982), was a distinguished member of the profession who spent most of his career at Howard University (Rankin-Hill & Blakey, 1994; Watkins, 2007). Of the four major figures in physical anthropology discussed—Hrdlička, Pearl, Hooton, Todd—Todd was probably the closest to Boas. Todd had great admiration and even affection for Boas as reflected by several letters sent to Boas with what was identified by Jones-Kern (1997, 367–370) as uncharacteristic sensitivity and emotional expression. Their friendship and mutual respect was reflected in Boas's failed attempt to see Todd elected to the NAS (because Todd was not a U.S. citizen; Jones-Kern, 1997, 242).

The last decade of Boas's life was devoted to many things, including continuation of his growth studies, the publication of major books and revisions (Boas, 1938a; 1938b; 1940b), and the heroic attempt to counter the national racism that arose in Germany after 1933 when Adolf Hitler and the Nazi Party came to power (Boas was 75 years of age in 1933). Boas had a commitment to racial equality and the separation of race and culture that dated back to his publication of *The Mind of Primitive Man* (Boas, 1911b). As early as the spring of 1933, "Boas and [Ruth] Benedict were already engaged in discussions with their colleagues about how best to attack the ideologies of fascism, racism, and anti-semitism" (Patterson, 2001, 90).

Barkan (1988; 1992, 279ff) chronicled the reactions of the scientific community to the rise of Nazi Germany from 1933 to WWII, including Boas's participation in this response. Boas was active in attempting to marshal support against Germany's policies from mid-1933, but his efforts intensified in July 1934 at the International Congress of Anthropological and Ethnological Sciences (ICAES) in London, where he unsuccessfully tried to get a resolution passed against the Aryan race concept (Barkan, 1988, 185). Since Boas believed that arguments against the racialism and anti-Semitism in Germany would carry more weight if presented by a non-Jew, he contacted Livingston Farrand, an old friend and colleague from Columbia University, who was then president of Cornell University, to solicit his help: Farrand declined. He next contacted Raymond Pearl, who also declined to become involved. Finally, Boas contacted Earnest Hooton because of his high position in the profession at Harvard, and despite Hooton's ambiguous views on race, he agreed to help Boas (Barkan, 1988, 186). Hooton prepared a statement on race (later published by Hooton, 1936) that was distributed to Aleš Hrdlička (U.S. National Museum), C. H. Danforth (Stanford University), William King Gregory (American Museum of Natural History), Raymond Pearl (Johns Hopkins University), Robert J. Terry (Washington University), and T. Wingate Todd (Western Reserve University). All but Hrdlička declined, either with the belief that scientists should not meddle in public policy or because of disagreement with the points in the statement. It is ironic that Pearl and Todd, who were much closer to Boas's beliefs, were unwilling to support the document, while Hooton and Hrdlička, whose beliefs were more distant, *were* willing. It is a tribute to Boas's diplomacy that the unwillingness of his colleagues to support his initiatives on such an important issue did not lead to his alienation with those colleagues, especially Todd (Jones-Kern, 1997, 371–373). Despite the failure of this effort, Boas continued to speak out against German policies. But it was not until 1938 that the American Anthropological Association at its annual meeting unanimously approved a resolution forwarded by Hooton and moved by Boas that refuted Nazi racialist distortions (Barkan, 1988, 202).

DISCUSSION

Boas was at the same time a *peripheral figure* and a *central figure* in the development of physical anthropology during the first half of the 20th century. He was *peripheral* because his views were in a distinct minority among his physical anthropology colleagues and he was somewhat marginalized in physical anthropology (but not in anthropology). He was *central* because his ideas and his research results were lasting and generally incorporated by late-20th-century physical anthropologists. He was truly a modern anthropological scientist who arose during the 19th century. As physical anthropology developed as a profession in the 20th century, it was built on at least two traditions. The first tradition was medical and anatomical and based on a model that Aleš Hrdlička represented—hard tissue anatomy and craniology. The second tradition was more closely tied to the behavioral and biobehavioral side of anthropology but with a scientific overlay with elements of natural science and was represented by Franz Boas. This biobehavioral anthropology is also linked to the humanities component of anthropology that in recent times has been in conflict with the scientific component. These multifaceted traditions persist in slightly different permutations up to the present. Physical anthropologists who are active members of the American Association of Physical Anthropologists are quite likely to be on the science side of the profession, while those who are members of the American Anthropological

Association are more likely to be more closely linked to the social sciences and humanities. This is, of course, a broad generalization, but those who are most committed to a science-based, biologically oriented physical anthropology are also those who are more willing to branch off from anthropology. The social scientists are more likely to favor the four-field approach and the value of integration in anthropology. Some of the same trajectories have occurred in the United Kingdom but with less tradition of integration in anthropology. Only in the latter part of the 20th century did some degree of integration in anthropology take place in England with the rise of human biology in the 1950s.

In physical anthropology, the professionalism and academic ties arose from anatomy and natural history, and it was only after Hooton's students moved into academia that this anatomical orientation became deflected to evolution, plasticity, and adaptation. Cultural anthropology and archaeology had an academic and professional head start over physical anthropology, since both cultural anthropologists and archaeologists were being trained in larger numbers during the first half of the 20th century. Boas contributed ideas but not bodies to this professionalism in physical anthropology—ideas that only began to be incorporated into physical anthropology and were recognized for their value several decades after his death.

REFERENCES

Baker, Paul T. (1976). Research Strategies in Population Biology and Environmental Stress. In *The Measures of Man: Methodologies in Biological Anthropology,* ed. by E. Giles & J. S. Friedlaender, pp. 230–259. Cambridge, MA: Peabody Museum Press.

Barkan, Elazar. (1988). Mobilizing Scientists Against Nazi Racism, 1933–1939. In *Bones, Bodies, and Behavior: Essays on Biological Anthropology,* ed. by George W. Stocking, Jr., pp. 180–205. Madison: University of Wisconsin Press.

———. (1992). *The Retreat of Scientific Racism: Changing Concepts of Race in Britain and the United States Between the World Wars.* Cambridge: Cambridge University Press.

Boas, Franz. (1884). The Half-Blood Indian, an Anthropometric Study. *Popular Science Monthly, 45,* 761–770.

———. (1894a). The Anthropology of the North American Indian. Memoirs of the International Congress of Anthropology, pp. 37–49. Chicago: Schulte. (Reprinted in Stocking 1974, 191-201).

———. (1894b). The Correlation of Anatomical or Physiological Measurements. *American Anthropologist, 7,* 313–324.

———. (1895). Zur Anthropologie der Nordamerikanischen Indianer. *Zeitschrift fur Ethnologie, 27,* 366–411.

———. (1897). The Growth of Children. *Science, 5,* 570–573.

———. (1898). The Growth of Toronto Children. Report of the U.S. Commission of Education for 1896-97, pp. 1541–1599. Washington, DC: U.S. Commission of Education.

———. (1899). The Cephalic Index. *American Anthropologist, 1*(n.s.), 448–461.

———. (1911a). Changes in the Bodily Form of Descendants of Immigrants. Senate Document 208, 61st Congress. Washington, DC: U.S. Government Printing Office.

———. (1911b). *The Mind of Primitive Man.* New York: Macmillan.

———. (1912a). *Changes in the Bodily Form of Descendants of Immigrants.* New York: Columbia University Press.

———. (1912b.) Changes in the Bodily Form of Descendants of Immigrants. *American Anthropologist, 14,* 530–562.

———. (1928). *Materials for the Study of Inheritance in Man.* New York: Columbia University Press.

———. (1930). Observations on the Growth of Children. *Science, 72,* 44–48.

———. (1932). Studies in Growth. *Human Biology, 4,* 307–350.

———. (1933). Studies in Growth II. *Human Biology, 5,* 429–444.

———. (1935). Studies in Growth III. *Human Biology, 7,* 303–318.

———. (1936). Effects of American Environment on Immigrants and Their Descendants. *Science, 84,* 522–525.

———. (1938a). *The Mind of Primitive Man, Revised Edition.* New York: Macmillan.

——— (ed.). (1938b). *General Anthropology.* Boston: D.C. Heath.

———. (1940a). Age Changes and Secular Changes in Anthropometric Measurements. *American Journal of Physical Anthropology, 26,* 63–68.

———. (1940b). *Race, Language, and Culture.* New York: Macmillan.

———. (1943). Recent Anthropology. *Science, 98,* 311–314, 334–337.

Boas, Norman F. (2004). *Franz Boas, 1858-1942: An Illustrated Biography.* Mystic, CT: Seaport Autographs Press.

Carter, Isabel Gordon. (1928). Reduction of Variability in an Inbred Population. *American Journal of Physical Anthropology, 11,* 457–471.

———. (1932). Physical Measurements of "Old American" College Women. *American Journal of Physical Anthropology, 16,* 497–514.

Cole, Douglas. (1999). *Franz Boas, The Early Years: 1858–1906.* Seattle: University of Washington Press.

Collins, June M. (1979). Ruth Sawtell Wallis, 1895–1978 [obituary]. *American Anthropologist, 81,* 85–87.

Darnell, Regna. (1982). Franz Boas and the Development of Physical Anthropology in North America. *Canadian Journal of Anthropology, 3*(1), 101112.

———. (2001). *Invisible Genealogies: A History of Americanist Anthropology.* Lincoln: University of Nebraska Press.

Fishberg, Maurice. (1905). Materials for the Physical Anthropology of the Eastern European Jews. *Annals of the New York Academy of Science, 16,* 155–297.

———. (1905–1907). Materials for the Physical Anthropology of the Eastern European Jews. *Memoirs of the American Anthropological Association, 1,* 1–146.

Fisher, Ronald A., & Gray, H. (1937). Boas's Data Studied by the Method of Analysis of Variance. *Annals of Genetics, 8,* 74–93.

Garn, Stanley M., & Giles, Eugene. (1995). Earnest Albert Hooton: November 20, 1887-May 3, 1954. *Biographical Memoirs of the National Academy of Sciences, 68,* 167–180.

Giles, Eugene. (1997). Earnest Albert Hooton (1887–1954). In *History of Physical Anthropology: An Encyclopedia, Vol. 1,* ed. by Frank Spencer, pp. 499–501. New York: Garland.

Goldstein, Marcus S. (1940). Recent Trends in Physical Anthropology. *American Journal of Physical Anthropology, 26,* 191–209.

———. (1943). *Demographic and Bodily Changes in Descendants of Mexican Immigrants.* Austin: University of Texas, Institute of Latin American Studies.

———. (1948). Franz Boas' Contributions to Physical Anthropology. *American Journal of Physical Anthropology, 4,* 145–161.

———. (1995). *An Odyssey in Anthropology and Public Health.* Department of Anatomy and Anthropology. Tel Aviv, Israel: Tel Aviv University.

Gravlee Clarence C., Bernard, H. Russell, & Leonard, William R. (2003a). Heredity, Environment, and Cranial Form: A Reanalysis of Boas's Immigrant Data. *American Anthropologist, 105*(1), 125–138.

Gravlee, Clarence C., Bernard, H. Russell, & Leonard, William R. (2003b). Boas's Changes in Bodily Form: The Immigrant Study, Cranial Plasticity, and Boas's Physical Anthropology. *American Anthropologist, 105*(2), 326–332.

Greulich, William W. (1957). A Comparison of the Physical Growth and Development of American-Born and Native Japanese Children. *American Journal of Physical Anthropology, 15,* 489–515.

Hall, Roberta L., & Hall, Don Alan. (1995). Geographic Variation of Native People Along the Pacific Coast. *Human Biology, 67*(3), 407–426.

Harris, Marvin. (1968). *The Rise of Anthropological Theory: A History of Theories of Culture.* New York: Crowell.

Harrison, G. Ainsworth. (1966). Human Adaptability with Reference to the IBP Proposals for High Altitude Research. In *The Biology of Human Adaptability,* ed. by P. T. Baker and J. S. Weiner, pp. 109–119. Oxford: Clarendon Press.

Hendricks, Melissa. (2006). Raymond Pearl's "Mingled Mess." *Johns Hopkins Magazine, 58*(2), 50–56.

Herskovits, Melville J. (1943). Franz Boas as Physical Anthropologist. In *Franz Boas: 1858–1942,* ed. by A. L. Kroeber, R. Benedict, M. B. Emeneau, M. J. Herkovits, G. A. Reichard, and J. A. Mason, pp. 39--1. *American Anthropologist* 45, No. 3, Part 2 (Memoir No. 61 of the American Anthropological Association).

———. (1953). *Franz Boas: The Science of Man in the Making.* New York: Charles Scribner's Sons.

Hooton, Earnest A. (1925). Louis Robert Sullivan [obituary]. *American Anthropologist, 27,* 357–358.

———. (1936). Plain Statements About Race. *Science, 83,* 511–513.

———. (1937). *Apes, Men, and Morons.* New York: Putnam.

———. (1942). *Man's Poor Relations*. Garden City, NY: Doubleday.

———. (1954). The Importance of Primate Studies in Anthropology. *Human Biology, 26*, 179–188.

Howells, William W. (1959). Boas as Statistician. In *The Anthropology of Franz Boas: Essays on the Centennial of His Birth*, ed. by Walter Goldschmidt, pp. 112–116. American Anthropologist 61, No. 5, Part 2 (Memoir No. 89 of the American Anthropological Association).

Hulse, Frederick S. (1957). Exogamie et Hétérosis. *Archive Suis d'Anthropologie Generale, 22*, 103–125.

———. (1968). Migration and Cultural Selection in Human Genetics. *Anthropologist* (Delhi) Special Vol. pp. 1–21.

———. (1979). Migration et Selection de Groupe: le Cas de Cuba. *Bulletin et Memoire de la Société d'Anthropologie*, Ser. 6, *13*, 137–146.

———. (1981). Habits, Habitats, and Heredity: A Brief History of Studies in Human Plasticity. *American Journal of Physical Anthropology, 56*(4), 495–501.

Ito P.K. (1942). Comparative Biometrical Study of Physique of Japanese Women Born and Reared Under Different Environments. *Human Biology, 14*, 279–351.

Jantz, Richard L. (1995). Franz Boas and Native American Biological Variability. *Human Biology, 67*(3), 345–353.

——— (2003). The Anthropometric Legacy of Franz Boas. *Economics and Human Biology, 1*, 277–284.

——— (2006). Anthropometry. In *Handbook of North American Indians, Vol. 3, Environment, Origins, and Population*, ed. by William C. Sturtevant, pp. 777–788. Washington, DC: Smithsonian Institution.

Jantz, Richard L., D.R. Hunt, Anthony B. Falsetti, and P.J. Key. (1992). Variation Among North Amerindians: Analysis of Boas's Anthropometric Data. *Human Biology, 64*(3), 435–461.

Jantz, Richard L., & Spencer, Frank. (1997). Franz Boas (1858–1942). In *History of Physical Anthropology: An Encyclopedia, Vol. 1*, ed. by Frank Spencer, pp. 186–190. New York: Garland.

Jones-Kern, Kevin. (1997). T. Wingate Todd and the Development of Modern American Physical Anthropology, 1900-1940. PhD Dissertation in History. Bowling Green, OH: Bowling Green State University.

Keeley, Elizabeth A., & Sussman, Robert W. (2007). An Academic Genealogy on the History of American Field Primatologists. *American Journal of Physical Anthropology, 132*, 406–425.

Kingsland, S. (1984). Raymond Pearl: On the Frontier in the 1920's. Raymond Pearl Memorial Lecture, 1983. *Human Biology, 56*(1), 1–18.

Konigsberg, Lyle W., & Ousley, Stephen D. (1995). Multivariate Quantitative Genetics of Anthropometric Traits from the Boas Data. *Human Biology, 67*(3), 481–498.

Kroeber, Alfred L. (1943). Franz Boas: The Man. In *Franz Boas: 1858–1942*, ed. by A. L. Kroeber, R. Benedict, M. B. Emeneau, M. J. Herkovits, G. A. Reichard, & J.

A. Mason, pp. 5–26. *American Anthropologist* 45, No. 3, Part 2 (Memoir No. 61 of the American Anthropological Association).

Lasker, Gabriel W. (1946). Migration and Physical Differentiation. A Comparison of Immigrant and American-Born Chinese. *American Journal of Physical Anthropology, 4,* 273–300.

———. (1954). The Question of Physical Selection of Mexican Migrants to the U.S.A. *Human Biology, 26,* 52–58.

———. (1999). *Happenings and Hearsay: Experiences of a Biological Anthropologist.* Detroit: Savoyard.

Lewis, Herbert S. (2001). Boas, Darwin, Science, and Anthropology. *Current Anthropology, 42*(3): 381–406.

Lewis, Sinclair. (1925). *Arrowsmith.* New York: Harcourt, Brace.

Little, M. A., & Baker, Paul T. (1988). Migration and Adaptation. In *Biological Aspects of Human Migration,* ed. by C. G. N. Mascie-Taylor & G. W. Lasker, pp. 167–215. Cambridge: Cambridge University Press.

Little, Michael A.,& Leslie, Paul W. (1993). Migration. In *Research Strategies in Human Biology: Field and Survey Studies,* ed. by G. W. Lasker & C. G. N. Mascie-Taylor, pp.62–91. Cambridge: Cambridge University Press.

Marks, Jonathan. (2000). Ashley Montagu, 1905–1999. *Evolutionary Anthropology, 9*(3), 111–112.

Mascie-Taylor, Nicholas, C. G. & Little, Michael A. (2004). History of Migration Studies in Biological Anthropology. *Human Biology, 16,* 365–378.

Montagu, Ashley. (1942). *Man's Most Dangerous Myth.* New York: Columbia University Press.

———. (1971). *The Elephant Man: A Study in Human Dignity.* New York: Dutton.

——— (ed.). (1975). *Race and IQ.* New York: Oxford University Press.

Morant, G. M., & Sampson, O. (1936). An Examination of Investigations by Dr. Maurice Fishberg and Professor Franz Boas Dealing with Measurements of Jews in New York. *Biometrika, 27,*1–31.

Patterson, Thomas C. (2001). *A Social History of Anthropology in the United States.* Oxford: Berg.

Pearl, Raymond. (1927). The Biology of Superiority. *American Mercury, 12* (November), 257–266.

Prince, Joseph M. (1995). Intersection of Economics, History, and Human Biology: Secular Trends in Stature in Nineteenth-Century Sioux Indians. *Human Biology, 67*(3), 387–406.

Rankin-Hill, Leslie M., & Blakey, Michael L. (1994). W. Montague Cobb (1904–1990): Physical Anthropologist, Anatomist, and Activist. *American Anthropologist, 96*(1), 74–96.

Relethford, John H. (2004). Boas and Beyond: Migration and Craniometric Variation. *American Journal of Human Biology, 16,* 379–386.

Sawtell, Ruth Otis. (1928). Sex Differences in the Bone Growth of Young Children. *American Journal of Physical Anthropology, 12,* 293–302.

———. (1929). Ossification and Growth of Children from One to Eight Years of Age. *American Journal of Diseases of Children, 37*, 61–87.

Shapiro Harry L. (1939). *Migration and Environment: A Study of the Physical Characteristics of the Japanese Immigrants to Hawaii and the Effects of Environment on Their Descendants.* Oxford: Oxford University Press.

Sparks, Corey S., & Jantz, Richard L. (2002). A Reassessment of Human Cranial Plasticity: Boas Revisited. *Proceedings of the National Academy of Sciences, 99,* 14636–14639.

Sparks, Corey S., & Jantz, Richard L. (2003). Changing Times, Changing Faces: Franz Boas's Immigrant Study in Modern Perspective. *American Anthropologist, 105*(2), 333–337.

Spencer, Frank. (1979). Aleš Hrdlička, M.D., 1869–1943: A Chronicle of the Life and Work of an American Physical Anthropologist (Volumes I and II). Dissertation in Anthropology. Ann Arbor, MI: University of Michigan.

———. (1981). The Rise of Academic Physical Anthropology in the United States (1880–1980): A Historical Overview. *American Journal of Physical Anthropology, 56*(4), 353–364.

———. (1982). Introduction. In *A History of American Physical Anthropology: 1930–1980,* ed by Frank Spencer, pp. 1–10. New York: Academic Press.

Spier, Leslie. (1929). Growth of Japanese Schoolchildren Born in America and Japan. *University of Washington Publications in Anthropology, 3,* 1–30.

Steckel, Richard H., & Prince, Joseph M. (2001). Tallest in the World: Native Americans in the Great Plains in the 19th Century. *American Economics Reviews, 91,* 287–294.

Stewart, T. Dale. (1973). *The People of America.* New York: Charles Scribner's Sons.

Stewart, T. Dale. (1981). Aleš Hrdlička, 1869–1943. *American Journal of Physical Anthropology, 56*(4), 347–351.

Stocking, George W., Jr. (1968). Chapter 8: The Critique of Racial Formalism. In *Race, Culture, and Evolution: Essays in the History of Anthropology,* by G. W. Stocking, Jr., pp. 161–194. New York: The Free Press.

———. (1974). *The Shaping of American Anthropology, 1883–1911: A Franz Boas Reader.* New York: Basic Books.

Szathmáry, Emőke J. E. (1995). Overview of the Boas Anthropometric Collection and Its Utility in Understanding the Biology of Native North Americans. *Human Biology, 67*(3), 337–344.

Tanner, James M. (1959). Boas' Contributions to the Knowledge of Human Growth and Form. In *The Anthropology of Franz Boas: Essays on the Centennial of His Birth,* ed. by Walter Goldschmidt, pp. 76–111. *American Anthropologist, 61,* No. 5, Part 2 (Memoir No. 89 of the American Anthropological Association).

———. (1962). *Growth at Adolescence, 2nd Edition.* Oxford: Blackwell.

———. (1981). *A History of the Study of Human Growth.* Cambridge: Cambridge University Press.

Thieme, Frederick P. (1957). A Comparison of Puerto Rico Migrants and Sedentes. *Michigan Academy of Science, Arts, and Letters, 42,* 249–267.

Todd, T. Wingate. (1930). Physical and Mental Adolescent Growth: Proceedings of the Conference of Adolescence, Cleveland, October 17 & 18, 1930. Cleveland: The Brush Foundation and Western Reserve University.

———. (1937). *Atlas of Skeletal Maturation.* St. Louis: C.V. Mosby.

Wallis, Ruth O.S. (1931). How Children Grow: An Anthropological Study of Private School Children from Two to Eight Years of Age. *University of Iowa Studies in Child Welfare,* Vol. 5, No. 1.

Washburn, Sherwood L. (1984). Book Review of *A History of American Physical Anthropology: 1930–1980,* ed. by Frank Spencer. *Human Biology, 56,* 393–402.

Watkins, Rachel J. (2007). Knowledge from the Margins: W. Montague Cobb's Pioneering Research in Biocultural Anthropology. *American Anthropologist* 109(1): 186-196.

White, Leslie A. (1963). The Ethnography and Ethnology of Franz Boas. *Bulletin of the Texas Memorial Museum, 6,* 1–76.

Chapter 4

Aleš Hrdlička and the Founding of the *American Journal of Physical Anthropology:* 1918
by
Donald J. Ortner

INTRODUCTION

Undoubtedly, the *American Journal of Physical Anthropology* (*AJPA*) has played a major role in defining the content and direction of biological (physical) anthropology, certainly in America and very likely in the rest of the world. It is also certain that the vision, philosophy of science, and scientific rigor of Aleš Hrdlička (1869–1943) dominated the content of the journal from the time he founded it in 1918 through the close of his tenure as editor following the publication of volume 29 in 1942. At that time his protégé, T. Dale Stewart (1901–1997), assumed the editorship and largely continued the editorial emphasis established by Hrdlička until Stewart resigned that responsibility in 1948. Hrdlička had also retired from his curatorial post in the National Museum of Natural History in 1942. However, he continued his research activities and remained the honorary editor of the journal until his death from a heart attack in September 1943.

Hrdlička understood very well the need for a journal to establish the legitimacy of a scientific discipline and its significance in defining the focus of that discipline. On more than one occasion he complained about the limitations inherent in publishing research on physical anthropology in more general anthropological and scientific journals. In a letter to John H. Kellogg (1852–1943), a prominent Michigan surgeon who was to become one of the first associate editors of the journal, asking for financial support to found the journal, he noted that there were three journals for publishing research in physical anthropology in France, another three in Germany, two in Italy, and one in England, but none in America (Hrdlička to Kellogg, July 13, 1917, National Anthropological Archives [NAA]). By this time there were, of course, American journals for general anthropology, such as the *American Anthropologist*, but none specifically devoted to physical anthropology.

His passion for establishing an American journal to publish research in physical anthropology was linked to his hope to establish a national center in America for physical anthropology that would have been similar to the Paris Anthropological Institute founded by Paul Broca (1824–1880). The latter goal was to elude Hrdlička, but the establishment of the *American Journal of Physical Anthropology* in 1918 created a permanent legacy for science and the discipline of physical anthropology that continues today.

A review of the history of the founding of the *AJPA* highlights the importance a single person can play in shaping a scientific discipline. Without doubt the journal reflected Hrdlička's vision for what should constitute the research endeavors associated with physical anthropology. The broad range of topics published by Hrdlička during his years as editor testifies to his inclusiveness (see Table 4.1).

Table 4.1.   General topics published in the *American Journal of Physical Anthropology* between 1918 and 1927.

Human variation in both living and dead samples
Anatomical features and human variation
History and role of physical anthropology
Methodological issues with an emphasis on anthropometry
Human development and genetics
Age changes in the human skeleton
Human evolution
Primatology

Looking back on some of the prevailing assumptions in the human sciences in the early 20th century that provided the context for research is a disturbing exercise. Few scientists escaped the influence of pervasive ethnic prejudice and the associated hierarchical biological relationship thought to exist between different ethnic groups that was widespread to the point of being a truism. Hrdlička was less influenced than most, probably because of his own early cultural heritage in Central Europe. He was born in Czechoslovakia in 1869 and lived there until the age of 12, when he immigrated with his father to the United States. Early in his professional life he studied under Léonce Manouvrier (1850–1927) at the Paris Anthropological Institute and Manouvrier had a major impact on Hrdlička. Manouvrier rejected the Neo-Lamarckian social philosophy of his mentor Paul Broca and championed the idea that human nature was greatly influenced by the social environment in which a person develops. Manouvrier also opposed the "scientific racism" that was pervasive in the human sciences. Much of the ethnic prejudice was embodied in the ideology associated with the eugenics movement of the late 19th and early 20th centuries. Like Manouvrier, Hrdlička rejected much of the social philosophy and biological assumptions of the eugenics tradition and related movements. In early issues of the *AJPA* he published scathing reviews (e.g., Boas, 1918) of some of the prominent eugenics literature. He also requested and published a remarkable paper by Castle (1926), who was a distinguished geneticist at Harvard University. In this paper Castle attacked the pseudoscience which argued that race mixture resulted in a biological detriment to both groups. The opposition by those supporting eugenics, including prominent scientists, to race mixture is surprising because hybrid vigor was a well-established principle in non-human genetics. Indeed, Castle emphasized that race mixture was certainly not harmful from a biological perspective in direct opposition to much of what was being written by those supporting the eugenics movement. Castle's conclusion undermined one of the major dogmas of the movement and must have been controversial at the time it was published. Since Hrdlička had invited Castle to publish this paper in the *AJPA*, he almost certainly supported the conclusions.

Inevitably some of the social biases prevalent at that time did affect the content of papers published in the journal. However, it is remarkable that papers with conclusions well ahead of the prevailing ideas of the time were also published. The influence of social bias on some publications reminds those of us who follow that, despite the rigors of the scientific method, science and scientists are affected by the social milieu of which they are a part. In looking back on ideas that provided the context of research in the human sciences 75 years ago, it is more than a little troubling to speculate on what our successors 75 years from now will point to as obvious defects in our present scientific objectivity as we develop the various hypotheses that define our discipline today.

THE SOCIAL CONTEXT OF SCIENCE AND ANTHROPOLOGY IN THE EARLY 20TH CENTURY

In the Western scientific community there were three related but distinct ideas that influenced the philosophy of human biological science in the early part of the 20th century, but whose roots extend back well into the 19th century. The human sciences of that time and the early foundation of physical anthropology in the United States need to be considered in the social and ideological context in which science was conducted. As with any of the human sciences, physical anthropology developed in a cultural milieu that affected the research conducted and the meaning attributed to the data acquired.

The first of these ideas was a pervasive ethnic prejudice in which Western white society and, for some, especially the Nordic people, were viewed as the highest achievement of human biological development. It was taken as self-evident fact that differences between ethnic groups ("races" to use the terminology of that time) were explained primarily by differences in the collective genetics of these groups. The question of the influence of nature versus nurture in determining social or physical achievement was an important issue in Western society but also in the human sciences, including both biological and psychological dimensions. It is clear that genetic heritage was viewed as the major determinant of human biological and cultural achievement. Neo-Lamarckian concepts about the inheritance of acquired mental and physical traits were widely taken seriously in Western scientific circles. With a few notable exceptions, the Darwinian view of the crucial importance of environmental factors in shaping the direction of human evolution was still being debated in the human sciences of continental Europe.

The second key idea was the assumption that physical traits of people were associated with mental characteristics. The skull was viewed as the location where these characteristics were manifest, and this gave rise to a preoccupation with a suite of observations and measurements of the skull that would allow "defective" people to be identified. For example, the insane were thought to have relatively unique and measurable physical characteristics. Similarly, criminals also were thought to have special, identifiable, physical characteristics that could be determined through careful measurement and observation of physical features. This idea was the major driving force behind the popular pseudoscience of phrenology, but was also important in developing the more scientifically rigorous methodology of anthropometry. Indeed, much of Hrdlička's early research experience involved the physical measurement particularly of the insane, but also of criminals in order to identify the physical characteristics associated with people categorized by society as belonging in one or both of these socially defined groups. It is very much to his credit that this research led Hrdlička to conclude that no such link could be made (Spencer, 1979, 99), despite research and publications by others suggesting otherwise (Gould, 1981).

The third idea was that human society could at least affect, if not control, the direction of human social and biological change. One of the early proponents of the idea that human biological change could be directed was Sir Francis Galton (1822–1911), the English biologist of the mid-19th century, and cousin of Charles Darwin (1809–1882), who created the concept of eugenics. For Galton, eugenics was simply a process by which human groups improved their physical and mental qualities through selective parenthood. Eugenics, and the societies that developed to promote the social and political policies inherent in it, became a major social and political force in the latter part of the 19th and early part of the 20th century. The ideas imbedded in eugenics provided the basis of social policies including draconian measures, such as sterilization of socially defined misfits that were promulgated and became the law in some American states. There are, of course, many social and scientific problems with eugenics. One was the assumption that people with the best genetic makeup could be identified physically. Another was that it required some social mechanism for enhancing the fecundity of those defined as particularly fit, while depressing the fecundity of those defined as being inadequate.

The Galton Society was a very influential society that was founded in America in 1918 by Madison Grant (1865–1937), a lawyer, to support eugenics research and promote social action mandated by eugenics. The society attracted some major scientists, including Charles B. Davenport (1866–1944), a geneticist who was the founder and director of the Carnegie Institute Station for Experimental Evolution at Cold Spring Harbor. Davenport was a charter member and the first chairman of the society. Henry Fairfield Osborn (1857–1935), a paleontologist and president of the American Museum of Natural History, was also a member and a very visible and active supporter of eugenics.

Although Darwin's evolutionary ideas had been present since the mid-19th century, they were not universally accepted as the mechanism for biological change through time. This was particularly true of the human sciences in Continental Europe. In France, Auguste Comte's positivism was a major element of French social philosophy, in which it was thought possible for human societies to direct social change in beneficial ways. This philosophy combined well with Neo-Lamarckian biology that provided a significant theoretical context for explaining biological variability and the changes apparent in the paleontological record. There was also a popular view, as well as a scientific opinion, that acquired characteristics could be passed to one's offspring. Thus, the children of a criminal were likely to be criminals themselves. Part of the horror of suicide was that the children of someone who committed such an act were viewed as defective themselves. These ideas were central to the teaching and research of the French school of anthropology championed by Paul Broca and many of his students. Léonce Manouvrier (see Figure 4.1), although a student and protégé of Broca, rejected the neo-Lamarckian scientific philosophy that pervaded French anthropology and much of European human biology as well. He vigorously opposed much of the racist ideology

Figure 4.1. Prof. Léonce Manouvrier, École and Laboratorie d'Anthropologie, Paris, France, 1927. He became a close friend of Aleš Hrdlička when Hrdlička studied under Manouvrier for a few months in 1896 (courtesy of the Smithsonian Institution).

that was linked with this philosophy. Manouvrier was to become a major influence on Hrdlička as Hrdlička developed the ideological context for the research he wanted to conduct.

HRDLIČKA'S EARLY PROFESSIONAL ACTIVITIES

Following his training as a physician, Hrdlička was appointed a staff physician at Middletown State Homeopathic Hospital for the Insane in New York where he worked from 1894 to 1896. He accepted this position with the understanding that he would be able to pursue his research on the anthropometry of criminals and the insane. It soon became apparent that the resources and collaborative connections for achieving this objective would not materialize.

During this period, a major initiative in the study of insanity was being developed with the creation of the Pathological Institute in New York, and Hrdlička was offered a research position once the Institute opened. Hrdlička accepted the offer, but before undertaking this role he decided to acquire further formal training in anthropometric methods. In January 1896, he sailed from New York for Southampton, England, from there to France and by land to Paris where he studied at the École and Laboratorie d'Anthropologie, both of which were part of the Institute of Anthropology founded by Paul Broca. It was during the few months in Paris that he was to develop the close relationship with Léonce Manouvrier that lasted until the death of Manouvrier in 1927. It is clear that this relationship had a major impact on Hrdlička's philosophy of science that would have a significant impact on the directions he chose to emphasize when he established the *AJPA*.

Manouvrier recognized, to some degree at least, the importance of the environment in influencing human cultural and biological diversity (Spencer, 1979, 117). He vigorously opposed much of the racist ideology prevalent in the human biology of the late 19th and early 20th centuries (Spencer, 1979, 118). This influence did not completely eliminate some of the prejudices and cultural biases that Hrdlička had, but it probably did ensure that he was much less taken with some of the socially driven racist ideas encountered, for example, in the eugenics movement.

Following his return to America, Hrdlička remained at the Pathological Institute from1896 to 1899 and left primarily because he was again unable to conduct the research he wanted to do and as he had been promised. Following his tenure at the Pathological Institute, Hrdlička was affiliated with the American Museum of Natural History in New York City from 1899 to 1902. The main emphasis during this phase of his career was field work where he learned the basics of archeology and collected anthropometric data on living Native American groups, particularly in the American Southwest. On May 1, 1903, he began an appointment as assistant curator and head of the new Division of Physical Anthropology at the National Museum of Natural History (NMNH). William Henry Holmes (1846–1933), head curator of the Department of Anthropology, NMNH, played a major role in creating the position for Hrdlička and remained a staunch supporter for the rest of Holmes's life.

HRDLIČKA THE PERSON

The personality of a scientist inevitably affects his or her work, as well as relationships with people and processes associated with the professional activities in which he or she engages. Without doubt, Hrdlička inspired respect for, as well as trust and confidence in, his ideas and his ways of doing scientific research. This did not always extend to his interpersonal relationships with colleagues, which, in some cases, were strained. He stimulated a fair amount of hostility because of his strong and vigorously defended opinions and his somewhat heavy-handed way of dealing with colleagues with whom he disagreed. Despite his admiration for Hrdlička, Earnest A. Hooton (1887–1954), who was early in his career at Harvard at that time, recognized that Hrdlička's personality did have a negative effect on his relationships with colleagues as well as his participation in professional organizations and on scientific committees (Spencer, 1979, 732). This sentiment was also expressed by Alfred L. Kroeber (1876–1960), Department of Anthropology, University of California, in the context of Hrdlička's possible appointment to the National Research Council (Spencer, 1979, 708).

His physical appearance (see Figure 4.2) and personality were intimidating. In his obituary of Hrdlička, Adolph H. Schultz (1891–1976), the legendary anatomist and primatologist, commented that "in regard to his own conclusions Hrdlička seems to have been rarely plagued by doubts" (Schultz, 1946, 312). Schultz had a well-developed although subtle sense of humor, and this opinion is a humorous understatement to say the least. Schultz further notes that "he [Hrdlička] had no special training in biology and his schooling in mathematics had not gone beyond elementary instruction" (Schultz, 1946, 313). This may have been a factor in Hrdlička's dim view of research based on statistical methodology, although Frederick L. Hoffman (1865–1946), one of the initial associate editors of the journal was, in part, chosen for his expertise in statistics. The fact that Hoffman was also the president of the Prudential Insurance Company of America and a potential donor to underwrite the cost of the journal undoubtedly was a factor as well.

Ethnic and gender prejudice were social norms during Hrdlička's lifetime and were widespread among the scientists specializing in various aspects of human biology. Hrdlička had particularly strong feelings against German society and German science (Spencer, 1979, 50) that undoubtedly were influenced by the repression of the Czechs by the Austro-Hungarian Empire. Hrdlička's patronizing attitude toward women was certainly part of the lore passed on to me when I arrived in the Department of Anthropology in 1963, 20 years after his death. There are more tangible manifestations of this attitude, such as the language in his will specifying that research support provided by the fund he established was to be limited to medically educated men (Spencer, 1979, 804). Despite this evidence, Hrdlička clearly had great respect and affection for his first wife Marie

Figure 4.2. A candid photograph of Aleš Hrdlička taken in 1920, two years after the founding of the *American Journal of Physical Anthropology* (courtesy of the Smithsonian Institution).

Strickler (Spencer, 1979, 63). Furthermore, on more than one occasion he sought to involve women professionals in his research endeavors (e.g., letter from Hrdlička to Kellogg, April 13, 1918, NAA). Hrdlička published 16 papers by the anatomist and physical anthropologist Mildred Trotter (1899–1991) and had a very active correspondence with her. Trotter was the first woman appointed as an associate editor of the *AJPA*, although she did not begin her tenure until 1943 after Hrdlička resigned as editor. However, he remained on as honorary editor and retained considerable influence with Stewart, who followed as editor. It is unlikely that Stewart would have appointed Trotter without the full support of Hrdlička.

Hrdlička was relatively unaffected by the pervasive anti-Semitism of his time. This attitude was probably influenced by his debt to Meyer Rosenbleuth, the Jewish physician who attended him when he had typhoid shortly after his arrival in the United States. Rosenbleuth also arranged for Hrdlička's initial entrance to medical school and provided him with practical training in medicine. Hrdlička also had positive relationships with Jewish colleagues, the most notable of whom was probably Franz Boas (1858–1942). Boas was one of the charter associate editors of the new journal. Correspondence between the two clearly demonstrates the respect Hrdlička had for Boas regardless of occasional differences on scientific and policy issues. A distinguished physical anthropologist, Marcus S. Goldstein (1906–1997), an orthodox Jew, began his training as an aide to Hrdlička.

The picture that emerges with careful review of Hrdlička's relationships with people is that he probably was less influenced by the social prejudices of his time than most people. He was, for example, probably somewhat ahead of his time in recognizing some of the social biases, the careless research, and weak logic that were pervasive in the eugenics movement. Although he had professional ties with several scientists who supported eugenics and other racist variants, and participated in some scientific meetings promoting eugenics research, he was generally unimpressed with the research they conducted and resisted publishing papers on the subject in the journal. However, his negative opinions about some scientists did not prevent him from inviting their participation in the enterprise of publishing the journal if he thought they had something to contribute. Despite Hrdlička's weakness in formal training in the biological sciences, he had a good sense of what constituted bad research design and methods, poor quality data, and weak arguments based on inadequate research. The general high quality of the papers published in the journal reflects this judgment.

EARLY ISSUES IN THE PUBLICATION OF THE *AJPA*

Editorial Policy

We have seen earlier in this paper that Hrdlička had very definite ideas about what should be the subject matter of the journal and, by extension, the discipline of physical anthropology. He did not hesitate to express his opinion on the subject and his view undoubtedly influenced his editorial decisions about what he published in the journal. Subject content was important, but equally important was his evaluation of the quality of the research represented by a manuscript. He also had definite opinions about English usage and regularly imposed his standard regarding how a paper was written.

Hrdlička was not reluctant to use the journal to oppose ideas that he found deficient in scientific rigor. He was particularly disturbed by much of what eugenics came to represent. One of the major players in American eugenics was Madison Grant, noted above, who published a book entitled *The Passing of the Great Race* (Grant, 1917), a second edition of which was published a few months later in 1918. The basic message of the book was that the "Nordic race" represented the pinnacle of human evolutionary achievement and was being destroyed by war to the great detriment of human society. Franz Boas wrote scathing reviews of both editions (Boas, 1917; 1918). Hrdlička shared Boas's opinion about Grant and his book and asked Boas to write a review for the *AJPA*, which he did (Boas, 1918).

Later, when informed by J. H. Kellogg (letter from Kellogg to Hrdlička, October 30, 1923, NAA) that Grant was a patient at Kellogg's sanitarium in Michigan where he was being treated for rheumatism, Hrdlička responded, "Madison Grant ought to be afflicted with everlasting rheumatism of all his writing organs, for he has done a great deal of mischief with his 'Nordicism'" (letter from Hrdlička to Kellogg, November 6, 1923, NAA). This exchange illustrates the intensity of Hrdlička's distaste for careless research and poor logic. This sentiment was expressed in the face of considerable enthusiasm for Grant's books within the scientific community, including, in all likelihood Kellogg, who was also very much engaged in the eugenics movement, but was also a major financial supporter of the journal.

Hrdlička's own participation in at least one of the eugenics conferences (the Third National Conference on Race Betterment organized by Kellogg in 1927) may indicate that his opposition to some aspects of the movement was less ideological and more based on the sense that the research and data supporting eugenics was of poor quality.

Another of Hrdlička's biases was his opposition to statistical hypothesis testing, which was legendary and continued throughout his tenure as journal editor. In a letter sent to some of the journal's associate editors, including Charles H. Danforth (1883–1969) (Hrdlička to Danforth January 8, 1942), who was affiliated with the Department of Anatomy at Stanford University, Hrdlička sought "any good non-statistical paper that would fit our journal." In a letter to Prof. Fabio Frassetto (1876–1953), Instituto de Antropologia, Italy, Hrdlička responds to the catalog of scientific meetings held in Vienna in 1937 sent to him by Frasseto. "Thank you for the catalogue of the Vienna session. Regrettably the bulk of the communications were evidently devoted to statistics and not anthropometry. There is, I am afraid, a spreading illusion that biometric procedures may bring more out of any work than there is in it; and especially a spreading tendency to use such easy methods instead of hard brain work" (letter from Hrdlička to Frasseto, February 24, 1937, NAA).

Although Hrdlička's opposition to statistical methodology was probably extreme even in his day when many of the methods were being introduced, his caution about careless use of statistics deserves some attention at a time when the use of advanced multivariate statistical methods has become widespread. I certainly do not agree that statistical hypothesis testing does not involve strenuous brain activity. Nevertheless, I do have a great deal of sympathy for what I perceive was Hrdlička's fundamental concern for the need to engage in rigorous exploration of the basic biology that is associated with statistical findings.

One of the scientists invited to be an associate editor of the *AJPA* was Charles B. Davenport, as noted, a distinguished human geneticist and a leader in the American eugenics movement. Hrdlička invited Davenport to fill this role in the new journal despite misgivings about Davenport's research. Shortly following the founding of the journal, Davenport submitted a paper on relative human fertility in different human groups. In commenting on the manuscript, Hrdlička noted that (1) there was no attention given to varying infant and child mortality, (2) no control for the number of unmarried women in the various social groups included in the study, and (3) no control for average age of marriage (letter from Hrdlička to Davenport, October 2, 1918, NAA). Davenport's role as an associate editor did not blunt Hrdlička's criticism of his paper. The points made are all important issues in demographic and epidemiological research. The comments provide an indication of Hrdlička's breadth of knowledge and his sensitivity to fundamental issues in research design, methods, and communication of results.

Fortunately, Davenport appears to have had a rather disarming sense of humor, a personality trait that seems to have eluded Hrdlička. In earlier correspondence with Hrdlička about Davenport's research on the genetics of albinism, he inquired about the presence of this condition among Native Americans. Hrdlička indicated that he had encountered the abnormality. In response, Davenport noted the importance for some of his research for both parents to be albino. He commented, "It is unfortunate that these albino Indians generally prefer to marry full color individuals of the other sex. If you would add to your services as scientist that of matchmaker to these albinos, the final result would be awaited with interest" (letter from Davenport to Hrdlička, December 6, 1908, NAA).

Davenport accepted Hrdlička's invitation to be a charter associate editor of the new journal (letter from Davenport to Hrdlička, December 16, 1917, National Anthropological Archives) and is listed on the masthead of the first issue of the journal (see Figure 4.3). An important component of the early issues of the *AJPA* was summaries of relevant papers published in other scientific journals, a major responsibility of the associate editors. Hrdlička was particularly interested in having Davenport report on human genetic research published in the major journals on that subject. Nevertheless, the relationship between the two men was uneasy at best. Davenport's outspoken support of the eugenics movement seems to be one problem, but differences in the rigor of their scientific methodology seems to be equally, if not more, important. This disquiet was shared by Franz Boas who, in a letter to Hrdlička, refers to Davenport as "the dreamer" (letter from Boas to Hrdlička, March 18, 1919, NAA).

Hrdlička clearly felt that the discipline of physical anthropology was important both for the greater understanding it could provide about the human biology of modern groups but also the evolution of the species. His passion for the discipline and the journal, combined with his very definite ideas about what constituted good science, led to a very engaged and intrusive style as editor.

A manuscript by one author was viewed by Hrdlička as having scientific merit, but was too long and in major need of editing. He basically rewrote the manuscript and incurred the displeasure of the author who complained to Franz Boas, one of the new journal's associate editors. Boas wrote to Hrdlička (Boas to Hrdlička, March 26, 1919, NAA) expressing a philosophy of editorial engagement and responsibility that was rather laissez faire, at least with respect to established scientists, and very much at variance with Hrdlička's rather intrusive editorial policy. There is no subsequent indication that Hrdlička changed his editorial style or the level of his intervention, although he did query all the associate editors about editorial policy issues and the standards of excellence he wanted to maintain (letter from Hrdlička to associate editors of the *AJPA*, May 28, 1918, NAA). Indeed, well into his tenure as editor of the journal, Hrdlička wrote to another author that "I shall be glad to assist your work by publishing this additional paper; but I trust that in future contributions the English will be such that it will not give us so much work" (letter from Hrdlička to N. Bushmakin, August 27, 1930, NAA).

Vol. I WASHINGTON, JANUARY–MARCH, 1918 No. 1

AMERICAN JOURNAL
OF
PHYSICAL ANTHROPOLOGY

PUBLISHED QUARTERLY

FOUNDER AND EDITOR

ALEŠ HRDLIČKA

ASSOCIATE EDITORS

PROFESSOR G. STANLEY HALL
President, Clark University

DR. E. A. HOOTON
Peabody Museum, Harvard University

PROFESSOR GEORGE GRANT MACCURDY
Yale University

DR. CHARLES B. DAVENPORT
Carnegie Institution of Washington

PROFESSOR FRANZ BOAS
Columbia University

DR. CLARK WISSLER
American Museum of Natural History

PROFESSOR J. HOWARD MCGREGOR
Columbia University

DR. FREDERICK L. HOFFMAN
The Prudential Insurance Company

PROFESSOR H. H. DONALDSON
Wistar Institute

DR. WILLIAM C. FARABEE
The University Museum of Philadelphia

DR. GEORGE M. KOBER
Dean of Medical Department, Georgetown University

DR. J. H. KELLOGG
Superintendent, Battle Creek Sanitarium

DR. BERTHOLD LAUFER
Field Museum of Natural History, Chicago

PROFESSOR J. C. MERRIAM
National Research Council

PROFESSOR A. L. KROEBER
University of California

PROFESSOR A. E. JENKS
University of Minnesota

DR. FRANCIS H. S. KNOWLES
Victoria Museum, Ottawa

Annual Subscription { Domestic and Canada, $5.00
Other Countries, $5.50

Application has been made for entry as second class matter at the Post Office at Washington, D. C., under the Act of March 3, 1879

Figure 4.3. The masthead of the first issue of the *American Journal of Physical Anthropology* published in 1918.

Financial Problems

The cost of printing and distributing the journal were major problems through the first few years after it was founded. Because of Hrdlička's tenacious insistence both on the independence of the journal and his control of its contents, options for support by a scientific society were limited. The creation of the American Association of Physical Anthropologists, which would eventually play a major oversight role for the journal, was 12 years away. Hrdlička approached the Wistar Institute about publishing the journal, but they declined initially, although in 1927 they did take over its management and publication. Boas urged Hrdlička to obtain financial support from the Galton Society (Spencer, 1979, 695), one of several American societies promoting eugenics. However, the Galton Society wanted more editorial control over the journal than Hrdlička was willing to grant and no support was forthcoming.

Boas's enthusiasm for the Galton Society seems strange given his outspoken opposition to much of what they supported. His paper in *The Scientific Monthly* on eugenics, addressing many of the theoretical, scientific, and practical inadequacies of the ideology, could, with very little change, be an effective statement against racism today (Boas, 1916, 471–478). The Galton Society was founded by Madison Grant, a lawyer who was one of the leading figures in the eugenics movement until it lost momentum as well as credibility and dissolved in 1935.

During the first three years the journal was published, the shortfall between income from subscriptions and the cost of publication was about $1,000.00 per year. This deficit diminished somewhat in subsequent years, but remained a significant expense, much of which was absorbed by Hrdlička, until taken over by the Wistar Institute in 1927. Hrdlička's initial salary at the National Museum of Natural History in 1903, when he began his career there, was $175.00 per month. It is likely that this had increased by 1918 but even so, his personal financial commitment to the success of the journal is both obvious and impressive. This expense would have been even greater but for the funds contributed by the associate editors, either directly or through their influence on other donors.

DISCUSSION AND CONCLUSIONS

National and international preoccupation with World War I did not provide an auspicious time to inaugurate a new scientific journal. Nevertheless, Hrdlička felt strongly that a niche in scholarly publications existed for papers on physical anthropology. There were several reasons for this, including a general social interest in the anatomical aspects of human diversity. Enhancing this interest was an assumption in Western governments that data on race provided by research in physical anthropology was crucial in defining some new boundaries between nations following the war.

Establishing the *AJPA* in 1918 is a tribute to Hrdlička's vision as well as his tenacity. He was able to attract an eclectic, but also rather remarkable, initial group of associate editors who lent their prestige and, in at least some cases, provided crucial supplemental funding that underwrote the cost of publication. As is the case for any editor of a scientific journal, a major preoccupation for Hrdlička was attracting manuscripts that met a high standard of scientific excellence as he defined it. He had a remarkable ability to identify flawed research design and methodology and to detect careless logic. He had little patience for any of these deficiencies. Not all of his editorial policies were well founded. His prejudice against statistical hypothesis testing was misguided; he would probably be dismayed at the central role this methodology plays in papers published today.

The content of scientific journals is inevitably influenced by the social climate in which these journals are published. Hrdlička avoided, at least partially, some of the social biases of his time because the scientific basis for these opinions was badly flawed and he recognized this defect. At least a partial defense against making mistakes because of social and/or scientific biases is to maintain high standards of scientific rigor. Testable hypotheses, careful research design, appropriate methods, not overextending the meaning of one's data, and the use of careful logic in interpreting results are basic to high-quality publications, and insistence on them remains the primary objective of journal editors today. Attention to these factors does not guarantee flawless research or publications, but it does minimize the effect of scientific and social biases. This is well illustrated in Hrdlička's early attempt to identify anatomical characteristics that would distinguish criminals or the insane from the normal members of a society. On the basis of his own research, Hrdlička correctly concluded that distinguishing characteristics simply did not exist, despite the prevailing opinion to the contrary.

It is not surprising that science and scientists in the early part of the 20th century were influenced by the social milieu in which they operated. Pervasive ethnic prejudice undoubtedly affected the social philosophy and policies inherent in the human sciences as evidenced by the eugenics movement in Europe and North America during the last half of the 19th and the early 20th centuries. It is hard to argue against the idea that human society can and should use its knowledge of human variation to promote healthier and more intelligent people. Indeed, the genetic counseling that is available today for couples who have the potential of producing children with serious genetic problems is a modern extension of the eugenics movement, but based on careful research. A major problem with the eugenics movement was the preoccupation with untenable assumptions and the careless research reported and used to support its assumptions (Gould, 1981). The harsh lessons we have learned from the Nazi pogroms during World War II and the additional human atrocities that have taken place since are a reminder of the horrible impact that incorrect and misguided concepts of human biological and cultural variation can have on political and social policy.

Two factors were significant in Hrdlička's ability to avoid some of the egregious excesses of the social philosophy of his time. The first of these is the influence of Léonce Manouvrier, who rejected the Neo-Lamarckian philosophy prevalent in France in the late 19th and early 20th centuries. He emphasized the plasticity of human nature and the role of the environment in determining human behavior and achievement. Although genetic heritage remains important in defining humanity, the role of culture is substantial and the potential of humans to transcend the influence of their genetic heritage is great.

The second factor was Hrdlička's remarkably clear perception of what constituted the best in scientific methods. His correspondence with authors of manuscripts submitted for publication in the *AJPA* reveals an exceptional ability to spot flaws in method, logic, and interpretation. Despite his deficiencies in formal scientific education, he understood very well the requirements of good scientific research. Hrdlička recognized poor research and consistently rejected or modified manuscripts that did not meet his high standard of scientific rigor and excellence.

This scientific rigor remains an important component of scientific research and publication today. The very high scientific standard Hrdlička had both for his own research and for the research of others that he published as editor of the *AJPA* established a strong tradition of scientific excellence that continues to contribute to the prestige and reputation of the *AJPA* in the world community of human scientists today.

Arguably, the *AJPA* continues to be the leading journal for publications in human biological anthropology. In today's scientific context, one can challenge the scientific merit of some papers published in the *AJPA* during Hrdlička's tenure as founding editor. Eugenics and related racist ideology was prominent in both scientific and general social circles and undoubtedly influenced the content of some publications on physical anthropology. However, this influence was at least limited in the *AJPA* due to Hrdlička's suspicion of research conducted by the scientists supporting these ideas and his own clear understanding of what constituted good research.

ACKNOWLEDGMENTS

The symposium in which this paper was presented in 2005 was primarily a celebration of the 75th anniversary of the founding of the American Association of Physical Anthropologists. However, the organizers of the symposium and editors of this book, along with the participants, paid tribute to the late Frank Spencer, whose remarkable scholarship both as a historian of physical anthropology and a physical anthropologist provided important insight and facts on which much of what I have written is based. His biography of Hrdlička (Spencer, 1979) provides a window into the culture of science that was prevalent in the late 19th and early 20th centuries. I also appreciate the assistance of the staff of the National Anthropological Archives, particularly Vyrtis Thomas, who facilitated my access to the relevant correspondence of Hrdlička.

REFERENCES

Boas, Franz. (1916). Eugenics. *Scientific Monthly, 3,* 471–478.
——. (1917). Inventing a Great Race. *The New Republic, 9,* 305–307.
——. (1918). *Review of* The Passing of the Great Race. *American Journal of Physical Anthropology, 1,* 363.
Castle, William E. (1926). Biological and Social Consequences of Race-Crossing. *American Journal of Physical Anthropology, 9,* 145–156.
Gould, Stephen Jay. (1981). *The Mismeasure of Man.* New York: W.W. Norton and Company.
Grant, Madison. (1917). *The Passing of the Great Race.* New York: Charles Scribner's Sons.
Schultz, Adolph H. (1946). Biographical Memoir of Aleš Hrdlička, 1869–1943. *Biographical Memoir, National Academy of Sciences* Vol. XXIII–Twelfth Memoir, pp. 305–336.
Spencer, Frank. (1979). Aleš Hrdlička, M.D.: A Chronical of the Life and Work of an American Physical Anthropologist. Ph.D. Dissertation, Department of Anthropology, University of Michigan.

Chapter 5

Principal Figures in Early 20th-Century Physical Anthropology: With Special Treatment of Forensic Anthropology

by

Kenneth A. R. Kennedy

ALEŠ HRDLIČKA'S CONTRIBUTIONS TO PHYSICAL ANTHROPOLOGY

In the first issue of the *American Journal of Physical Anthropology* published in 1918, its founder, Aleš Hrdlička (1869–1943; 1918, 3), asserted that "the actual birth of a new science may be counted from the commencement of substantial research work in a new field, which in due time is followed by differentiation of concepts, advanced organization of forces and plans, standardization of procedures and gradual development of regular instruction and means of publication." Hrdlička set the starting date of American physical anthropology at 1866 (the year of the founding of the Army Medical Museum at Washington, DC, and the Peabody Museum in Boston). However, it was not until the first half of the 20th century that North American physical anthropologists became recognized by European anthropologists as adherents to an "American School," which differed in some aspects from the perspectives and methodologies of European scholars. British and continental anthropologists gained a closer acquaintance with their trans-Atlantic associates after Hrdlička's founding of the American Association of Physical Anthropologists in 1930 (Hrdlička, 1929). Foreign attendance increased at the annual meetings of these organizations, and scholarly interactions with students of human biological diversity and evolution were promoted.

CURRICULA OF PHYSICAL ANTHROPOLOGY
AT AMERICAN UNIVERSITIES

Given the title of this paper, "Principal Figures in Early 20th-Century Anthropology," I hope that readers will not feel deceived when they discover that my "Principal Figures" include numerical ones. Accounts of the lives and anthropological contributions of some of our learned predecessors are appropriately considered by other writers of chapters in this volume. The present author discusses the scientific significance of Hrdlička's outlook, during the early years of the 20th century, that the advancement of American physical anthropology demanded "[the] gradual development of regular instruction and means of publication" (Hrdlička, 1918, 3). Using departmental records and published sources revealing the progress of teaching programs and student fieldwork, several earlier members of our profession put together a rostrum of physical anthropology college and university courses for the years 1902, 1940, and 1950. Most recent records of curricula and listings of instructors in various academic departments in North America are published in the annually up-dated *Guide: A Guide to Programs (and) a Directory of Members*. This is available to members of the American Anthropological Association. The data cited in this study are from the 2004–2005 guide. The materials for this sample series were collected from 54 to 600 institutions of higher learning, where the canon of instruction included racial identification and classification, racial paleontology, eugenics, human anatomy and physiology, and various interpretations of the nature of heredity and phylogeny commonly held prior to the "Modern Synthesis" of Darwinian evolution and genetics, an integration that emerged in the 1940s. There was an excessive dependence upon anthropometry of living populations and skeletal remains of prehistoric fossil specimens. Numerous anthropometric instruments were engineered and manufactured for the purpose of taking precision measurements of human skeletons and living people in the quest to identify and classify human "races." There was a "craniocentric" attention to morphometric variables of skulls.

Most of the courses in American physical anthropology were at one time offered in departments of anatomy and social sciences (Kroeber, 1954, 764), a career choice still available to doctoral students who have had training in physical anthropology. Courses in our discipline continue to be offered outside of anthropology departments as a comparison of three studies conducted over a 48-year period demonstrate (see Table 5.1). Writing in 1902, George MacCurdy (1863–1947; 1902, 211) recorded that in his sample of 54 American universities, 31 (57%) offered courses in physical anthropology: 10 in departments of anthropology, 9 in departments of sociology, and 12 courses scattered throughout departments of anatomy, psychology, zoology, biology, and a category that he labeled "unclassified."

Table 5.1.   Distribution of physical anthropology courses by departments in U.S. academic institutions from 1902 (MacCurdy, 1902, 211), 1940 (Goldstein, 1940, 207) and 1950 (Voegelin, 1950, 387).

Department	1902 (54) [31]	1940 (149) [20]	1950 (600) [128]
Anthropology	10	12	88
Sociology	9	-	-
Anatomy	-	5	-
Zoology	3	1	-
Biology	1	1	39
Psychology	5	-	-
History	1	-	-

Values in parentheses are the number of institutions in the series; values in brackets are the number of institutions in which courses in physical anthropology were offered.

In 1940, Marcus Goldstein (1906–1997; 1940, 207) surveyed curricula of 149 universities. He noted a drop to 20 (13%) offering courses in physical anthropology. Then there was a slight rise of 12 courses in departments of anthropology, 5 in anatomy, and the remaining courses in departments of sociology, biology, and zoology. Ten years later, Ermine W. Voegelin (1903–1988; 1950, 387), using a sample of 600 colleges and universities, found that 128 (21%) listed courses in physical anthropology, but 39 (6.5%) had homes in other departments, as noted by MacCurdy and Goldstein. These statistical efforts to measure progress in the discipline were undertaken by a fourth study published in 1942 by Lucy J. Chamberlain (1893–1969) and E. Adamson Hoebel (1907–1993; 1942, 387). They reported that among 273 institutions, some167 (61.2%) offered courses in general anthropology, but of these only 58 (21.4%) listed offerings in physical anthropology (see Table 5.2).

A good honors thesis topic for an undergraduate student with a calling to be a physical anthropologist would be to calculate the annual course frequencies in his/her field of research from 1950 to the present day. The survey undertaken by the present author was based upon listings in the AAA guide for 2004–2005. A total of greater than 529 physical anthropologists are currently teaching their discipline at colleges and universities. It may be assumed

Table 5.2.   Number of offerings of course topics in physical anthropology for 167 colleges and university in 1942 (Chamberlain & Hoebel, 1942, 527).

Course Topics	Course Offerings
Human Evolution	17
General Physical Anthropology	20
Fossil and Living Races	20
Criminal and Constitutional Anthropology	1
Totals	58

that individual instructors teach an average of three to six courses per academic year, thus suggesting an estimate of 3,000 classes and laboratories offered annually in the United States. This survey did not include Canadian and Mexican universities. These figures are a fraction of the numbers of physical anthropologists teaching at museums, research institutions, medical facilities, and in applied aspects of the field where they may identify themselves as forensic anthropologists, nutritional anthropologists, specialists in molecular-genetic research, and members of modern health-related sciences.

If the apparent "racism" of physical anthropology of the pre-1950s seems to characterize a very different discipline from the one we practice today, this should not evoke embarrassment. Western astronomy has its origins in astrology; early chemistry was alchemy; medicine emerged from shamanism; and biology had its early home in natural theology and the concept of the chain-of-being. There are skeletons in every field of science. The dictates of instruction and research in our discipline have undergone dramatic changes over time, as should be expected. One may compare what had been taught in 1950 with what is offered to students today in laboratories, lecture rooms, and field trips within and outside the Ivory Tower and research institutions (McCown, 1952).

The study by Voegelin (1950, 387) helps us to perceive frequencies of the primary topics in research and teaching in 1950 (see Table 5.3). Today, constitutional anthropology (somatotypology) and racial classifications survive mainly in some anthropology textbooks, popular novels, and television, but not in today's classrooms. Film and television portrayals of forensic anthropologists at work in the field or laboratory are usually grossly inaccurate (one actor in the role of a medical examiner attempted to describe how a deceased victim of assault had parted his hair by observing his femur!). There are romantic depictions of our science with their heroic forensic anthropologists. We all enjoy the entertaining novels by Aaron Elkins (1987) and Kathleen Reichs (2005), both of whom have received training in forensic anthropology. Also available are biographies and details of individual case studies by practicing forensic anthropologists: Mary Manhein (1999), William Maples and M. Browning (1994) Stanley Rhine (1998), Douglas Ubelaker, H. Scammell (1992), and Dawnie Steadman (2002). These sources serve to enlighten some undergraduate students in a pursuit of forensic anthropology at the professional level.

Table 5.3. Frequencies of course topics in physical anthropology for 128 colleges and universities in 1950 (Voegelin, 1950, 387).

Course Topics	Independent Departments	Programs	Combined Departments	Host Departments and Isolated Courses	Totals
General Physical Anthropology	21	4	9	2	36
Fossil and Living Races	31	1	4	4	40
Human Evolution and Genetics	19	1	8	2	30
Morphology and Somatology	9	-	3	-	12
Constitutional Anthropology	2	-	1	3	6
Populations	2	-	-	-	2
Growth and Development	2	-	-	-	2
Laboratory	2	-	1	3	6
Totals	88	6	26	14	134

Physical anthropology at the dawn of the third millennium reveals some striking contrasts with what was taught during the first 50 years of the preceding century. For example, phylogenetic trees with hominid fossils and representatives of "living races" suspended from the branches have withered away. Eugenics lost its respectability. But the Piltdown chimera was still hanging around in this era of a relatively meager and poorly understood paleontological record of our fossilized primate ancestors. Primatology, growth and development studies, DNA analyses and molecular genetics, nutritional anthropology, and forensic anthropology were in their infancy, although a few pioneers were sensitive to the research potential of these areas of anthropological investigation before 1950.

The *Weltanschauung* of American physical anthropologists in the first half of the 20th century must be difficult for present-day students to comprehend, especially as vestiges of the earlier canon of what every physical anthropology student should know continue to clank about as chained ghosts in our discipline. Yet, without an awareness of our intellectual history, how can we interpret the configurations of 21st-millennium research and instruction? As the late Gerald W. Johnson (1890–1980; 1943, 1), the distinguished political journalist, reminds us, "Nothing changes more constantly than the past; for the past that influences our lives does not consist of what actually happened but what men believe happened." Thus the present author offers his interpretations as to what he believes happened in physical anthropology from 1901 to 1950.

RESEARCH ORIENTATIONS, INSTRUCTION, AND FUNDING

Those of us who have been practicing and teaching physical anthropology over several decades may nurse a wistful remembrance "For old unhappy far-off things and battles long ago," to paraphrase the English poet William Wordsworth's (1770–1850; 1807) passage in "A Solitary Reaper." But our reminiscences of venerable mentors and their lessons and impassioned arguments in which they provoked their colleagues have been transcended by new methods and research projects in the arena of molecular biology, DNA analysis of living and prehistoric populations, a more sophisticated knowledge of human growth and development, and accurate recognition of markers of pathology trauma and stress agents of bone remodeling.

These recent research innovations have served to question a plethora of traditional "ecological myths" loaded with interpretations of how climate, diet, and geographical latitude are the most critical agents accounting for variables of human body size and shape under tropical and cold-stress environments. These, and other anthropological myths, were once taken for granted by physical anthropologists. For example, some ancient and modern populations habitually perform activities demanding stamina and muscular-skeletal robusticity. Enthesopathic lesions on bones and tooth modifications may be markers of occupational stress (often misidentified as pathological lesions). These consequences of bone remodeling are seldom considered in some of these overly simplified environmental hypotheses. This is only one of our scientific legacies. Others are shadowed by a traditional race concept with its multiple hierarchial classifications of ancient and modern human populations. Nor have the ravages of the battlefield of eugenics wrought peace in some programs of anthropological instruction today. Vestiges of a preoccupation with anthropometric measurements and morphological analyses survive in criminal anthropology, criminal profiling, and in efforts to create a national or group identity encumbered with political and social class implications.

But apart from these residues of an earlier anthropology, there has been a positive reorientation of curricula. William Boyd's (1903–1983; 1950) book *Genetics and the Races of Man* was published in 1950 and in the same year as the conference of geneticists, anthropologists, paleontologists, and other evolutionary biologists at Cold Spring Harbor (Warren, 1951). These are significant historical signposts marking the dramatic changes in research and teaching of physical anthropology in the latter half of the twentieth century. This shift in academic curricula prompted Sherwood Washburn (1911–2000; 1951) to write "The New Physical Anthropology," published in 1951 in the *Transactions of the New York Academy of Sciences.*

By the late 1950s, research funding was provided by business contributors outside the Ivory Tower, including the Viking Fund/Wenner-Gren Foundation beginning in 1941. Governmental sources of funding include the National Science Foundation, National Institute of Mental Health, National Endowment for the Humanities, Howard Foundation, Smithsonian Institution, and research grants from universities and other scientific institutions. The American Anthropological Association is the largest organization of North American anthropologists, including physical anthropologists in one of its more than 30 units. Since its founding in 1902, with the merger of other societies of anthropologists located in the United States, it has organized annual meetings and publishes the *American Anthropologist,* the foremost journal for the discipline. Hrdlička was one of the presidents of the AAA from 1925 to 1926.

The discovery of fossil hominid remains in Europe, the Near East, and Asia initiated a strong impetus for North American scholars to expand programs in paleoanthropology beyond the borders of the Western Hemisphere. Living and prehistoric Native American populations were foci of study made feasible by the geographical availability of mounds, burial sites, and ruins. But when the hominid paleontological treasures of Africa were forthcoming in the second half of the 20th century, attention was directed to discoveries of fossil hominids and consequent changes of interpretations about the antiquity and course of human evolution.

Paramount among these advances of American physical anthropology was the publication in 1918 of the first issue of the *American Journal of Physical Anthropology* and the foundation of the American Association of Physical

Anthropologists 12 years later. Hrdlička established both the journal and the association in the course of his long tenure as director of the Department of Physical Anthropology at the Smithsonian Institution. His contemporaries among physical anthropologists included Franz Boas (1858–1942) of Columbia University, Thomas Dwight (1843–1911), a Bostonian surgeon and anatomist, Earnest A. Hooton (1887–1954) of Harvard University, Harris H. Wilder (1864–1928) of Smith College, T. Wingate Todd (1885–1938) of Western Reserve Medical School, Frederick S. Hulse (1906–1990) of the University of Arizona), James E. Anderson (1926-1995) of the University of Toronto, Georg K. Neumann (1908–1971) of the University of Indiana, Theodore D. McCown (1908–1969) of the University of California at Berkeley, Wilton M. Krogman (1903–1988) of the University of Pennsylvania, Mildred Trotter (1899–1991) of Washington University Medical School in St, Louis, and Alice Brues (1913–2007) of Colorado University. While this is not an exhaustive list of physical anthropologists practicing between 1901 and 1950, their names are included here because they were the highly honored "grandparents" or "great grandparents" of the present generation of American physical anthropologists. Of these scholars, a majority were the American pioneers of the applied discipline of forensic anthropology. A discussion of this relatively new component within the broader field of physical anthropology serves as a realization of Hrdlička's vision of the "actual birth" of a new science.

FORENSIC ANTHROPOLOGY

Forensic anthropology involves the application of field, laboratory, and statistical procedures to human skeletal biology for purposes of establishing personal identification of human remains that come within the jurisdiction of judicial and medical agencies. Forensic anthropologists are newcomers to the community of forensic sciences, which today includes specialists in the American Academy of Forensic Sciences (AAFS). They are active in one or more of the sections of pathology and biology, toxicology, jurisprudence, questioned documents, criminalistics, odontology, forensic engineering, and psychology and behavioral sciences. As T. Dale Stewart (1901–1997; 1979, 17) noted in his book *Essentials of Forensic Anthropology: Especially as Developed in the United States,* "Prior to the formal organization of the Section of Physical Anthropology in the Academy the expressions 'forensic anthropology' and 'forensic anthropologist' were seldom heard. This is no longer the case." Physical anthropologists of the pre–World War II period did not form any self-determined unit within the emerging field of forensic sciences, although they shared with the international community of physical anthropologists studies of variations and identifying features of the skeletons: estimations of age at time of death, sex, ancestry ("race"), determinations of living stature, and markers on bones that could be identified as the results of trauma, pathology, and unique features of bones and teeth of individual subjects (individuation).

The majority of cases encountered by forensic anthropologists involves personal identification of human remains, skeletal or decomposed, of individuals of historical significance—identification of the "eminent dead." Cases of this kind arise when there is a question that the human remains in a tomb, grave, or in other kinds of disposition are actually those of an individual whose name appears on a burial marker or when local tradition ascribes a burial site to a person who enjoyed some level of distinction during his or her life. Or the identity of the deceased may be known, but an understanding of his or her manner of death (homicide, pathological condition, suicide, accident?) is critical for survivors, particularly when an inheritance is involved. Hypothetically, a citizen might ask "Who is buried in Grant's tomb?" In a number of situations this issue has been raised under more serious circumstances, such as the identification of the individual members of the royal Russian Romanoff family, who were executed in 1918 and their bodies buried (Maples & Browning, 1994). A mummy in its sarcophagus was identified as a scribe from ancient Egypt, his personal name "Penpi" appearing on his coffin. Examination of the bones, teeth, and preserved soft tissues of Penpi allowed the forensic anthropologists to determine his sex, age at time of death, an estimation of his living stature, and the pathological conditions which he had suffered (Kennedy et al., 1986).

It should be helpful at this point in this study to provide an example of the forensic anthropology contributions of one of the discipline's principle figures. Theodore D. McCown was a professor in the Department of Anthropology, with a joint appointment in the Department of Criminology at the University of California at Berkeley (see Figure 5.1). He is best known for his collaboration with Sir Arthur Keith (1866–1955) and their co-researched and co-written volume *The Stone Age of Mount Carmel: The Fossil Human Remains from the Levalloiso-Mousterian* (Keith & McCown, 1939). The majority of McCown's publications were about the Neanderthal fossils from the caves of Skhūl and Tabūn, his accounts about his two field expeditions to Middle Pleistocene archaeological localities in India, and related topics about hominid evolution. But he was active in teaching an annual lecture-laboratory course in which human osteology and anthropometry were oriented to forensic anthropology. During World War II, his military service was in Graves Registration of the U.S. Army

Chapter 5

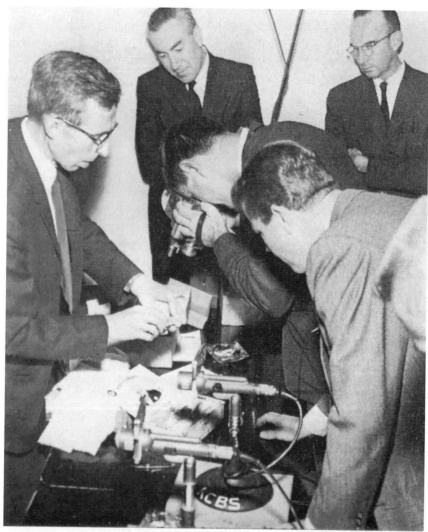

Figure 5.1. Theodore Doney McCown (left) examining the human skeletal remains which were reputed to be those of Amelia Earhart (1908–1937), the American aviatrix whose airplane went down somewhere in the Pacific. Presumably she and her flying companion, Fred Noonan, were killed. McCown concluded that the bones could not have been those of Earhart or Noonan, but were likely to be those of a prehistoric Micronesian. The photograph was taken in December 1961 (courtesy of the *San Francisco Examiner*). In the center background is Jules Dundes, CBS Vice-President and General Manager of KCBS Radio, San Francisco.

Quartermaster Corps at the San Francisco Presidio. His duties included efforts to make personal identifications of the war dead from both the European and Asian theaters.

Upon returning to his *alma mater* at Berkeley, McCown served as chair or minor member to a number of graduate students who became professional forensic anthropologists—Russell W. Newman (PhD 1949), Sheilagh T. Brooks (1951), John G. Roney (1955), Thomas W. McKern (1955), Kenneth A. R. Kennedy (1962), and John M. Whitehead (1968). He was the chair or minor member of other Berkeley graduate students who have careers in other areas of physical anthropology: William D. Hohenthal (1951), Chester Chard (1953), Clement W. Meighan (1953), Dwight T. Wallace (1957), Edward P. Lanning (1960), Clara S. Hall (1962), Paul E. Simonds (1963), Theodore I. Grand (1964), Mary R. W. Marzke (1964), Ralph L. Holloway (1964), Russell H. Tuttle (1965), Adrienne L. Zihlman (1967), Vincent M. Sarich (1967), Jane B. Lancaster (1967), and Alan E. Mann (1968). These are only a few of the 44 graduate students who received training in physical anthropology from McCown (Kennedy, 2000, 255).

McCown's casework in forensic anthropology was unique since it focused upon identification of the "eminent dead." Among the most notable of his cases was the positive identification of the Franciscan missionary Father Junipero Serra (1718–1784). The skeletal and dental remains of this man, who established many of the missions in western California, were beatified by the Roman Catholic Church in 1988. He is buried at the Carmel Mission Church near Monterey. In collaboration with Mark Harrington (1882–1971), McCown was able to identify Serra's remains in a grave in which two other persons had been buried (Morgado, 1987). McCown identified the bones of Juan Bautista de Anza (1735–1788), founder of the city of San Francisco under the flag of Spain in 1776. The reputed remains of the American aviatrix Amelia Earhart (1898–1937) were brought from a Pacific island and presented to McCown for identification under the auspices of Fred Groener (1966) of KCBS News. Alas, a negative identification resulted, McCown reporting that these were the vestiges of a prehistoric Micronesian adult male with severe dental attrition, a condition unlikely to be encountered in a 20th-century female who died in her fourth decade of life.

McCown did not take part in medical-legal cases involving homicides, determination of manner of death, time elapsed since death, and the examination of decomposed bodies. He was never subpoenaed as an expert witness in court. Rather, his value to forensic anthropology was in his teaching and cases involving the "eminent dead," and in training his students in the applications of human skeletal biology to the forensic sciences (Brooks, 1970; Hammel, 1969; Kennedy, 1997; 2000; 2005; Kennedy & Brooks, 1984).

McCown's premature death from heart failure in 1969 prevented him from experiencing the immense progress in forensic anthropology that began in the 1970s. But, indeed, he was one of the scholars who established the intellectual and methodological foundation of the exciting discipline practiced today.

HOW DID WE GET TO WHERE WE ARE?

The anatomical variables and the progress of scientific methods for taking accurate measurements and defining non-metric (morphological) traits encountered in human skeletal remains were of keen interest to paleontologists in their discoveries and examinations of the hominid fossil record. Thus, it was a short step to applying these methods to medical-legal problems by the second half of the 20th century. Although the Academy had been established in 1948, almost a quarter of a century was to pass before a Physical Anthropology Section was introduced.

It is rewarding to look at past developments of forensic anthropology in order to understand its changes since the first half of the 20th century and its present status in science. There exist a number of good "histories" of this field (Bass, 1979; Işcan, 1988; Joyce & Stover, 1991; Kennedy, 2000; Kerley, 1978; Reichs, 1998; Rhine, 1998; Snow, 1973; 1982; Spencer, 1981; 1982; 1997; Stewart, 1970; 1979; Thompson, 1982; Ubelaker & Scammell, 1992; Ubelaker, 1997). These document the American origins of forensic anthropology since the end of the 18th century, as well as the past and current practices of our European peers.

Important early cases include personal identification of a slain American Revolutionary War officer by Paul Revere (1735–1818), who had made his false teeth for him. Revere recognized his handiwork among the other vestiges of the decedent. A mid-19th-century case of personal identification of human remains is the one at Harvard University where Professor George Parkman was murdered by his colleague, Professor Webster, over a dispute concerning an unpaid loan of money. A trial ensued when Parkman's remains were identified, and Webster became the first Harvard professor to be hung for his sins. Then there was the infamous Luetgert murder case that took place in Chicago in 1897. Adolf Luetgert was a sausage manufacturer who, in a moment of pique, disposed of Mrs. Luetgert in one of his meat processing vats. Rumors that Mrs. Luetgert became an ingredient in his delicious bratwurst remain unsubstantiated, but discovery by the police of bone fragments on the factory premises and their identification as human by George Amos Dorsey (1868–1931), anthropologist and curator of the Field Columbian Museum in Chicago, neither enhanced Mr. Luetgert's business nor extended his life.

When we look at the careers of "principal figures" in American physical anthropology who, in the first half of the last century, assisted medical and legal investigators in personal identification cases, almost all of them offered courses in human osteology at their academic or research institutions. Hooton taught osteology at Harvard University, but did not prepare published reports about the occasional identification cases that came his way. Nor did Hrdlička publish any of the cases brought to him by law enforcement personnel from the time of his appointment as curator of the United States National Museum (Smithsonian Institution) in 1910. However, these two prominent anthropologists—Hrdlička and Hooton—trained a generation of students who came to identify themselves as forensic anthropologists: Alice Brues, J. Lawrence Angel (1915–1986), Harry L. Shapiro (1902–1990) and Frederick S. Hulse among others. Hrdlička's successor at the Smithsonian was T. Dale Stewart. He did write reports, often in association with the FBI with its headquarters in Washington, DC.

Wilton M. Krogman gained his education of methods in forensic anthropology while working in the laboratory of T. Wingate Todd (1885–1938), professor of anatomy at Western Reserve University in Cleveland. A major turning point in the progress of forensic anthropology occurred in 1939 when Krogman published a paper that appeared in the *FBI Law Enforcement Bulletin* (Krogman, 1939). This was followed in 1962 with his book *The Human Skeleton in Forensic Medicine* (Krogman, 1962). These influential publications, along with others appearing before the outbreak of World War II, encouraged other physical anthropologists to write about the applied aspects of their discipline. These included Krogman's colleague Mildred Trotter (1899–1991; Trotter & Gieser, 1958) of Washington University, St. Louis, who examined skeletons of World War II and the Korean War dead and created formulae for estimation of stature in life from military records and her measurements of postcranial bones of the deceased.

During the first half of the 20th century, forensic anthropology remained a peripheral activity for those physical anthropologists who were willing to assist in law enforcement investigations. The majority who did venture forth into this applied aspect of their discipline risked the biases held by some of their fellow professors and researchers that "police work," with its consequent newspaper publicity, was incompatible with the mores of the academic life. Reports of analyses of skeletons and decomposed bodies were not published in scientific journals, not even in the *American Journal of Physical Anthropology* prior to 1940, although articles about human and non-human primates were abundant. Nor did these academics working with medical-legal agencies receive or expect financial compensation for their labors beyond travel costs.

Three approaches to the teaching and practice of forensic anthropology are discernible by mid-century: (1) instruction in human osteology was offered by physical anthropologists at colleges, universities, and research institutions who undertook some forensic work outside of their major research and teaching programs, but publication was rare and payment for services was nonexistent; (2) there were minimal experimental endeavors; and (3) employment of some physical anthropologists in military and governmental research institutes offered them a broader field for publication and engagement in the development of new methodologies and scientific instrumentation for precise measurements of bones and teeth, and also sound preparation for serving as an expert witness in a court of law. Articles about how to teach physical anthropology, including its applied side in the forensic sciences, were published in major journals (Brooks, 1981; McCown, 1952).

We must look at the second half of the 20th century and the first decade of the present century to see the flowering of forensic anthropology, today recognized by academics and the public as a legitimate field of science. The first symposium focusing upon this discipline was held at Washington, DC, in 1948 at the annual meeting of the American Association of Physical Anthropologists. There were only four speakers discussing forensic anthropology: Krogman, Shapiro, Stewart, and Charles Snow. Eight years later, the Wenner-Gren Foundation for Anthropological Research sponsored a summer seminar on forensic anthropology in New York City. By the late 1960s, J. L. Angel of the Smithsonian Institution directed a course for law enforcement officers that was held at his institution, a program continued by Douglas H. Ubelaker following Angel's death in 1986.

The catalyst that has created the modern era of forensic anthropology was the founding of its separate section at the 1972 annual meeting of the American Academy of Forensic Sciences (AAFS), as noted above. Attending this gathering of forensic scientists in Atlanta were 14 forensic anthropologists; at the time of the meeting held in Seattle in 2006, there were over 300 forensic anthropologists participating, of whom about 70 are "Diplomates" certified by the American Board of Forensic Anthropology (ABFA). Since 1986, qualification and maintenance of the high professional standards demanded by the board have been conferred upon some 70 "Diplomates," those PhD applicants who have passed the rigorous practical and written board examinations for Diplomate status. There is a yearly recertification requirement that records teaching, research, field trips, publications, and courtroom appearances as an expert witness. One-third of the members of the section are students who have received training at colleges, universities, and research institutions that offer the requisite laboratory and lecture courses about forensic anthropology. They are ranked in the association as student affiliate, trainee affiliate, member, associate member, fellow, retired fellow, retired member, and honorary member. These titles are based upon frequency of attendance at annual AAFS meetings and academic degrees (MA, MS, PhD). Since the 1970s, there have been regional-level meetings held yearly which are attended by students and professionals: The Northeast Forensic Anthropology Association; the Mountain, Desert, and Coastal Forensic Anthropologists; the Mountain, Swamp, and Beach Group; and the Mid-West Bioarchaeology and Forensic Anthropology Group.

While these markers of achievement of the discipline since 1950 fall outside the timeframe of this paper, students and their mentors should know that there is an increasing number of forensic anthropologists participating in personal identification at sites of mass disasters (the Twin Towers, the Oklahoma City bombing, the fire at the Branch Dravidian compound, airplane disasters of PanAm 103, TWA 943, and Egyptian Airline 990, flooded regions of the American southeastern region, mass graves of victims of genocide in Bosnia, Kosovo, Argentina, Chile, and in other countries). Many forensic anthropologists work with the National Disaster Medical System and Disaster Mortuary Teams (D-MORT), which have been active since 1993, as well as with the FBI.

Education in forensic anthropology is offered at relatively few American colleges and universities. Those listed by Clyde Snow (1982, 112) in his study of 1982 included the Universities of Tennessee, Arizona, Nevada–Las Vegas, Maryland, Florida, New Mexico, and the California State University at Fullerton. Some of these institutions have maintained their programs while others have arisen more recently: Arizona State University, Florida Atlantic University, University of Wyoming, San Diego State University, Cornell University–Ithaca, New York, Kansas State University, University of Indianapolis, Michigan State University, University of Southern Florida, University of South Carolina, Indiana University, State University of California–Chico, State University of Louisiana–New Orleans, Binghamton University of the State University of New York, Mercyhurst College in Pennsylvania, and the University of Maine. This is not a complete list at the date of this paper since changes reflect retirements, deaths, or transience of faculty, of whom the greatest numbers are in departments of anthropology. However, these listings are significant when considering that in 1940 graduate-level training in forensic anthropology was offered by so few scholars: Theodore D. McCown of the University of California at Berkeley, T. Wingate Todd of Western Reserve University, Wilton M. Krogman at the University of Pennsylvania, and Earnest A. Hooton of Harvard University.

Curriculum changes and training in forensic anthropology reflect the increase of younger scholars entering the field, retirements and deaths of their mentors and grand-mentors, and transition of some forensic anthropologists to other academic or research institutions. Any of these factors may mean the departure of qualified scholars and their programs and the hiring of new and experienced teachers who develop their laboratories, teaching materials, and curricula. In short, forensic anthropology today is an exciting and expanding discipline. Textbooks with case histories and instructions for performing the many aspects of a forensic anthropology study appear on the market every year, although the more detailed research reports are published in key journals of the discipline—for example, *American Journal of Forensic Sciences, American Journal of Physical Anthropology, Science, Nature.* Edited books with multiple chapters, each written by a professional forensic anthropologist or with several co-authors and addressing specific topics, are legion (e.g., Reichs, 1986; 1998). Access to all of these various sources is critical in allowing the professional forensic anthropologists to "keep up" with new developments in the discipline. Today, remuneration for services carried out at the request of medical and legal clients is the rule, the amount set by the individual forensic anthropologist for an hourly rate and for travel, lodging, and other expenses. This is as it should be for services of any professional practitioner, and this is a reflection of the present status of a forensic anthropologist.

HOW DOES THE FUTURE LOOK FOR YOUNG PHYSICAL ANTHROPOLOGISTS?

If left with this description of the present-day health and vigor of forensic anthropology, the reader might conclude that there are no foreseeable problems at the dawn of the 21st century. Such is not the case. Challenges the author perceives for the years ahead are as follows:

1. Younger members of the discipline are unlikely to find positions within the Ivory Tower that advertise for forensic anthropologists without training in other areas of physical anthropology. Therefore, those professionals who offer graduate-level instruction in this aspect of the broader field of anthropology must assure that their students acquire a broad background in those areas that will allow them to teach courses in the human biology of living populations, paleoanthropology, paleodemography, genetics and molecular biology, comparative human and non-human primate anatomy, statistics, and some background in the other fields of physical anthropology.
2. Newly appointed instructors and assistant professors at academic institutions must seek funding to build their teaching and research facilities. Space, instruments, osteological collections, and computers are among the essentials for teaching and research, particularly in those departments

of anthropology oriented to the socio-cultural part of the field where conflicts of interest with physical anthropologists (sometimes labeled as "racists" since they study human biological variations in time and space) may take root.

3. Since the years of the war in Viet Nam, when "applied anthropology" became linked to protests against the "industrial, capitalist, and military establishment" and the actual or rumored CIA operations, many anthropologists question the political correctness or scholarly merits of any practical applications of their discipline. When this bias thrives in a department of anthropology, it is not overcome by the odor of a decomposing corpse next door where a forensic anthropologist conducts his or her laboratory investigations.

4. It is the responsibility of forensic anthropologists to get the word to medical examiners and law enforcement agencies that no investigation of human remains is complete without the collaboration of a well-trained forensic anthropologist. This prospect is enhanced when the anthropologist in a town, city, or county offers training to local and state police as to proper methods of treating human remains at the time of their discovery. Ideally, a forensic anthropologist with training in "forensic archaeology" is present at the scene of investigation and supervises removal of buried bones and teeth prior to their removal and shipping to the laboratory where the remains await identification.

5. Anthropology in its multiple facets of research and teaching, including forensic anthropology, undergoes continual change over time. As new methods evolve, such as DNA analysis and molecular biology, they supplement, rather than replace, some methods with longer practical histories. These are welcome additions to the discipline, of course, but do not compel "revisions of all the textbooks" as claimed by many journalists in their regional newspapers. Recent discoveries of fossil hominids take the prize in sensational reporting with today's murder victim following as a close second!

6. More field schools are needed to teach students techniques for recovery of human remains, how to deal with multiple bodies in cases of mass disasters, autopsy and laboratory procedures, establishment of relations with medical examiners and the agents of law enforcement, and the most effective requirements of teaching.

7. The forces that drive forensic anthropology are crimes, mass disasters, and identification of skeletal remains which may be encountered in remote places by hunters and hikers, and the application of laboratory methods to the relatively recent, as well as prehistoric palaeontological specimens, and to the "eminent dead."

8. The assumption of some anthropologists that forensic studies have no theoretical component requires correction. As forensic anthropologists, we are examining anatomical variables of modern *Homo sapiens* within the context of Darwinian evolutionary theory. As noted above, most of the techniques we apply in the identification of a deceased individual include many of the analytical and statistical techniques applied to pre-historic subjects. This is because of the diversity of physically expressed adaptations, which may be attributed to ancient or modern effects of geographical location, climate and temperature, and lifeways. Human responses for natural and cultural stresses under different and changing ecological settings are subject to natural selection.

9. Students must understand that the estimated ancestry of a decomposed body or skeleton is not for the purpose of supporting the traditional prac-tice of racial classification. The assumption of the existence of human races as natural entities is maintained only in a social context in Europe and the Americas. Among biologists today, the former race theory is re-garded as defunct when considering subspecies (breeds, varieties, races below the taxonomic level of species) for all living things, including past and present *Homo sapiens*.

10. Finally, forensic anthropology, with other subfields of the discipline, is not a purely descriptive exercise best represented by tables of measure-ments, photographs, and short texts on a poster. It is a humanistic as well as a scientific field of study within democracies where accountability of the dead is recognized as the most effective counter-position to the phi-losophies motivating genocide and falsification of historic events.

One of my graduate students at Cornell University asked me if it is feasible for a practicing forensic anthropologist to contribute to the advancement of knowledge in the other research areas of physical anthropology and still remain up-to-date and effective in his or her practice. This is a thoughtful question, par-ticularly as most of us in academic life do not have the freedom of our colleagues who are affiliated with the military, are in government departments, or are retired from their teaching positions whose status allows them to devote more time to the forensic side of their careers. This doubling-up of research interests may become a problem in the 21st century. However, the present writer ventures to suggest that we may be better forensic anthropologists and more enlightened scholars in a general sense by having a broad exposure to other research foci of anthropology. Is this not what Hrdlička and Boas had in mind in making physi-cal anthropology a respected and multifaceted discipline? And did we not decide to have a career in anthropology because we were attracted to the challenges facing modern practitioners of this discipline and their successors?

ACKNOWLEDGMENTS

The author thanks the Darwin Fund of Cornell University for research support for this study. Ms. Dale Davis, formerly an undergraduate student in the Human Biology Laboratory, is thanked for her excellent assistance in many aspects of the project. My beloved wife, Margaret Carrick Fairlie-Kennedy, devoted her time to proofread the draft of this chapter, and I am most grateful to her.

REFERENCES

American Anthropological Association. (2004–2006). *Guide: A Guide to Programs and a Directory of Members*. Arlington: American Anthropological Association (AAA).

Bass, William M. (1979). Developments in the Identification of Human Skeletal Material, 1968–1978. *American Journal of Physical Anthropology, 51*, 555–562.

Boyd, William C. (1950). *Genetics and the Races of Man*. Boston: Little, Brown.

Brooks, Sheilagh T. (1970). Theodore D. McCown, 1908–1969. *American Journal of Physical Anthropology, 32*, 165–166.

———. (1981). Teaching of Forensic Anthropology in the United States. *Journal of Forensic Sciences, 26*, 627–631.

Chamberlain, L. J., & Adamson-Hoebel, J. (1942). Anthropological Offerings in American Undergraduate Colleges. *American Anthropologist, 44*, 527–530.

Elkins, Aaron. (1987). *Old Bones*. New York: Berkley Crime.

Goldstein, Marcus S. (1940). Recent Trends in Physical Anthropology. *American Journal of Physical Anthropology, 26*, 191–209.

Goerner, F. (1966). *The Search for Amelia Earhart*. Garden City: Doubleday.

Hammel, Eugene. (1969). Theodore Dibey McCown, June 18, 1908–August 17, 1969. *Papers of the Kroeber Anthropological Society, 41*, 1–7.

Hrdlička, Aleš. (1918). Physical Anthropology: Its History and Present Status in America. *American Journal of Physical Anthropology, 1*, 3–23, 133–182, 267–304, 377–414.

———. (1929). Notes: American Association of Physical Anthropologists. *American Journal of Physical Anthropology, 12*, 519–521.

İşcan, M. Yaşar. (1988). Rise of Forensic Anthropology. *Yearbook of Physical Anthropology, 31*, 203–230.

Johnson, G.W. (1943). *American Heroes and Hero-Worship*. New York: Harper and Brothers.

Joyce, C., & Stover, E. (1991). *Witness from the Grave: The Stories Bones Tell*. Boston: Little, Brown.

Keith, Arthur, & McCown, Theodore D. (1939). *The Stone Age of Mount Carmel II: The Fossil Human Remains from the Levalloiso-Mousterian*. Oxford: Clarendon.

Kennedy, Kenneth A. R. (1997). McCown, Theodore (Doney) (1908–1969). In *History of Physical Anthropology, Vol II*, ed. by Frank Spencer, pp. 627–629. New York: Garland.

———. (2000). Becoming Respectable: T. Dale Stewart and the Acceptance of Forensic Anthropology in the Academic Community. *Journal of Forensic Sciences, 45,* 253–257.

———. (2005). McCown, Theodore D. In *Encyclopaedia of Anthropology,* ed. by J. Birx, pp. 1563–1564. Thousand Oaks: Sage.

Kennedy, Kenneth A. R., & Brooks, Sheilagh T. (1984). Theodore D. McCown: A Perception of a Physical Anthropologist. *Current Anthropology, 25,* 99–103.

Kennedy, Kenneth A. R., Plummer, T. P., & Chiment, J. (1986). Identification of the Eminent Dead: Penpi, a Scribe of Ancient Egypt. In *Forensic Osteology: The Recovery and Analysis of Unknown Skeletal Remains,* K. Reichs, pp. 290–307. Springfield, IL: Charles C. Thomas.

Kerley, E. R. (1978). Recent Developments in Forensic Anthropology. *Yearbook of Physical Anthropology, 21,* 160–173.

Krogman, Wilton M. (1939). A Guide to the Identification of Human Skeletal Material. *FBI Law Enforcement Bulletin, 8*(8), 3–31.

———. (1962). *The Human Skeleton in Forensic Medicine.* Springfield, IL: Charles C. Thomas.

Kroeber, Alfred L. (1954). The Place of Anthropology in Universities. *American Anthropologist, 56,* 764–767.

MacCurdy, George G. (1902). The Teaching of Anthropology in the United States. *Science, 15,* 211–216.

Manhein, Mary H. (1999). *The Bone Lady: Life as a Forensic Anthropologist.* Baton Rouge. Louisiana State University.

Maples, William R, & Browning, M. (1994). *Dead Men Do Tell Tales.* New York: Doubleday.

McCown, Theodore D. (1952). The Training and Education of the Professional Physical Anthropologist. *American Anthropologist, 54,* 313–317.

Morgado, M. J. (1987). *Junipero Serra's Legacy.* Pacific Grove: Carmel.

Reichs, Kathleen J. (ed.). (1986). *Forensic Osteology: Advances in the Identification of Human Remains.* Springfield, IL: Charles C. Thomas.

———. (1998). *Forensic Osteology: A Decade of Progress.* Springfield, IL: Charles C. Thomas.

———. (2005). *Cross Bones.* New York: Pocket Star.

Rhine, Stanley. (1998). *Bone Voyage: A Journey in Forensic Anthropology.* Albuquerque: University of New Mexico Press.

Snow, Clyde C. (1973). Forensic Anthology. In *Anthropology Beyond the University,* ed. by A. Redfield, pp. 4–17. Athens: University of Georgia.

———. (1982). Forensic Anthropology. *Annual Review of Anthropology, 11,* 97–131.

Spencer, Frank. (1981). The Rise of Academic Physical Anthropology in the United States, 1880–1980: A Historical Review. *American Journal of Physical Anthropology, 56,* 353–364.

——— (ed.). (1982). *A History of American Physical Anthropology, 1930–1980.* New York: Academic Press.

—— (ed.). (1997). *History of Physical Anthropology: An Encyclopedia, 2 Vols.* New York: Garland.

Steadman, Dawnie Wolf (ed.). (2002). *Hard Evidence: Case Studies in Forensic Anthropology.* Upper Saddle River, NJ: Prentice-Hall.

Stewart, T. Dale (ed.). (1970). *Personal Identification in Mass Disasters.* Washington, DC: National Museum of Natural History.

——. (1979). *Essentials of Forensic Anthropology Especially as Developed in the United States.* Springfield, IL: Charles C. Thomas.

Thompson, D. D. (1982). Forensic Anthropology. In *A History of American Physical Anthropology, 1930–1980,* ed. by Frank Spencer, pp. 357–369. New York: Academic Press.

Trotter, Mildred, & Gieser, G. C. (1958). A Re-evaluation of Stature Based on Measurements Taken During Life and of Long Bones after Death. *American Journal of Physical Anthropology, 16,* 79–123.

Ubelaker, Douglas. (1997). Forensic Anthropology: History of Physical Anthropology. In *History of Physical Anthropology: An Encyclopedia, Vol. 1,* ed. by Frank Spencer, pp. 392–396. New York: Garland.

Ubelaker, Douglas, & Scammell, H. (1992). *Bones: A Forensic Detective's Casebook.* New York: Harper Collins.

Voegelin, E.W. (1950). Anthropology in American Universities. *American Anthropologist, 52,* 350–391.

Warren, Katherine B. (ed.). (1951). *Origin and Evolution of Man.* Cold Spring Harbor Symposia on Quantitative Biology, Vol. XV. New York: The Biological Laboratory, Cold Spring Harbor.

Washburn, Sherwood L. (1951). The New Physical Anthropology. *Transactions of the New York Academy of Sciences, 13,* 298–304.

Wordsworth, William. (1807). The Solitary Reaper. In *The Oxford Book of English Verse, 1250–1900,* ed. by A. Quiller-Coach, pp. 602–603. Oxford: Clarendon.

Chapter 6

The Founding of the American Association of Physical Anthropologists: 1930

by

Emőke J. E. Szathmáry

INTRODUCTION

In 2005, the Web site of the American Association of Physical Anthropologists stated that physical anthropology is both a biological and a social science. It observed that from its founding in 1930, with 83 claimed charter members, it has grown into an international organization with over 1700 members, and that more than 1,000 scientists from around the world take part in its annual meetings (see contribution by Brown & Cartmill in this volume).

What relevance might a re-examination and/or re-interpretation of the origin of this association have to its members as well as those outside it? For some, articulation of a history is intrinsically interesting, but more generally, it permits us to see how the development of a given discipline has been shaped by social and scientific forces as well as by individual personalities. Such findings have explanatory power that can be applied and put to use within and beyond a discipline's domain of knowledge. The founders of the American Association of Physical Anthropologists (AAPA) were aware of this, and the organization they put into place has been successful as judged by longevity and membership. This chapter reviews the context and process through which the AAPA came into being, and describes the impact of the founding forces on the development of the discipline of physical anthropology.

BACKGROUND

The establishment of the AAPA and the area of knowledge now called physical anthropology (or biological anthropology) is the result of events set into motion in the mid-19th century. Spencer (1981) noted that the period following the American Civil War (1861–1865) was marked by the tendency of various occupational groups to professionalize. This implied that during this period opportunities for training were available or were created, and that employment opportunities existed for sustainable lifetime careers. As the numbers of professionals grew, practitioners established associations to promote their disciplines and achieve collective, as well as individual, professional goals.

The professionalization of anthropologists was part of this trend. The Bureau of American Ethnology, established in 1879 by the federal government, was the first American entity to offer stable employment to anthropologists (Judd, 1967). However, its focus was ethnology and allied fields (e.g., ethnolinguistics) that could inform federal Indian policy, and the bureau did not offer formal training. Education in anthropology was increasingly seen as the province of universities, though most were reluctant to add a discipline that they believed overlapped with others already in the array that they supported (Spencer, 1981). Accordingly, in 1901 only two American universities had independent departments of anthropology (Harvard and the University of California–Berkeley), and where the discipline existed, the tendency was to focus less on physical anthropology than on archaeology and ethnology. For example, in the four departments that offered graduate study (UC–Berkeley, Columbia, Harvard, Pennsylvania) fewer than 11% of doctoral theses completed in the period 1900–1925 focused on topics in physical anthropology, and no such theses were completed at either the University of California–Berkeley or at Columbia University during that time (Spencer, 1981, 1982). This situation had consequences for American physical anthropology.

At the onset of 1928, there was no anglophone association that focused exclusively on issues that mattered to physical anthropologists. The Anthropological Institute of Great Britain and Ireland, which had been established in 1871 and was granted the right to add "Royal" to its name in 1907, focused on "anthropology as a whole" (www.therai.org.uk/history.html). It provided a forum for physical anthropology, though Aleš Hrdlička, the first physical anthropologist appointed (1903) to the U.S. National Museum of Natural History (now part of the Smithsonian Institution), regarded the institute as "little more than a clubhouse" (Stewart, 1981, 348). The Anthropological Society of Washington, established in 1879, and the American

Anthropological Association, established in 1902, were also "holistic" in their orientations, and for these groups physical anthropology was consistently a minority interest. In contrast, on the continent of Europe, where the term "anthropology" was synonymous with "physical anthropology" (Spencer, 1981), the Société d'Antropologie had been publishing its *Bulletins et Mémoirs* since 1860, and there were no less than three French centers that provided training in physical anthropology between 1869 and 1896 (Stewart, 1981).

In the United States, the individual arguing the most for the establishment of a training center in physical anthropology was Aleš Hrdlička. Czech by origin, he held an American degree in medicine and had practiced as a physician until he obtained training in 1896 in physical anthropology under Léonce Manouvrier, Paul Broca's student and successor at the École d'Anthropologie in Paris, France (Stewart, 1981). Hrdlička's specific role in the development of the AAPA will be detailed more fully below. It is sufficient to note here that though he met obstacles regarding the establishment of his proposed institute, Hrdlička amassed a large osteological collection at the Smithsonian, undertook several field expeditions, and began training others in physical anthropology. Almost all were physicians and or professional anatomists, given his view that physical anthropology is a biomedical discipline (Spencer, 1981). To serve his and their needs for a periodical that focused on their interests, in 1918 Hrdlička established the *American Journal of Physical Anthropology* at the Smithsonian Institution. By 1929, although those who identified themselves as physical anthropologists were few, their number was augmented manyfold by a number of anatomists who had been attracted to physical anthropology by Hrdlička. The group recognized not only a need for a disciplinary identity, but also the need to establish a recognized research tradition with appropriate funding support.

The first meeting of the American Association of Physical Anthropologists was held at Charlottesville, Virginia, with 84 charter members recorded (AAPA Proceedings, 1930, 327), rather than the 83 customarily mentioned (Spencer, 1981; Spencer & Erickson, 1981, 531–532). However, of these, only 21% described themselves as anthropologists, and fewer than 10% of the membership was made up of full-time professional physical anthropologists. On the other hand, more than half the membership was comprised of anatomists. It is arguable that most members of the AAPA at the organization's inception were not interested in promoting education in physical anthropology, and most would *not* have regarded anthropology departments as providing suitable training for practitioners; they would likely have proposed medical or anatomical training. Such perspectives would have impact on the discipline of physical anthropology.

THE 1930 CHARLOTTESVILLE, VIRGINIA, MEETING

The formation of the American Association of Physical Anthropologists is said to have occurred in 1930, whether one consults the AAPA Web site (www.physanth.org) or Spencer (1996, 62). Strictly speaking, it was the inaugural meeting of the American Association of Physical Anthropologists that occurred in 1930, between April 17 and 18 at Charlottesville, Virginia. It was there that the man who chaired the meeting, Aleš Hrdlička, was confirmed as president, Dudley J. Morton, an anatomist in the School of Medicine and Surgery at Columbia University was confirmed as secretary-treasurer, the Association's first Constitution and By-Laws were drafted and approved, and the cost of annual membership was confirmed at $2.00. Two committees had been appointed the day before Hrdlička and Morton were confirmed: William K. Gregory chaired the Committee on By-Laws and Robert J. Terry chaired the Committee on Nominations. Two additional committees were established: the Committee on Anthropoid Material, chaired by James H. McGregor, and the Committee on Human Material, chaired by T. Wingate Todd. The AAPA appointment of a representative to the National Research Council was referred to the Executive Committee, the members of which had also been elected on the first day of the meeting (William King Gregory, Earnest A. Hooton, and Robert J. Terry). Franz Boas was appointed to chair a small committee "to consider the future relations of the Society [AAPA] to the Journal [AJPA]" (AAPA Proceedings, 1930). Even 30 papers were read, including those by the core anthropologists and anatomist/anthropologists: Boas, Davenport, Gregory, Hrdlička, Shapiro, Stewart, Straus, Terry, Todd, and Trotter (AAPA Proceedings, 1930). Twenty abstracts from the meetings were published in the *AJPA* (AAPA Abstracts, 1930) along with several papers from the meetings (Comas, 1969, Alfonso & Little, 2005).

Table 6.1 is a revised and updated version of Frank Spencer and G. E. Erikson's (1981) Appendix 1, "Charter Members of the AAPA," published in the "Jubilee Issue" of the *American Journal of Physical Anthropology*. How and why did the original 84 charter members—of whom two were women (Ruth O. Sawtell [later Wallis] and Mildred Trotter)—get together in 1930? Only eight of them were called "physical anthropologists," though not all of the six shown as having PhDs were holders of doctorates in physical anthropology. By education, 28 were doctors of medicine, 23 were PhDs in anatomy, another 8 were PhDs in zoology, and 10 held doctorates in archaeology or ethnology. The eight functioning physical anthropologists and 10 PhD ethnologists/archaeologists were outnumbered 3:1 by biomedical scientists. Institutional representation was weighted heavily in favor of Columbia University

Table 6.1.   84 Charter Members of the American Association of Physical Anthropologists (modified* and updated from Spencer and Erikson 1981).

Name (born-died, age in 1930)	Institutional Affiliation
Alvarez, Walter C. (1884–1952, 46)	U. Chicago
Bean, Robert Bennett (1874–1944, 56)	U. Virginia
Bensley, Benjamin A. (1875–1934, 55)	U. Toronto
Black, Davidson (1884–1934, 46)	Peking Union Med. Col.
Boas, Franz (1858–1942, 72)	Columbia U.
Brewer, George E. (1861–1939, 69)	Columbia U.
Cameron, John (1873– , 57)	Dalhousie U.
Carey, Eben James (1889–1947, 41)	Marquette U.
Cates, Harry A. (1890– , 40)	U. Toronto
Cattell, James McKeen (1860–1944, 70)	Columbia U.
Cole, Fay-Cooper (1881–1961, 49)	U. Chicago
Collins, Henry Bascom (1899–1987, 31)	Smithsonian Institution
Connolly, Cornelius (1883–c1955, 47)	Catholic U.
Cummins, Harold (1893–1976, 37)	Tulane U.
Danforth, Charles H. (1883–1969, 47)	Stanford U.
Davenport, Charles B. (1866–1944, 64)	Cold Spring Harbor
Dixon, Roland B. (1875–1934, 55)	Harvard U.
Dorsey, George Amos (1868–1931, 62)	U. Chicago
Elftman, Herbert O. (1902–1989, 28)	Columbia U.
Engle, Earl T. (1896–1957, 34)	Columbia U.
Ferris, Harry B. (1865–1940, 65)	Yale U.
Field, Henry (1902–1986, 28)	
Fortuyn	
Freeman, Rowland G. (1894–c1959, 36)	Tufts U.
Goss, Charles Mayo (1899–1981, 31)	Louisiana State U.
Grant, J.C. Boileau (1886–1973, 44)	U. Toronto
Graves, William W. (1865–1949, 65)	Washington U.
Greenman, Milton J. (1866–1937, 64)	Wistar Institute
Gregory, William K. (1876–1970, 54)	American Museum
Hellman, Milo (1872–1947, 58)	Columbia U.
Herskovits, Melville (1895–1963, 35)	Northwestern U.
Hooton, Earnest A. (1887–1954, 43)	Harvard U.
Hrdlička, Aleš (1869–1943, 61)	Smithsonian Institution
Huber, Ernst (1892–1932, 38)	Johns Hopkins U.
Jackson, Clarence M. (1875–1947, 55)	U. Minnesota
Jenks, Albert E. (1869–1953, 61)	U. Minnesota
Job, T. Theodore (1885–1976, 45)	Loyola U.
Kelly, Arthur R. (1900–1979, 30)	U.S. Government
Kroeber, Alfred L. (1876–1960, 54)	U.C. Berkeley
Krogman, Wilton Marion (1903–1987, 27)	U. Chicago
Loo, Yu Tao	
Love, Albert G. (1877– , 53)	U.S. Army
Lull, Richard Swan (1867–1957, 63)	Yale U.
MacCurdy, George Grant (1863–1947, 67)	Yale U.

(Continued)

Table 6.1. **(Continued)**

Name (born-died, age in 1930)	Institutional Affiliation
McGregor, James H. (1872–1954, 58)	Columbia U.
McMurrich, James P. (1859–1939, 71)	U. Toronto
Meyer, Arthur W. (1873–1966, 57)	Stanford U.
Michelson, Truman (1879–1938, 51)	Smithsonian Institution
Miller, Gerrit Smith, Jr. (1869–1956, 61)	Smithsonian Institution
Morton, Dudley Joy (1884–1961, 46)	Columbia U.
Noback, Charles V. (1888–1937, 42)	Cornell U.
Noback, Gustave J. (1890–1955, 40)	
Oetteking, Bruno (1871–1960, 59)	
Osborn, Frederick H. (1889–1981, 41)	American Museum
Osborn, Henry Fairfield (1857–1935, 73)	American Museum
Papez, James W. (1883–1958, 47)	Cornell U.
Pearl, Raymond (1879–1940, 51)	Johns Hopkins U.
Post, Richard H. (1904– , 26)	
Pryor, Joseph W. (1856–1956, 74)	U. Kentucky
Redway, Laurance (1890–1960, 40)	
Royster, Lawrence T. (1874–1953, 56)	U. Virginia
Sankas, Sngiam Hata	Siriraj Hospital, Bangkok
Sawtell, Ruth O. (1895–1978, 35)	U. Iowa
Scammon, Richard E. (1883–1952, 47)	U. Chicago
Schulte, H.V.W. (1876–1932, 54)	Creighton U.
Schultz, Adolph H. (1891–1976, 39)	Johns Hopkins U. & Zürich
Shapiro, H.H. (1892–1958, 38)	Columbia U.
Shapiro, Harry L. (1902–1990, 28)	American Museum
Smith, Maurice G. (ca.1900–1930, 30)	U. Oklahoma
Stevenson, Paul H. (1890–1971, 40)	Peking Union Med. Col.
Stewart, Thomas Dale (1901–1997, 29)	Smithsonian Institution
Stockard, Charles R. (1879–1939, 51)	Cornell University
Straus, William L. (1900–1981, 30)	Johns Hopkins U.
Tello, Julio C. (1880–1947, 50)	Museo de Arqueología, Callao
Terry, Robert J. (1871–1966, 59)	Washington U.
Tilney, Frederick (1875–1938, 55)	Columbia U.
Todd, Thomas Wingate (1885–1938, 45)	Western Reserve U.
Trotter, Mildred (1899–1991, 31)	Washington U.
Weed, Lewis H. (1886–1952, 44)	Johns Hopkins U.
Welch, William H. (1850–1934, 80)	Johns Hopkins U.
Williams, George D. (1898–1961, 32)	U. Arizona
Williams, Herbert H. (1866–1938, 64)	U. Buffalo
Wissler, Clark (1870–1947, 60)	American Museum
Zwemer, Raymond Lull (1902–1981, 28)	U.S. Government

* Dr. Eugene Giles assisted with the correction of the Spencer and Erickson (1981) compilation of the charter membership. They had left off two of the original charter members—one DV Fortyun, whose actual initials were ABD, and who was located in Peking Union Medical College, and Julio C. Tello, from Peru. They had also included Sidney A. Fox, who was an ophthalmologist and benefactor of Brown University's Medical School, but who had not been listed by Hrdlička as a charter member.

(10 members), Johns Hopkins (6), Chicago (5), the Smithsonian Institution (5), and the American Museum of Natural History (5). Other charter members were from institutions in the United States, Canada, Peru, Thailand (then called "Siam"), and China.

THE CRUCIAL 1928 AAAS MEETING

Why would such an assemblage come together? These individuals were deliberately recruited by Hrdlička and Morton and six others as charter members to attend the inaugural meeting of the AAPA, which had been convened to coincide with the annual meeting of the American Association of Anatomists at Charlottesville at that time. The association of physical anthropologists had already been formed two years earlier, in 1928 at a meeting of Section H (anthropology) of the American Association for the Advancement of Science, held between December 28 and 29 (Hrdlička, 1929).

Hrdlička, who had proposed such an organization as early as 1924, had faced resistance and so Spencer (1979, 738) and Stewart (1981) suggested that until 1928 Hrdlička bide his time in the face of opposition to a formal society. Two major figures were opposed to the formation of the American Association of Physical Anthropologists as envisioned by Hrdlička—Franz Boas and T. Wingate Todd. In 1924, when Hrdlička began to gain modest support for the formation of the AAPA, Todd actively opposed the formation of this association on the grounds that anatomy and physical anthropology should not be divided because of their common goals (Jones-Kern 1997, 273–275; Kern, 2006). In a letter from Todd to Hrdlička (December 19, 1924; cited in Jones-Kern, 1997, appendix D), Todd argued that there would never be many positions in physical anthropology, that physical anthropologists would lose their identity as anatomists, that there is no difference between gross anatomy and physical anthropology, that special societies encourage "amateurish work," and that a special society would not provide support for the *AJPA*. Spencer (1979, 738) suggested that Todd's opposition might also have been related to his active membership in the Galton Society, and that a new physical anthropology society might have competed for members. Boas also opposed the formation of the association because he felt that it would draw members away from the parent organization, the AAA.

It was at the 1928 meeting of the AAAS, Section H (anthropology) that Hrdlička proposed the formation of the new society. Fortunately, Todd did not attend the 1928 Section H, AAAS meetings, since he surely would have argued persuasively against launching the AAPA. And it was only in January 1930 that Todd was persuaded to support the new association (Spencer, 1979,

749). This is where interpretation becomes problematic, however, regarding Hrdlička's motives in this endeavour. Hrdlička's reason for the establishment of the American Association of Physical Anthropologists was linked with another purpose, in which he was ultimately unsuccessful—that is, the establishment of an Institute of Physical Anthropology.

HRDLIČKA'S IDEAS AND MOTIVES

The context for the formation of the AAPA has to take into account three factors: (1) the formal mechanisms that existed for teaching and research in physical anthropology at the onset of the 20th century in America, (2) the definition of anthropology in terms of the branches of knowledge that were its elements and its proponents, and (3) the dreams of Aleš Hrdlička, an MD who had studied anthropology in 1896 at Paul Broca's Institute d'Anthropologie in Paris, and who became the Curator of the Division of Physical Anthropology at the National Museum of Natural History in 1903.

Hrdlička's conceptualization of anthropology was formed in France under the leading physical anthropologist of that time, whose influence linked the (1) French anthropological society (Société d'Anthropologie), (2) the Laboratory of Anthropology (Laboratoire d'Anthropologie) at a free-standing School of Advanced Studies (École pratique des Hautes Études), and (3) the School of Anthropology into an unofficial union called "Broca's Institute." Hrdlička returned to America to discover that though "anthropology" on the European continent meant "physical anthropology"—as it still does today—in the United States it was claimed to be a four-field amalgam of ethnology, linguistics, archaeology, and physical anthropology. Further, at research institutions, and most specifically in the American government's Bureau of American Ethnology, ethnolinguistics was rapidly becoming the field to be reckoned with. The impact, in Hrdlička's view, of this increasingly entrenched view of the nature of anthropology in America and the kinds of research skills favored by employing institutions was that there were few people in America who were properly educated as physical anthropologists: that is, their education was grounded in the biomedical sciences and their subsequent training in the techniques of physical anthropology met a desired standard of competence. Three years after he left Paris for New York, Hrdlička proposed an Anthropological Institute after the French model, and after his appointment at the Division of Physical Anthropology at the National Museum of Natural History, he pursued with vigor his dream of a teaching and research institute on the banks of the Potomac. He was able to obtain funding between 1914 and 1920 to train physical anthropologists at the National Museum of Natural History

(NMNH). The group included men such as Davidson Black, Fay-Cooper Cole, Ralph Linton, and Earnest A. Hooton. However, Hrdlička was unable to attain his principal goal for neither his masters nor the National Research Council of the National Academy of Sciences, which he also approached in the 1920s, was willing to establish an Institute of Anthropology as he envisioned it (Spencer, 1981).

By the mid-1920s, Hrdlička was of the view that a bias was operating in the Unites States against physical anthropology, given that in the first quarter of the 20th century, only four physical anthropology PhDs were conferred at institutions offering doctorates in anthropology: three at Harvard (1900, 1905, 1915) and one at Pennsylvania (1915) out of a total of 39 doctorates awarded at UC–Berkeley, Columbia University, Harvard University, and the University of Pennsylvania combined. Further, it was known that former students of Franz Boas controlled the National Research Council of the NAS, which was unsympathetic to Hrdlička's ideas about establishing an Institute of Anthropology to undertake research and to teach in physical anthropology (Spencer, 1981). One might have expected something different from students of Boas, for their mentor at Columbia University had established a new field of research that focused on defining the limits of human plasticity (Szathmáry, 1991). Boas's treatment of growth and of statistical methods was sophisticated, he had a "masterful integration of facts pertaining to race" (Goldstein, 1940, 202), and he wanted to develop links between cultural and physical anthropology. However, because of his circumstances at Columbia, during all the years that Hrdlička was trying to legitimize physical anthropology and define its character as had been done in France, Boas directed his attention, and those of his students, to cultural anthropology. Faced with opposition, Hrdlička concentrated on building a network of anatomists across the United States by encouraging publication in the *AJPA,* which he had founded in 1918 and had edited ever since. Though he did not abandon his dream of an Institute, the next best thing for Hrdlička was the establishment of a society, which indeed came into being under the auspices of Section H of the AAAS in December 1928 in New York City.

As Spencer described (1979, 745ff), Charles H. Danforth, who was secretary of Section H of the AAAS, wrote to Hrdlička, asking if he wished to present a paper at the December 1928 meeting. Hrdlička responded positively, indicating that he wanted to present a paper on "The Needs of Physical Anthropology," and he indicated the time and date that he wished to be included on the program (second paper of the first afternoon). As a reflection of his good relations with Danforth, the program organizer, Hrdlička was given a 45-minute slot, whereas all other papers were allotted 25 minutes. Hrdlička's paper was a strong statement on why a new society of physical anthropology was needed, and included in the argument were the 12 objectives which later became a part of the Constitution of the AAPA. There was enthusiastic support for Hrdlička's proposal, and the first step involved some 20 anatomists and anthropologists to establish an organizing committee with power to act on December 28. This seven-member committee—Hrdlička, Fay-Cooper Cole, Charles H. Danforth, George A. Dorsey, William K. Gregory, Earnest A. Hooton, and Robert J. Terry—brought forth two resolutions the following day:

> I: That there should be, and hereby is founded an organization of American and allied scientific men and women active or interested in physical anthropology, to be known as the American Association of Physical Anthropologists; and
>
> II: That the general object of this organization will be the promotion, by all legitimate means, of the interests and serviceability of physical anthropology. (Hrdlička 1929)

The next day, on December 29, 1928, the group adopted these resolutions and elected Aleš Hrdlička as its chairman and Dudley J. Morton as its secretary-treasurer. The group further agreed that it would try to follow the American Anthropological Association in "its essentials," and that the AAPA would cooperate as much as possible with the AAA, with section H of the AAAS, and with the American Association of Anatomists. The *American Journal of Physical Anthropology* was named as the official medium of communication of the new society, and the eight "initial members" were charged with preparing a platform of objectives for the new organization. Twelve objectives were devised and identified as the basic Constitution of the Association. The preamble and objectives follow (Proceedings, *AJPA*, 1930):

> In recognition of the steadily progressive development in this country of Physical Anthropology, as a distinct branch of science, which has been manifested in its advancing research studies, increasing personnel, more numerous and meritorious publications, and in its prospects for still greater advances in knowledge and in practical benefits to mankind, an organization of the workers in this line has been deemed a necessity and is herewith instituted.

The objects of this organization are given in the following paragraphs:

1. To the promotion of contacts, of cooperation, and of service in this and other countries, with all branches of anthropology; with the anatomists and physiologists; with the biologists, and with medicine and dentistry.
2. To the promotion, in the broadest sense, of research and publication in physical anthropology.

3. To the promotion of sound anthropological teaching in universities, colleges, medical schools, art institutes, and all other establishments of learning where such instruction, in suitable forms, would be useful.

4. To the preparation of proper text-books, charts, and other aids to anthropological instruction.

5. To the promotion and harmonization of anthropometric instruction, and to that of standardization and production of anthropometric instruments in this country.

6. To the extension of standardized methods of measuring with proper metric instruments, into all colleges and other establishments where measurements of many subjects are being taken, such as institutions for children, institutions for special classes of defectives and abnormals, insurance companies, and the recruiting stations of the army and navy.

7. To the furtherance of the same methods, instruments, etc., in other countries.

8. To the development of physical anthropology as a well-organized branch of science in order to ensure its greatest practical value and educational benefits for future generations.

9. To the popular dissemination of the results of scientific research in physical anthropology.

10. To the furthering and assisting, in our museums, universities, and colleges, of the best possible exhibits in human phylogeny, ontogeny, variation, and differentiation.

11. To the aid of advanced and worthy students in original research and field work.

12. To the eventual establishment, in the most favorable location, of the "American Institute of Physical Anthropology," which would serve both as the home and library of the association, and as the center of anthropometric instruction and of dissemination of anthropological knowledge.

At the inaugural meeting of the AAPA in April 1930, the two principles and the 12 objectives were adopted. However, a proposal that "cheap" life memberships ($25) be offered to raise funds to build the Institute was rejected. After that, despite the 12th objective of the Constitution, Hrdlička ceased promoting his Institute, and the American Association of Physical Anthropologists got on with their task of promoting its science.

Whether or not there was, even at that date, a single science, however, is highly questionable. For example, the third president of the AAPA was Raymond Pearl, a professor of biometry and vital statistics at Johns Hopkins University, whose view of human biology included a cultural component. Pearl was the founder of the journal *Human Biology* in 1929, and the content of this journal was contrasted with the content of the *AJPA* in 1940 by Marcus Goldstein (1940). Goldstein found that over 50% of the articles published in the *AJPA* were anatomical in nature, very few were in "group [population] biology," and the largest group of authors were comprised of anatomists. In *Human Biology,* by contrast, the proportion of article topics were reversed, and the largest single group of authors were anthropologists, including ethnologists and archaeologists. Clearly, a decade after the establishment of the AAPA, "a split remained among physical anthropologists between those who focussed on anatomical issues and those who studied the living" (Szathmáry, 1991, 19).

Which view of physical anthropology prevails in the AAPA today? In Spencer's (1981) view the profession's scientific direction was determined not by Hrdlička's anatomical orientation but by the legion of PhDs produced by Hooton at Harvard, by Krogman at the University of Pennsylvania, and at the University of California–Berkeley by McCown. Certainly, the orientation has shifted, though new associations for human biologists and anthropological geneticists came into being in the last quarter of the 20th century. What remains is a dogged linkage between the AAPA and these other associations, reminiscent of the desire in 1929 to maintain cooperation with the social and scientific sides of knowledge, reminding us that the explanatory power of physical anthropology shifts according to new evidence and new understandings, but its power remains, nonetheless.

ACKNOWLEDGMENTS

I am grateful to Dr. Michael Little and to Dr. Eugene Giles for their assistance with this manuscript. Any errors of fact that may remain are mine.

REFERENCES

Alfonso, Marta P., & Little, Michael A. (tran. & ed.). (2005). Juan Comas's Summary History of the American Association of Physical Anthropologists (1928–1968). *Yearbook of Physical Anthropology, 48,*163–195.

AAPA Abstracts. (1930). Abstracts of Communications to Be Presented at the First Meeting of the American Association of Physical Anthropologists, April 17–19, 1930 and at the Joint Meeting of the Anthropologists and Anatomists, April 18, 1930 at the University of Virginia. *American Journal of Physical Anthropology, 14*(1), 83–90.

AAPA Proceedings. (1930). Meeting of the American Association of Physical Anthropologists, University of Virginia, Charlottesville, Virginia. *American Journal of Physical Anthropology, 14*(2), 321–329.

Comas, Juan. (1969). *Historia Sumaria de la Asociación Americana de Antropólogos Físicos, (1928–1968)*. Departamento de Investigaciones Antropológicas, Publication 22. Mexico: Instituto Nacional de Antropología e Historia.

Goldstein, Marcus S. (1940). Recent Trends in Physical Anthropology. *American Journal of Physical Anthropology, 26*, 191–209.

Hrdlička, Aleš. (1929). American Association of Physical Anthropologists. *Science, 69*, 304–305.

Jones-Kern, Kevin. (1997). T. Wingate Todd and the Development of Modern American Physical Anthropology, 1900–1940. PhD Dissertation in History. Bowling Green, OH: Bowling Green State University.

Judd, Neil M. (1967). *The Bureau of American Ethnology: A Partial History.* Norman: University of Oklahoma Press.

Kern, Kevin F. (2006). T. Wingate Todd: Pioneer of Modern American Physical Anthropology. *Kirtlandia* (Cleveland), *55*, 1–42.

Royal Anthropological Institute of Great Britain and Ireland 2008. History. www.therai.org.uk/history.html.

Spencer, Frank. (1979). Aleš Hrdlička, M.D., 1869–1943: A Chronicle of the Life and Work of an American Physical Anthropologist (Volumes I and II). Dissertation in Anthropology. Ann Arbor, MI: University of Michigan.

———. (1981). The Rise of Academic Physical Anthropology in the United States (1880–1980): A Historical Overview. *American Journal of Physical Anthropology, 56*(4), 353–364.

———. (1982). Introduction. In *A History of American Physical Anthropology: 1930–1980*, ed. by Frank Spencer, pp. 1–10. New York: Academic Press.

———. (1996). *History of Physical Anthropology: An Encyclopedia.* New York: Routledge.

Spencer, Frank, & Erickson, G. E. (1981). Appendix 1. *American Journal of Physical Anthropology, 56*(4), 531–532.

Stewart, T. Dale. (1981). Aleš Hrdlička, 1869–1943. *American Journal of Physical Anthropology, 56*, 347–351.

Szathmáry, Emőke J.E. (1991). Biological Anthropology. In *Fiftieth Anniversary Issue. Report for 1990 and 1991*, pp. 18–30. New York: The Wenner-Gren Foundation for Anthropological Research.

Chapter 7

Principal Figures in Physical Anthropology Before and During World War II

by

Eugene Giles

INTRODUCTION

Selecting Earnest A. Hooton and Aleš Hrdlička as the principal figures in American physical anthropology before and during World War II is not intended to slight others whose importance is unquestioned. Nevertheless, for a 25-year period, the contributions of Hooton and Hrdlička laid the foundations for the remarkable scope of physical anthropology today.

Both men were the sons of immigrants to the United States, but beyond that it is difficult to discern similarities in their backgrounds and education. Any seeming shorting in this brief recounting of Hrdlička's role in American physical anthropology only reflects that other chapters deal specifically with his accomplishments with the AAPA and the *AJPA*. Briefly, then, Aleš Hrdlička was born in the town of Humpolec in Bohemia (now the Czech Republic) in 1869 but came to the United States with his parents at the age of 13. After he earned a medical degree in New York City in 1892, he gradually evolved from being a medical practitioner to being a physical anthropology researcher—one so successful that he was chosen to head the newly created Division of Physical Anthropology at the National Museum of Natural History at the Smithsonian Institution in 1903. There he stayed until he resigned his curatorship in 1942. He died a year later. In recognition of his contributions to anthropology while at the Smithsonian, he was given a testimonial dinner at the occasion of his 70th birthday at the 1939 meeting of the American Association of Physical Anthropologists, the organization he had founded a decade earlier. As an indication of the reputation he held "inside the Beltway," as we might now say, a year after his death a wartime Liberty ship was named the Aleš Hrdlička in his honor.

Hooton's father was an immigrant, from England by way of Canada, and his mother a Canadian schoolteacher, but Hooton was born in 1887 in the United States in a tiny Wisconsin town, now vanished. As a Methodist minister, his father was assigned a series of pulpits around the state, so Hooton was educated in a variety of public schools, but obtained his baccalaureate degree from Lawrence University, a small, private liberal arts school in Appleton, Wisconsin. While at Lawrence, two academic activities foreshadowed aspects of his subsequent anthropological career; his nonacademic activities essentially secured his entrance into the University of Wisconsin's doctoral program in the Classics. One of these sidelines was minor: he honed his abilities as a cartoonist-illustrator on the Lawrence yearbook, the *Ariel*. His drawings later illustrated some of his writings, including the doggerel that he inserted into several of his papers and books.

The second was more serious. During vacation periods, he obtained a job at the State Penitentiary at Waupun, working for a knitting company that had a contract to make socks for inmates around the state utilizing prison labor. The semester before, he had read Havelock Ellis's *The Criminal* in a psychology course. Although initially skeptical about the Lombrosian approach that permeated it, he began, while carrying out his modest duties, observing the variety of humankind among the 600-odd prisoners. After some time, he started agreeing with some of the old "trusties" that you could tell the nature of the crime committed by physical aspects of the prisoner. As he wrote later, "Nothing that I ever stumbled into has affected my anthropological viewpoint and the direction taken by my research as those two summers in the Wisconsin penitentiary, when I really knew nothing of the science of man and could have defined 'anthropology' only by reference to my knowledge of Greek and etymology."

The sequelae of those two summers were to come much later. Meanwhile, he entered the University of Wisconsin at Madison in the Department of the Classics and began working on a dissertation that became titled, "The Evolution of Literary Art in Pre–Hellenic Rome." That by this time he was aware of what anthropology was all about is evidenced by the very first sentence in the dissertation's introduction: "The application of anthropological methods to the study of the culture of Greece and Rome is the most important innovation in classical research since the archaeological discoveries of Schliemann" (Hooton, 1911, i). Hooton was awarded a Rhodes scholarship to Oxford a year before he received his PhD in 1911. There he gravitated into the orbit of R. R. Marett, a classicist-turned-anthropologist. Hooton soon, however, with Marett's blessing, turned toward a more biological pursuit of anthropology under the tutelage of Sir Arthur Keith, a human paleontologist and anatomist at the Museum of the Royal College of Surgeons in London. During his stay at Oxford he examined archaeological skeletal material and even conducted an excavation at a Saxon graveyard (Peake & Hooton, 1915).

In 1913, during Hooton's last year at Oxford, the converted classicist made first contact with the converted medico. Hooton wrote Hrdlička asking for a job, saying he was both a cultural and a physical anthropologist, but leaning toward physical. Hrdlička had no position for him, but within a few months Hooton was offered beginning professorships at both the University of California at Berkeley and at Harvard. He chose the latter, and there he stayed until his death in 1954. His tenure at Harvard, and Hrdlička's at the Smithsonian, were virtually identical in length, but offset by a decade.

Hooton and Hrdlička interacted frequently, but usually by correspondence: Hooton did not particularly like to travel. The sort of expeditions mounted by Hrdlička in the Arctic (to say nothing of his world-wide travel to research collections) would have been anathema to Hooton, whose only field work amounted to less that two months in the Canary Islands in 1915 and the 1920 summer at the Pecos Pueblo archaeological excavations in New Mexico. On those occasions when he visited Harvard, however, Hrdlička stayed with the Hootons. Hooton realized Hrdlička could be difficult—when he invited both Hrdlička and a physiologist from the University of Illinois, the keynote speaker, to stay with him during a meeting of the American Association of Physical Anthropologists, he wondered in a letter to a colleague whether they would kill each other. They didn't.

Hooton had great respect for Hrdlička: as he said in dedicating his 1931 book, *The Indians of Pecos Pueblo,* to Hrdlička, "Great student of the physical anthropology of the American Indian." Early in his career, Hooton wrote Hrdlička saying that "I can't refrain from telling you how fortunate I think we are in having a man of your attainments and executive ability to promote the course of physical anthropology in the U.S." (Hooton, 1917). Late in his career, Hrdlička wrote Hooton that he was "one of the bulwarks of American anthropology. . . . You must feel that I have but the highest regard for you. Before long you are destined to be the sole leader of American physical anthropology, and I wish to aid you all I can towards the proper assumption of that position" (Hrdlička, 1938). One might be suspicious of all this mutual admiration, but in fact they did agree on some matters. For example, in 1935 when the American Association of Physical Anthropologists was trying to issue a statement on race, a dozen drafts were solicited from distinguished anthropologists; Hooton said he could only agree with Hrdlička's. Ultimately, none was approved by the Association's membership, and Hooton went on to publish his effort in *Science* under the title, "Plain Statements About Race" (Hooton, 1936).

On other matters, though, they didn't agree. Hooton supported quantitative and statistical approaches to analysis; Hrdlička didn't. As an associate editor of the *American Journal of Physical Anthropology,* "Hrdlička's Journal," as many called it, Hooton locked horns with Hrdlička on a number of occasions. Late in Hrdlička's editorship, Hooton resigned the post over one of these, but it didn't end their friendship. For many years before World War II, Hooton's wife Mary provided financial support to the *AJPA,* the equivalent of about $3,000 annually in today's dollars. Hrdlička was greatly appreciative of this.

ALEŠ HRDLIČKA

Although Hrdlička was a prodigious writer and organizer (the catalog to the Hrdlička archival collection at the Smithsonian is itself a 79-page paperbound book), perhaps it is possible to summarize his primary contributions to American physical anthropology as four. In terms of research, primary among these was his untiring effort to document the origin and antiquity of Native Americans and to see that others' claims had, on the one hand, a rigorously factual basis, and on the other, that the origin was relatively recent, about 10,000 years ago. Hooton did not agree; he wrote to a colleague three days after Hrdlička's death that he mourned his loss since he was an old and valued friend, but went on to say that Hrdlička's attitude on the date of New World peopling was "wrong-headed and obsolete." Nevertheless, for 30 years Hrdlička's criteria were those that had to be met for credibility. (see Figure 7.1)

Hrdlička was an early and persuasive advocate for, as the title of his paper put it, "The Neanderthal Phase of Man" (Hrdlička, 1927). Although published a year before Franz Weidenreich's own paper adopting this view of the continuity between Neanderthals and modern humans, both acknowledged their indebtedness to the anatomist Gustav Schwalbe. Hrdlička was quite willing to travel to the ends of the earth and undertake arduous archaeological excavations, particularly in the Arctic, in search of tangible evidence to bolster his viewpoints.

Hrdlička's third major accomplishment in this assessment was the development of the Division of Physical Anthropology at the Smithsonian to world stature in terms of collections and research. Although he never managed to organize the Division into a more independent American Institute of Physical Anthropology along the lines he so admired in France, he deserves credit for the creation of the premier museum operation devoted to physical anthropology in the United States.

Figure 7.1. Aleš Hrdlička as a young man about the turn of the 20th century (courtesy of the Smithsonian Institution).

And finally, of course, Hrdlička is directly responsible for the origination of the *American Journal of Physical Anthropology* in 1918 and the American Association of Physical Anthropologists in 1930, both achievements discussed at length elsewhere. It should be mentioned, however, that the founding of the AAPA was not just a bright idea easily accomplished. Hrdlička needed to overcome considerable resistance on the part of established physical anthropologists. For example, Franz Boas, well-known for his research on change in cranial shape before moving substantially into cultural anthropology, opposed the AAPA on the grounds that it would be better to have it as a subdivision of the American Anthropological Association in which he was active (Boas, 1924). For quite opposite reasons, T. Wingate Todd, professor of anatomy at Western Reserve University was vigorous in his opposition, seeing little difference between gross anatomy and physical anthropology — the former descriptive, the latter quantitative. His obstruction was effective for some years, but he was finally outflanked. Once Hrdlička's maneuvering made the AAPA a *fait accompli,* Todd became a charter member as well as an active one, bringing new emphasis on growth and development studies, as well as an enlightened view on race, to the organization. In fact, he became its president just before his death at age 53 (Jones-Kern, 1997).

Hrdlička died during World War II, but early on his anthropological expertise was elicited in an unusual form by none other than the president himself. He was asked by President Franklin Delano Roosevelt to work on a private study of the effect of racial crossing. Hrdlička said a Japanese-European mixture was bad, as was a Chinese-European one. Roosevelt disagreed, saying that experience had shown that while the Japanese-European mixture was thoroughly bad, the Chinese-European one was not bad at all. Roosevelt also asked about the Ainu. Hrdlička said their skulls were about 2,000 years less developed than "ours," and agreed with Roosevelt that an Ainu background might account for what Roosevelt saw as the nefariousness of the Japanese (Thorne, 1978).

EARNEST A. HOOTON

Hooton's principal contribution to American physical anthropology, was, above all else, his teaching. He enjoyed it. He took only two sabbatical semesters in 41 years. His undergraduate courses were immensely popular and lured a number of students into the field. But it is with his graduate students that he left his greatest mark. Although he may have participated in the training of earlier Harvard doctoral students, such as the Chinese scholar Li Chi, the first PhD that Hooton claimed was Harry Shapiro in 1926. Twenty-eight followed, if Paul T. Baker is included, even though he completed his PhD shortly after Hooton's death (for a complete list of names and dissertation titles, see Giles, 1997). This is an amazing number of PhDs in anthropology in this approximately 30-year period. And even more amazing is the fact that no fewer than seven became members of the National Academy of Science. Although not all of his PhD students ended up in academic or other anthropological research settings (one made a career in the CIA), Hooton indeed seeded a large number of institutions with their first physical anthropologist. And those trained many more (see Figure 7.2).

It was characteristic of Hooton's mentoring that students followed research paths of their choosing. Hooton had a broad, encompassing view of what constituted physical anthropology, even though he may not himself have conducted such research. He encouraged, for example, Frederick Hulse and Alice Brues to pursue genetic-oriented research, and they did. His final

Figure 7.2.   Earnest A. Hooton (photo by Arthur Griffin).

paper, published the year he died, was titled, "The Importance of Primate Studies in Anthropology" (Hooton, 1954). Consequently, the number of his students actually enhanced subject matter diversity within the field of physical anthropology.

Student diversity in terms of gender was not a Hooton strong point. He had only one female PhD, Alice Brues. He did encourage female students, however, after a fashion. Ruth O. Sawtell (Wallis) took an AM with him and has reported that although Hooton believed most young women in graduate work abandoned it if they married, he would help her in every way if she had serious intentions to study (Collins, 1979). She left Harvard after her AM and completed a PhD at Columbia under Franz Boas. Boas, incidentally, produced six PhDs in physical anthropology, four of whom were women.

Hooton also mentored Carolyn Bond Day, one of the earliest African-American students in anthropology, let alone physical anthropology. Day was one of just four African-American women to receive Harvard/Radcliffe degrees before World War II (two ABs, one AM, and one PhD; Sollors et al., 1993). Day received her Radcliffe AM in 1930 under Hooton, and Hooton arranged to publish her thesis, "A Study of Some Negro-White Families in the United States" in 1932 as volume 10 in the *Harvard African Studies* series of which he was in charge (it was reprinted in 1970 by Negro Universities Press). Hooton and Day appear to have had a good working relationship and continued corresponding long after she left the University. Hooton encouraged Day to pursue a PhD, but Day's deteriorating health precluded this; Day, on her part, encouraged Hooton and his wife to visit her and her family in North Carolina. Day bought a silver belt buckle on the Cherokee reservation (she claimed some Cherokee ancestry) and sent it to Mary Hooton in appreciation of the kindnesses she had shown her while in Cambridge.

Hooton's research, taken as a whole, has not withstood the test of time well, however competently done for its day. Early in his career he focused on skeletal analysis, first with the skeletons of the extinct inhabitants of the Canary Islands, the Guanches. Ronald Ley (1979) has written an entertaining account of Hooton's travails on Tenerife, but ultimately he did obtain many measurements and Harvard received many skeletons. These were analyzed and published in 1925 as *The Ancient Inhabitants of the Canary Islands.* Subsequently he examined, with more statistical sophistication, skeletal material recovered from the Pecos Pueblo excavations in New Mexico and published his results in 1930 as *The Indians of Pecos Pueblo.*

In the 1930s, Hooton's research moved away from human osteology toward the examination of anthropometric variation in living populations. He recalled his prison days in Wisconsin and set out to prove, in effect, that there were physical correlations between criminals and the crimes they commit, as well as physical differences between criminals and the non-criminal population. His growing prestige helped him gain enough research funding to conduct a massive study with measurements taken on about 13,000 prisoners (and a control sample of 3,200 civilians) in 10 states. At the very least, this project provided dissertation research support for a number of his graduate students during the Depression. Although he collected data on African-American prisoners as well as Caucasian ones, only the latter were analyzed for his research volume, *The American Criminal* (1939). Two other research volumes were to be supported by the royalties from a popular book, replete with his cartoon drawings, titled *Crime and the Man* (1939). The popular book was not popular enough to fund further publication, and professional reviews of his work were discouraging. He ended up believing that he had "convinced virtually no one else" of the relationships but he still was confident he had seen.

Around the same time as the criminal study, he organized, in part by mobilizing the Boston Irish community, an anthropological study of Ireland that had archaeological, sociocultural, and physical anthropology components. The project was, in many ways and given the funding difficulties, quite successful as a whole. Hooton's portion, the examination of measurements of more than 10,000 Irish males, was completed but published posthumously in 1955 as *The Physical Anthropology of Ireland* with C. W. Dupertuis.

Toward the end of World War II, Hooton entered into a contract with the Heywood-Wakefield Company of Gardner, Massachusetts, to design new seats for railway coach cars. This effort probably ranks as the first applied physical anthropology research for the private sector. With widespread publicity, he set up measuring chairs in Boston's North Station and Chicago's North Western Station where his students and assistants measured some 3,800 people who happened by while his team was there. His results were published by the company as *A Survey in Seating* (1945), and were the basis for the "Sleepy Hollow" railway seat that was used for many years (Byron, 2003). Although Hooton recommended 19 inches for what he termed "hip breadth," his research found that the 95th percentile for accommodating male hip breadth was 17.4 inches and for females 17.2. It is surprising that this 1940s study became the criterion for seat breadth on many Boeing and AirBus jets (including the new, huge A380), where 18 inches became the accepted width. When Boeing introduced its new 737s, seat width was reduced to 17 inches, yielding unhappiness that Hooton might have predicted (McCartney, 1999; Lander, 2007).

Hooton's research following World War II pursued a tack he called "anthropology of the individual." He was initially attracted to the concept of somatotype that was promulgated by William H. Sheldon. This involved the quantification of physique on a seven-point scale determined visually from full-length nude photographs. Sheldon's bizarre views and refusal to submit his technique to testing or a mensurational approach led to Hooton's disengagement, but he continued applied research along somewhat similar lines under several contracts with the U.S. Army. Little was published other than in government reports.

Probably next to his range of doctoral students, Hooton's greatest contribution was placing a human, if somewhat dyspeptic, face on physical anthropology. He developed a public persona, captured by the actress and author Ilka Chase in her 1941 book, *Past Imperfect:* "tall, shaggy, a little stooped, [holding] forth on mankind with penetrating insight and malice." He seemed perpetually ready with a pungent quote for an inquiring reporter on almost any topic. He authored a number of books that were scientifically sound but accessible to a lay person, and gave them intriguing titles, such as *Up From the Ape,*

Man's Poor Relations, Twilight of Man, "Young Man You Are Normal," Apes, Men and Morons, and *Why Men Behave Like Apes and Vice Versa.*

More than with the books, he addressed the public with a stream of articles in magazines, widely popular ones like *Good Housekeeping* (1944, "A Woman for President"), *Ladies' Home Journal* (1946, "Is Your Man Normal?"), *Woman's Home Companion* (1943, "Morons Into What?") and smaller circulation ones such as *'47, The Magazine of the Year* ("Spare the Twaddle, Save the Child"), *Forum* (1937, "Apology for Man"), *The Churchman* (1943, "Litters of Illiterates"), and *The Atlantic Monthly* (1939, "Wages of Biological Sin"; Hooton, magazines). One of his more off-beat articles, "Science Debunks That Pure Race Theory of the Nazis," was published in 1942 in the Hearst newspapers' rather lurid Sunday supplement, the *American Weekly* (its most famous headline: NAILED HER FATHER'S HEAD TO THE FRONT DOOR). Since it was inserted in the Sunday edition of every Hearst newspaper, it had in its heyday the largest circulation of anything published in the United States with over eight million copies each week.

Hooton's views hardly met with universal approbation. They so enraged one legislator in the Massachusetts House of Representatives, Edmond J. Donlan, that in January 1943 he filed a resolution attacking Hooton:

RESOLUTION condemning the teaching and publishing of inhuman doctrines by the professor of anthropology at Harvard University.

WHEREAS, America was founded upon the ideal that man is a sacred and inviolate creature endowed by the Creator with the right to life, liberty and the pursuit of happiness; and

WHEREAS, we are now engaged in a holy crusade for the protection and perpetuation of that ideal; and

WHEREAS, the enemies of God and man, seeking to enslave mankind, and having conspired behind the Nazi mask and myth of Blood and Super-Race, seek to destroy that ideal; and

WHEREAS, the spreading of such Nazi doctrines at home while American boys are fighting and dying for human ideals abroad, is unfair and unpatriotic; and

WHEREAS, the professor of anthropology at Harvard University has taught and published that the Declaration of Independence is a pathetic document; that democracy is making the world safe for morons; that it is a government of the unfit, by the unfit, for the unfit; that our senile and diseased leaders have inflicted upon us financial crises, wars and new deals. . . .

The resolution continues with 26 more "thats" and concludes:

THEREFORE, BE IT RESOLVED that the Massachusetts House of Representatives condemns the teaching and publishing of such inhuman doctrines as contrary to the spirit of American institutions and as tending to be destructive of our liberties.

The House of Representatives first adopted, then rescinded, the resolution. Curiously, just after filing the resolution, Donlan wrote a note to Hooton, saying among other things, "I hope that this action of mine will not cause you or your family any embarrassment" (Donlan, 1943).

Meanwhile, in Nazi Germany, Hooton wasn't so well received either. For example,

Ein sogenannter Anthropologe an der
Harvard Üniversität namens Nooten verlangte
man müsse aus den Deutschen ein Mischvolk
machen und zu diesem Zweck die deutschen
Armeen zu Formationen von Arbeitssklaven
umgestalten denen die Rückkehr nach
Deutschland verboten sei. Die schmutzige
Phantasie gewisser Yankees ist offenbar
unerschöpflich in sadistischen Projekten.
Wie unsere Antwort darauf aussieht können
die amerikanischen Soldaten den Nooten und
Genossen schildern.

Völkischer Beobachter

(A so-called anthropologist from Harvard
University by the name of Nooten [*sic*] has
demanded that Germans must be made into a
mixed race, and to do this the German army
would be changed into units of worker-slaves
whose return to Germany would be forbidden.
The dirty imagination of certain Yankees is
obviously inexhaustible in [supplying] sadistic
projects. The American soldiers can describe to
Nooten and his ilk what our answer to this looks
like.)

Peoples Observer

During World War II Hooton continued to teach, and in fact taught a much heavier schedule since so many faculty members had joined the military. The "E" word has to be part of the vocabulary describing Hooton, but Hooton's eugenics was specifically non-racist. He sought the biological "improvement" of all races as he saw them. He rejected any idea of a hierarchy of races or ethnic groups, and was widely seen in this sense. For example, the National Association for the Advancement of Colored People asked him to present its Spingarn medal to Dr. Charles R. Drew for his research in blood transfusion at its Wartime Conference in Chicago in 1944. "Dr. Hooton Assails Racial Prejudice" is the way the *New York Times* (July 17) headlined its story on Hooton's speech, which was given in Chicago's Washington Park before an audience estimated at 20,000.

In addition to writing anti-Nazi articles like the one mentioned in *The American Weekly*, and being an air-raid warden in Cambridge, Hooton aided the U.S. war effort by responding to a request for help by the Army Air Forces Aero Medical Research Unit in early 1941. Sizing standards for the design of cockpits and gun turrets appear to have been based, at least in part, on old British research, and the misfit with American pilots and gunners had become dangerous. Hooton generated an anthropometric survey of cadets that was used to modify equipment and screen candidates. The effort's success so impressed the military that a permanent applied anthropology unit was established at, as it is now called, Wright-Patterson Air Force Base in Ohio.

CONCLUSION

The contributions of Earnest A. Hooton and Aleš Hrdlička to American physical anthropology might, with little exaggeration, be said to be contrapuntal. In so many ways they differed in what they did and how they did it, but together they built a truly multi-faceted, distinctive American physical anthropology, one reflected well in the American Association of Physical Anthropologists and the *American Journal of Physical Anthropology* that one originated but both nurtured.

ACKNOWLEDGMENTS

I want to acknowledge my great indebtedness to the Hooton archives in the Peabody Museum, Harvard University, and the Hrdlička archives at the National Anthropological Archives of the Smithsonian Institution for access to their materials. Much assistance was also provided by the Massachusetts Archives at Columbia Point, Boston, and the University of Illinois Interlibrary Loan Department, Urbana, by Margrith Mistry (German translation), E. H. Robbins (unpublished material on Hooton's prisoner work), and my wife Inga. Support was provided by the Wenner-Gren Foundation for Anthropological Research, the National Endowment for the Humanities, and the American Philosophical Society.

REFERENCES

Boas, F. (1924). Letter to Hrdlička, 24 December. Hrdlička archives, Smithsonian Institution.

Byron, C. R. (2003). Dr. Hooten [*sic*] and His Sleepy Hollow Seats. Dream Trains. Classic Trains Special Edition No. 1. Waukesha, WI: Kalmbach Publishing, pp. 3–39.

Chase, Ilka. (1941). *Past Imperfect*. Garden City, NY: Doubleday.

Collins, J. M. (1979). Ruth Sawtell Wallis, 1895–1978. *American Anthropologist, 81*, 85–87.

Donlan, E. J. (1943). Letter to Hooton, 14 January. Hooton archives, Peabody Museum, Harvard University.

Giles, E. (1997). Hooton, E(arnest) A(lbert) (1887–1954). In *History of Physical Anthropology: An Encyclopedia, Vol. 1*, ed. by F. Spencer, pp. 499–501. New York: Garland Publishing.

Hooton, E. A. (1911). The Evolution of Literary Art in Pre–Hellenic Rome. PhD Dissertation, University of Wisconsin, Madison.

———. (1917). Letter to Hrdlička, 27 November. Hrdlička archives, Smithsonian Institution.

———. (1936). Plain Statements about Race. *Science, 83*, 511–513.

———. (1954). The Importance of Primate Studies in Anthropology. *Human Biology, 26*, 179–188.

———. Magazine articles:

Good Housekeeping (October, 1944), pp. 97, 99–100.

Ladies' Home Journal (April, 1946), pp. 167–170.

Woman's Home Companion (August, 1943), pp. 4, 96.

'47, The Magazine of the Year (June, 1947), pp. 22–24.

Forum (1937), 97: 332–338.

The Churchman (1943), 15 February, pp. 7–8.

Atlantic Monthly (1939), October, pp. 435–445.

American Weekly (1942), 12 April, p. 7.

Hrdlička, A. (1927). The Neanderthal Phase of Man. *Journal of the Royal Anthropological Institute of Great Britain and Ireland, 57*, 249–274.

———. (1938). Letter to Hooton, 11 February. Hrdlička archives, Smithsonian Institution.

Jones-Kern, K. F. (1997). T. Wingate Todd and the Development of Modern American Physical Anthropology, 1900–1940. PhD Dissertation, Bowling Green State University, Ohio.

Lander, M. (2007). A380 Test Flight: 2 Bars, 15 Lavatories and 200 Reporters. *New York Times*, 8 February.

Ley, R. (1979). From the Caves of Tenerife to the Stores of the Peabody Museum. *Anthropological Quarterly, 52*, 159–164.

McCartney, S. (1999). Feeling Confined? You May Be Flying in One of Boeing's New 737s. *Wall Street Journal*, 2 August.

Peake, H., & Hooton, E. A. (1915). Saxon Graveyard at East Stafford, Berks. *Journal of the Royal Anthropological Institute of Great Britain and Ireland, 45,* 92–130.

Sollors, W., Titcomb, C., & Underwood, T. A. (eds.). (1993). *Blacks at Harvard: A Documentary History of African-American Experience at Harvard and Radcliffe.* New York: New York University Press.

Thorne, C. (1978). *Allies of a Kind: The United States, Britain and the War Against Japan, 1941–1945.* London: Hamish Hamilton.

Chapter 8

The Immediate Postwar Years: The *Yearbook of Physical Anthropology* and the Summer Seminars

by

Michael A. Little and Bernice A. Kaplan

INTRODUCTION

The period immediately following the Second World War saw dramatic changes in academic professions and the growth of colleges and universities in the United States. Military personnel were able to take advantage of the 1944 GI Bill to attend college, and this led to an expansion of higher education. As an example, by 1947, 49% of college students were WWII veterans (www.gibill.va.gov). At this time, anthropology had not yet expanded much at the graduate and professional level, but the end of the war did enable anthropologists to begin to redirect their efforts from wartime activities to academic research and graduate training.

In physical anthropology, the annual meetings of the American Association of Physical Anthropologists (AAPA), which had been discontinued in 1943 and 1944 as a result of the war, were resumed in March 1945 in Philadelphia. At that meeting, however, only 23 papers were presented (Comas, 1969). During this period of recovery after the war, Sherwood L. Washburn, who was secretary-treasurer of the AAPA, conceived of two projects to stimulate the exchange of ideas in physical anthropology beyond those of the annual meetings: the Summer Seminar in Physical Anthropology and the *Yearbook of Physical Anthropology* (see Figure 8.1).

The Summer Seminars in Physical Anthropology were based on the idea of bringing together professionals and students to discuss and explore new ideas in the profession. There were six Summer Seminars in New York City between 1946 and 1951 that fundamentally set the stage for the growth of

Figure 8.1. A young Sherwood L. Washburn in the early 1940s.

a modern, scientific physical anthropology during the second half of the 20th century. The first Seminar in 1946 was held under the auspices of the Columbia University Summer School (Washburn taught at Columbia during this period), and all of the Summer Seminars were supported by Paul Fejos, as the director of research (later president) of the Viking Fund, Inc., which became the Wenner-Gren Foundation for Anthropological Research, Inc. in 1951. Washburn and Fejos had developed a very close relationship, and Washburn's vision of physical anthropology certainly inspired Fejos to support the project for six summers, as well as an additional two seminars. These two later Summer Seminars were held outside of New York City in 1953 and 1955: the first was held in Boston and the second in Washington, DC. A synopsis of the eight Summer Seminars from 1946 to 1955 is given in Table 8.1.

The *Yearbook of Physical Anthropology* was founded also in 1946 (Volume 1, 1945) under the editorship of Gabriel W. Lasker. Sherwood Washburn appointed Lasker editor of the new annual publication, believing that physical anthropology needed a vehicle to report on the Summer Seminars, to

Table 8.1.   Summer Seminars from 1946 through 1955.

Year	Themes and Key Issues	Special Guests
1946	Specific problems, causality, statistics, methods and measurements, a move away from essentialism, collaborative and multidisciplinary field teams, genetics, racial classification, evolution as a theoretical focus	————————
1947	Classification, constitutional anthropology, adaptation, genetics, human evolution	Franz Weidenreich, H.R. von Koenigswald, Wilton M. Krogman
1948	Study of growth, evolution of man	James M. Tanner, Wilfrid E. Le Gros Clark
1949	Recently found Australopithecine specimens, current methods of study of the American Indian	Raymond Dart, Alexander Galloway, Solly Zuckerman
1950	New techniques and methods (dating, fossils, photography, statistical tools, objectives for the future)	Kenneth P. Oakley
1951	Scope of physical anthropology, what is to be taught (evolution, fossil studies, primate studies, anthropometry and other measurements, genetics and typology, human ecology, human growth and development, constitution, applied physical anthropology)	John T. Robinson, Marston Bates
1953	Analysis of bodily components in growth, the skeleton, application of genetic principles, dental-facial complex in growth	Earnest A. Hooton Wilton M. Krogman (organizer)
1955	Human skeletal identification, early forensic anthropology	T. Dale Stewart (organizer)

summarize the state of physical anthropology, and to reprint important papers that had been published in the preceding year (Lasker, 1999, 97). The Summer Seminars and the yearbook were linked in several ways, and it was believed that the yearbook would serve also to inform those who were unable to attend the Summer Seminars. Bernice Kaplan, Elizabeth Richards, and Gabriel Lasker prepared the proceedings of the first Summer Seminar, and Lasker spent the rest of the summer working on other contributions to the yearbook at the Viking Fund headquarters on East 71st Street in New York City (see Figure 8.2). The Viking Fund also supported the publication of the yearbook, which was distributed to interested anthropologists at no charge during these early years.

Figure 8.2. Gabriel W. Lasker during the time when he was editor of the *Yearbook of Physical Anthropology* (courtesy of Bernice A. Kaplan).

THE EARLY SUMMER SEMINARS IN NEW YORK CITY

The proposal for the first Summer Seminar was presented by Washburn at a Viking Fund supper-conference for anthropologists on October 5, 1945, in New York City. At this supper-conference, Washburn suggested a six-week summer session that "would provide an opportunity a) for physical anthropologists to convene; [and] b) for students to become acquainted with the field." Washburn's proposal focused on the fact that "physical anthropologists are not numerous.

The majority are employed in anatomy departments . . . [and there is] . . . a high degree of intellectual isolation. [What is needed is] . . . to launch a cooperative attack on important problems." The proposal included five points that (1) the summer session be held in New York City; (2) the principal activity be a professional seminar; (3) the courses be offered in the Columbia University Summer Session; (4) the faculty be composed primarily of younger physical anthropologists; and (5) the "great men" of physical anthropology and experts from other fields be invited to attend for short periods (W-G Archives, 1945).

In late October 1945, Washburn sent letters of invitation to 23 physical anthropologists and others throughout the United States, encouraging their participation. They included James M. Andrews, J. Lawrence Angel, Robert S. Benton, Joseph B. Birdsell, R. B. Cummings, Albert Damon, C. Wesley Dupertuis, Loren Eiseley, Marcus Goldstein, William W. Howells, Byron Hughes, Frederick Hulse, Gabriel W. Lasker, Theodore D. McCown, Georg K. Neumann, Marshall T. Newman, Francis E. Randall, Earle R. Reynolds, R. M. Snodgrass, and Charles E. Snow. Of these, 15 responded, and 8 indicated that they were very much interested in participating. Several of those who responded were either recently discharged from or still members of the military services. In late November 1945, Washburn requested $5,200 to support the Summer Seminar in a letter to Paul Fejos. In a letter to Washburn from Fejos dated January 2, 1946, $4,000 was granted for the project. Of these funds, between $500 and $600 each was allocated to Lawrence Angel, Joseph Birdsell, Georg Neumann, Theodore McCown, and Marshall Newman for their active participation. (W-G Archives, 1945, 1946)

It is difficult to overestimate the value of the late 1940s Summer Seminars on the development of physical anthropology as a mature science. The 1946 Summer Seminar met twice a week for six weeks at the Viking Fund building on East 71st Street in New York City (Kaplan et al., 1946). This must have been a busy year for physical anthropologists because there were two meetings of the AAPA that same year: the 15th Meeting on April 2–3 in Cleveland and the 16th Meeting in Chicago on December 27–29. During the 1946 Summer Seminar, there were 11 papers presented, 14 regular attendees, and an additional 22 who attended occasionally to participate in the discussions on a variety of topics. Much of the discussion was progressive in the context of pre–WWII ideas, and some effort was devoted to defining how physical anthropology could contribute to scientific inquiry. For example, there was interest in moving away from description to analysis and problem solving, with an emphasis on more narrowly conceived scientific problems. Some participants, who argued that typologies and other classificatory schemes were based on unproven assumptions, criticized essentialism. Collaborative field research was encouraged, with specialists from a variety of biological sciences working together as part of a cooperative unit. Racial classification was not disputed as a preliminary technique, but it was agreed that "further studies of this sort might lead to a useless and confusing proliferation of classificatory schemes" (Kaplan et al., 1946, 7). Nearly all those regular participants were young professionals who had had the PhD in hand for less than 10 years. Loren Eiseley was the oldest with the PhD in 1937; Stanley Garn was the youngest with his PhD being awarded in 1948.

The second Summer Seminar of 1947 met twice a week for four weeks at the Viking Fund offices in New York City (Kaplan, 1947). Attendance was up substantially from the previous year to 93, with 34 of these participating in all of the sessions. This was the only major meeting of physical anthropologists in 1947, since the 16th Annual Meeting of the AAPA was held in December 1946, and there was no Annual AAPA Meeting the next year. Classification, one of the key issues of discussion, was challenged and defended on a number of occasions, especially in the context of constitutional anthropology. Since attendance was higher than the 1946 seminar, some old issues were reviewed. "There was agreement . . . on the need for a more penetrating analysis of adaptive characteristics" (Kaplan, 1947, 10), especially within genetics. Human evolution continued to be a major focus, with most of the papers centering on human origins and fossils. Krogman provided an evaluation of the Seminar, and there were several demonstrations of fossil specimens, x-ray, photography, somatology, blood grouping, and other techniques.

The 1948 Summer Seminar met daily for two weeks, again at the Viking Fund offices (Kaplan, 1948). There were 84 attendees with special guests James M. Tanner and Wilfrid E. Le Gros Clark. The seminar was organized into two sections: (1) the study of growth and (2) the evolution of man. There were nine talks and discussions and two round-table discussions held at the Viking Fund building, and a public lecture at Hunter College by Le Gros Clark. During the growth sessions, two of the papers drew on studies conducted on WWII military personnel. Le Gros Clark discussed Miocene primates, *Australopithecus,* and more advanced hominids in three lectures.

The fourth Summer Seminar in 1949 was held from August 29 to September 3, with sessions held daily for a full week at the Viking Fund offices (Kaplan, 1949). Alexander Galloway from Kampala, Uganda, Raymond Dart from South Africa, and Solly Zuckerman from the United Kingdom were special guests from overseas. There were two main themes: (1) "Significance of recently found Australopithecine materials" and (2) "Current methods in the study of the American Indian." Galloway, Dart, Zuckerman, and William King Gregory gave papers or participated in discussions on the Australopithecines. William Boyd, James Spuhler, Albert Dahlberg, Joseph Birdsell, Morris Steggerda, Charles Snow, Marshall Newman, Theodore

McCown, William Laughlin, and T. Dale Stewart gave papers on the American Indian. Attendance at this seminar was the highest of the six summers with 116 participants, including the distinguished visitors Juan Comas and Daniel F. Rubin de la Borbolla from Mexico, Carlos Monge from Peru, P. O. Pederson from Denmark, Martin Gusinde from Austria, and Ernst Mayr from the United States.

The 1950 Summer Seminar was held, again at the Viking Fund office, during the week of June 19–24 (Kaplan, 1950). With 35 papers delivered and 88 in attendance, the focus was on "New Techniques in Physical Anthropology." Kenneth Oakley was a special guest from the United Kingdom and gave talks on the fluorine-dating method (this was three years before Joseph Weiner and Oakley dispelled the Piltdown hoax) and the Broken Hill specimen. Other papers were given on fossil dating; casting, staining, and blood-typing techniques; standard, Polaroid, and X-ray photography; and statistical applications. In terms of participation, there were more papers presented at this Summer Session than any of the others. What is most remarkable is this Summer Session followed, almost immediately, the June 9–17 Cold Spring Harbor Fifteenth Annual Symposium on Quantitative Biology on the *Origin and Evolution of Man* that was jointly organized by Theodosius Dobzhansky and Sherwood Washburn (Warren, 1951). Hence, many of the Summer Seminar participants had already attended an intense, groundbreaking nine-day conference on Long Island.

The sixth and last Summer Seminar in New York City was held the last week of June 1951 at the newly named Wenner-Gren Foundation for Anthropological Research office in New York City (Kaplan, 1951). The format of the Summer Seminar was different from that in the past, in that papers were not presented. Rather, only a few formal presentations were made, and the principal activities were members of the seminar meeting in small discussion groups, where the chairman of each committee made a report to the whole group. The general theme of the seminar was to define the field of physical anthropology and, accordingly, to define what breadth of materials graduate students should be expected to cover in order to be well trained in the profession. The scope of physical anthropology, as defined at this meeting foreshadowed contemporary subareas: evolution, fossil studies, primate studies, anthropometry and measurements, genetics and typology, human ecology, human growth, constitution, and applied physical anthropology. Two special presentations/demonstrations by Carleton Coon on the Hotu site in Iran and by John Robinson on the Australopithecines were given under the fossil studies topic. Some of the issues discussed underlined transition in physical anthropology: (1) too much concern with techniques and not enough with problems; (2) less time spent on anthropometry; (3) many traditional methods no longer apply to contemporary studies; (4) the value of historical, ecological, experimental, and applied studies was emphasized; (5) contributions of anatomy, human ecology, and human genetics must be incorporated into a holistic physical anthropology, with ecology forming a bridge among these and other fields; (6) evolution is the unifying, theoretical framework for physical anthropology.

Attendance at the Summer Seminars was good and probably not too different from the AAPA Annual Meetings during those years. Those attending five or six of the Seminars who were the core participants included J. Lawrence Angel, Earl Count, Loren Eiseley, Paul Fejos, Stanley Garn, Bernice A. Kaplan, Gabriel W. Lasker, T. Dale Stewart, Frederick Thieme, and Sherwood L. Washburn. Earnest Hooton only attended two of the seminars, although William Sheldon attended three seminars, and C. Wesley Dupertuis, who was a supporter of Sheldon, attended four seminars. Numerous anthropologists from other subfields were in attendance from time to time, including Conrad Arensberg, David Bidney, Junius Bird, Donald Collier, Louis Dupree, John Gillin, James Griffin, Melville Herskovits, Alfred Kroeber, Ralph Linton, Richard MacNeish, J. Alden Mason, Ellman Service, William Duncan Strong, and Charles Wagley. In contrast to the AAPA Annual Meetings, which were broadly based in physical anthropology, the Summer Seminars attracted many younger members of the profession who were interested in more modern approaches to physical anthropology.

It is quite clear that, although Washburn had considerable assistance from colleagues, he *was* the driving force in organizing and managing the six Summer Seminars. The only Summer Seminar that he missed was the third in 1948, when he was traveling in East and South Africa with Viking Fund support (Haraway, 1988). J. Lawrence Angel and Gabriel W. Lasker organized that 1948 seminar. Washburn, probably more than anyone else from this post–WWII era, was responsible for the transformation of physical anthropology from a descriptive, typologically oriented science to one in which modern scientific principles were applied. The Summer Seminars helped to define this transition and enriched the ideas that were published in Washburn's seminal paper on the "New Physical Anthropology" in 1951.

THE LATER SUMMER SEMINARS

There were two Summer Seminars held outside of New York City in the early- to mid-1950s. The Wenner-Gren foundation continued to sponsor these last of the Summer Seminars. The first was held at the Forsyth Dental Infirmary for Children in Boston, June 22–25, 1953 (Tappen & Goodale, 1954).

The second was held at the Smithsonian Institution in Washington, DC, September 6–9, 1955 (Stewart & Trotter, 1955). There were no summer seminars in 1952 and 1954. In 1952, the Wenner-Gren Foundation was occupied with the International Symposium on Anthropology, which it sponsored and organized. Originally, the idea of Paul Fejos, the International Symposium ran from June 9–20 and was held at the foundation offices in New York City (Kroeber, 1952). It was presided over by Alfred L. Kroeber, and led to the important published compendium from the symposium, *Anthropology Today* (Kroeber, 1953). Sherwood Washburn, who was then president of the American Association of Physical Anthropologists, was a member of the planning committee and an active participant in the symposium activities (see Figure 9.1). Other physical anthropologists participated as well.

Wilton M. Krogman, a University of Chicago–trained specialist in growth and forensics and who was currently at the University of Pennsylvania, organized the 1953 Boston Seminar. Edward E. Hunt, Jr., who was a researcher at the Forsyth Dental Infirmary, was in charge of the local arrangements. The seminar was entitled, "The Role of Physical Anthropology in Medical and Dental Research." There were 90 who attended this Summer Seminar, the first one in which Washburn neither organized nor played a seminal role in its organization. Earnest A. Hooton, who would certainly not have been Washburn's first choice, gave the Keynote Address. It was to be one of his last major addresses as he died the following year. Hooton's address centered on the contributions that physical anthropologists could make to medical and dental research. His identification of the expertise of physical anthropologists fell into the traditional topics that Washburn was attempting to transcend in his "new physical anthropology": body typing, racial diagnosis, anthropometry, and anthroposcopy. On a more positive side, Hooton did emphasize the need for more statistical analyses of groups of individuals, the importance of anthropological contributions to medical science, and the importance of integrating sociological, economic, and psychological data in medical practice. Following Hooton's address, four major themes were developed through papers and discussion: (1) analysis of bodily components in growth, (2) the skeleton, (3) the application of genetic principles, and (4) the dental-facial complex in growth. Each of these themes was consistent with Krogman's interests and contained appropriate topics for the meeting site at the Forsyth Dental Infirmary.

Despite the traditional lead-in by Hooton, many of the papers were really quite progressive in their new approaches to the study of physical anthropology. Ancel Keys, who just a few years earlier had published a major work on World War II studies of starvation (Keys et al., 1950), gave a paper on the methods of assessment of body composition. Other papers included those by

Stanley Garn on subcutaneous fat analysis, Pauline Mack on bone densitometry, Edna Sobel on endocrines and growth, and papers by anthropologists from the Quartermaster Climatic Research Laboratory in Natick, Massachusetts (Russell Newman, Paul Baker). James Spuhler and James Neel reported on the most current approaches to population genetics, a field that had been introduced at the 1950 Cold Spring Harbor Symposium on the *Origin and Evolution of Man* (Warren, 1951). As an interesting historical note, Neel's discussion of sickle cell anemia made no mention of the association of sickle cell with malaria that was to be dramatically reported in the literature the next year by Anthony Allison (1954).

Several important indicators of trends in physical anthropology were apparent at this summer seminar. First, the climatic and physiological research arising from studies in the military were described. In the summary of the First Theme, Ancel Keys and Russell Newman suggested the need for greater cooperation among anthropologists and physiologists in studies of body composition. Second, the importance of anthropology to the medical and dental sciences was emphasized and demonstrated in several papers. Third, Marcus Goldstein's encouragement of demography to serve as a bridge to anthropology in population studies was viewed positively by the geneticists. Finally, in an "impromptu panel discussion of constitution studies," Carleton Coon, William Sheldon, Ancel Keys, and Sherwood Washburn discussed the pros and cons of somatotyping, reflecting some of the concerns of the procedures that continue up to the present.

There is less information about the last Summer Seminar that was held at the U.S. National Museum of the Smithsonian Institution in September 1955. T. Dale Stewart and Mildred Trotter (1955), who were the organizers, published a brief report in *Science* that described some of the highlights of the four-day seminar entitled "The Role of Physical Anthropology in the Field of Human Identification." Whereas the previous Summer Seminar in 1953 drew participants heavily from the Boston area, this 1955 seminar drew participants widely from the Washington, DC, area, including many from the Smithsonian Institution and U.S. government agencies. In addition to anthropologists from the District of Columbia and elsewhere, there were representatives from the Federal Bureau of Investigation (FBI), U.S. Public Health Service, National Institute of Dental Research, Eastman Kodak Company, Quartermaster Research and Development Command (Massachusetts), Wright-Patterson Air Force Base (Ohio), and the Offices of the Maryland and Virginia Medical Examiners. This last Summer Seminar was the most "applied" of all the previous seven seminars and might be identified as the transitional conference leading to modern forensic anthropology studies. It came at the end of the Korean War when a number of physical anthropologists were working in the identification of war dead. Several years later, Krogman (1962) wrote the pioneering volume, *The Human Skeleton in Forensic Medicine* that must have been stimulated by this important Summer Seminar.

The seminar began with T. Dale Stewart, who gave a dinner talk on anthropological participation in medico-legal matters on the first evening. This was followed by five panel sessions over the next three days. The first, chaired by Krogman, was "Physical anthropologists as specialists in human identification." William S. Laughlin chaired the second panel on "Identification of small remnants of the human body," and the third panel was led by Steward and J. Lawrence Angel to discuss methods of determination of "Sex and age of the skeleton." Mildred Trotter headed the fourth panel "On construction of stature, body build, and facial features." The final panel was chaired by Theodore D. McCown, in which "Education and administrative aspects" were discussed, particularly the need to incorporate "identification" as a part of the physical anthropology curriculum. Closing discussion at the seminar emphasized the importance of applied physical anthropology in human identification work.

THE *YEARBOOK OF PHYSICAL ANTHROPOLOGY*

If Washburn was the initiator of the yearbook, then Gabriel Lasker was the editor who made it a success. As noted, the early yearbooks each focused on (1) a summary of the Summer Seminar, (2) a review of the year's contributions to physical anthropology by the editor, and (3) reprinted papers not accessible in the major U.S. journals in physical anthropology. In addition, original papers from Summer Seminar talks and review papers were published; however, the bulk of the yearbook pages were devoted to reprinted articles published in the previous year, many from overseas journals. In the early volumes, the issue year referred to the period in which the reprinted articles were originally published. For example, the first yearbook was labeled as 1945 but was published in 1946 and included the review of the 1946 Summer Seminar: most of the papers reprinted in this first 1946 issue were originally published in 1945.

Lasker's policy was not to reprint articles from the *American Journal of Physical Anthropology* on the grounds that this was accessible to most physical anthropologists. The variety of journals surveyed was quite remarkable and reflected the hard work of literature review in marked contrast to modern electronic methods of survey on the Web. In the 1945 yearbook there was no review of the year's literature and most of the 26 reprinted articles were on the traditional topics of skeletal biology, dentition, and evolution from the fossil record. A classic article by Adolph H. Schultz and William L. Straus, Jr. on "The Number of Vertebrae in Primates" and two articles by Alexander S. Wiener on blood groups highlighted this first issue. Lasker, who surveyed the literature in "Physical Anthropology During the Year" by reviewing more than 100 references, put substantial effort into the 1946 volume. His categories were primates, evolution, race, human inheritance, bones, growth, effects of diet, constitution, metabolism, and demography. This volume had articles by W. E. Le Gros Clark, A. S. Weiner, L. S. B. Leakey, E. A. Hooton, S. L. Washburn, L. W. Sontag and E. L. Reynolds, and N. Bayley, and represented a better-balanced coverage of the literature for that year than the previous one. The 1947 volume incorporated 22 reprinted papers that included two each by James Tanner and Theodosius Dobzhansky, and others by R. Broom, Le Gros Clark, and W. C. Boyd. J. Lawrence Angel reviewed the literature for the year with the title "Physical Anthropology in 1947: A Time of Transition." Lasker prepared the review of the literature again in the 1948 volume, but the papers surveyed were well over 200, reflecting the postwar expansion of research and writing. Charles I. Shade reviewed nearly 200 papers for the 1949 volume. Reprinted papers include authors such as Mildred Trotter, Kenneth Oakley, Robert Broom, John Robinson, Le Gros Clark, Ernst Mayr, Earle Reynolds, and Wilton Krogman. Lasker, again, did masterful surveys of the literature, citing 447 references in the 1950 review and 549 references in the 1951 review. James N. Spuhler compiled a bibliography of nearly 1,000 references for the 1952 volume.

The history of publication of the yearbook from its inception to the present might be divided into three stages. The first stage was from 1945 (Vol. 1) to 1952 (Vol. 8), when Gabriel Lasker was the primary editor, except for 1952, when Lasker was working in Mexico and James Spuhler was the editor (Lasker, 1989). During this period, the Viking Fund/Wenner-Gren Founda-

Table 8.2.   The *Yearbook of Physical Anthropology:* 1945–1952.

Year	Volume	Editor(s)	Publisher/Supporter
1945–46	1–2	G.W. Lasker	Viking Fund
1947	3	G.W. Lasker & J.L. Angel	Viking Fund
1948	4	G.W. Lasker & F.P. Thieme	Viking Fund
1949	5	G.W. Lasker & C.I. Shade	Viking Fund
1950	6	G.W. Lasker & J.L. Angel	Wenner-Gren Foundation
1951	7	G.W. Lasker & W.L. Straus, Jr.	Wenner-Gren Foundation
1952	8	J.N. Spuhler	Wenner-Gren Foundation

Table 8.3. The *Yearbook of Physical Anthropology*: 1953–1967.

Year	Volume	Editor(s)	Publisher/Supporter
1953–61	9	G.W. Lasker	American Association of Physical Anthropologists, Instituto de Investigaciones Históricas, UNAM, Instituto Nacional de Antropología e Historia, Wenner-Gren Foundation
1962	10	J. Kelso & G.W. Lasker	Same
1963	11	J. Kelso, G.W. Lasker & S.T. Brooks	American Association of Physical Anthropologists, Instituto de Investigaciones Históricas, UNAM, Instituto Nacional de Antropología e Historia
1964–65	12–13	S. Genovés T., S.T. Brooks & G.W. Lasker	Same
1966–67	14–15	S. Genovés, G.W. Lasker & J.H. Prost	Same

tion funded publication, and the volumes were distributed without charge (see Table 8.2). The second stage was 1953–1961 (Vol. 9) to 1967 (Vol. 15), when Gabriel Lasker, Jack Kelso, Santiago Genovés, Sheilagh Brooks, and Jack Prost edited the volumes in various editorial combinations. Lasker had revived the yearbook with some start-up funds from the Wenner-Gren Foundation (Lasker, 1964). The Instituto de Investigaciones Históricas at the Universidad Nacional Autónomica and the Instituto Nacional de Antropología e Historia in Mexico published these volumes for the AAPA at a nominal cost (see Table 8.3). The first volume of the third stage is the modern pattern that began in 1972 with Volume 16 when the practice of publishing original review articles began. Volume 16 was published after a hiatus of four years (1968–1971) with John Buettner-Janusch as the editor. Earlier, Buettner-Janusch (1967) had written a very critical review of Volume 13 of the yearbook, arguing that reprinted articles were no longer needed and that review articles were more appropriate for this publication. Serving as the editor of the 1972 volume gave him an opportunity to put these ideas into practice (see Table 8.4).

Table 8.4.   The Yearbook of Physical Anthropology: 1972–2004.

Year	Volume	Editor(s)	Publisher/Supporter
1972–76	16–20	J. Buettner-Janusch	American Association of Physical Anthropologists, Wenner-Gren Foundation
1978–81	21–24	K. A. Bennett	American Association of Physical Anthropologists
1982–86	25–29	R. M. Malina	Same
1987–91	30–34	E. J. E. Szathmáry	Same
1992	35	J. S. Friedlaender	Same
1993–97	36–40	A. T. Steegmann, Jr.	Same
1998–2003	41–46	C. Ruff	Same
2004–	47–	S. Stinson	Same

THE ROLE OF THE VIKING FUND/WENNER-GREN FOUNDATION IN THE POSTWAR DEVELOPMENT OF PHYSICAL ANTHROPOLOGY

It is difficult to exaggerate the impact that the Viking Fund/Wenner-Gren Foundation had on the post–World War II development of physical anthropology and of anthropology more broadly. This is especially the case, since federal funding was very limited and museums, universities, and private foundations were the only source of conference and research funds (Baker & Eveleth, 1982). Paul Fejos, its founder and early director, who was born in 1897 in Budapest, was trained as a physician, but later became a filmmaker, an explorer, and an anthropologist (see Figure 8.3). He persuaded Axel Wenner-Gren, the Swedish industrialist, to endow the Viking Fund, which was dedicated to the promotion of anthropology (Dodds, 1973). Fejos, who was a charismatic and brilliant person, based much of his direction of the foundation on judgment of an individual's creativity and character, and he established special relationships with many anthropologists who were leaders in the profession. One of these special relationships was with Sherwood Washburn, as testified by the continued support that the director, through the foundation, provided to Washburn. While at Columbia University, Washburn was a regular attendee at the supper-conferences that were held biweekly at the foundation headquarters in New York City. It was at the October 5, 1945, supper-conference that Washburn proposed the first Summer Seminar.

Figure 8.3. Paul Fejos in the early 1940s (Reprinted by permission of the Wenner-Gren Foundation for Anthropological Research, Inc., New York, New York).

In addition to physical anthropologists attending the regular supper-conferences in New York City, during the postwar years the Viking Fund/Wenner-Gren Foundation supported the following activities that benefited physical anthropology directly:

1. several supper-conferences devoted exclusively to physical anthropology (Szathmáry 1991)
2. the Summer Seminars (from 1946 to 1955)
3. the *Yearbook of Physical Anthropology*
4. the 1950 Cold Spring Harbor Symposium XV on *Origin and Evolution of Man* (joint support)
5. fourteen of the 51 papers presented in 1952 at the First International Symposium—"A World Survey of the Status of Anthropology"—were in physical anthropology (Kroeber 1953)

Emőke Szathmáry (1991) prepared an excellent comprehensive review of the contributions of the Viking Fund/Wenner-Gren Foundation to biological anthropology for their 50th Anniversary Report.

DISCUSSION

The postwar years in physical anthropology as characterized by the Summer Seminars were akin, in some ways, to a Kuhnian paradigm shift in the profession (Kuhn, 1962). And as Szathmáry (1991, 21–22) suggested, "Although it is likely that such a shift would have occurred anyway as the conservative, older generation died away, the Summer Seminars permitted the transformation to be much more rapid than might otherwise have been the case." Most of those physical anthropologists who attended the Summer Seminars were former students of Earnest A. Hooton at Harvard. Despite the fact that Hooton was well liked by most of his students, his perspectives were traditional and typological. These relatively new PhDs were considerably different in their receptivity to the spectrum of Hooton's and Washburn's ideas, and some of the well indoctrinated to the more traditional beliefs dug in their heels and were often inflexible and unreceptive to the new ideas. Racial typologizing and the need for an anthropometric laundry list of measurements for each population studied were outmoded practices debated at the Summer Seminars. Washburn was in the vanguard of this argument, pushing to have all studies problem-focussed with methods designed specifically for the scientific problem at hand.

The intellectual climate of the Summer Seminars was an exciting one and marked by the relative youth and enthusiasm of the participants and the social welding together of the group by post-seminar meetings at the local pub. The "honored" guests accompanied the other regular attendees and there was an open exchange, both among the established professionals and between them and the younger cohort. For younger members of the profession and students, these experiences contributed exciting new ideas, but also contributed to their professional socialization and commitment to physical anthropology.

Finally, during these postwar years, the *Yearbook of Physical Anthropology* was the vehicle designed to communicate these new ideas in the context of current research. The Viking Fund/Wenner-Gren Foundation and its director Paul Fejos must be acknowledged also as recognizing the value of this pioneering endeavor and as crucial the effort to promote it.

REFERENCES

Allison, Anthony. (1954). The Distribution of the Sickle-Cell Trait in East Africa and Elsewhere, and Its Apparent Relationship to the Incidence of Subtertian Malaria. *Transactions of the Royal Society of Tropical Medicine and Hygiene, 48*, 312–318.

Baker, Thelma S., & Eveleth, Phyllis B. (1982). The Effects of Funding Patterns on the Development of Physical Anthropology. In *A History of American Physical Anthropology:1930–1980*, ed. by Frank Spencer, pp. 31–48. New York: Academic Press.

Buettner-Janusch, John. (1967). Review of *Yearbook of Physical Anthropology* 13 (1965), ed. by Santiago Genovés T., Sheilagh Brooks, & Gabriel W. Lasker. *American Journal of Physical Anthropology, 27*(3), 403–405.

Comas, Juan. (1969). *Historia Sumaria de la Asociación Americana de Antropólogos Físicos (1928–1968)*. Mexico City: Instituto Nacional de Antropología e Historia. (See also the English translation by Marta P. Alfonso, and Michael A. Little. 2005. *Yearbook of Physical Anthropology, 48*, 163–195.)

Dodds, John W. (1973). *The Several Lives of Paul Fejos: A Hungarian-American Odyssey*. New York: The Wenner-Gren Foundation.

Haraway, Donna J. (1988). Remodeling the Human Way of Life: Sherwood Washburn and the New Physical Anthropology, 1950–1980. In *Bones, Bodies, and Behavior: Essays on Biological Anthropology*, ed. by G.W. Stocking, Jr., pp. 206–259. Madison: University of Wisconsin Press.

Kaplan, Bernice A., Richards, Elizabeth, & Lasker, Gabriel W. (1946). A Seminar in Physical Anthropology. *Yearbook of Physical Anthropology, 1*, 5–11.

———. (1947). Second Summer Seminar in Physical Anthropology. *Yearbook of Physical Anthropology, 2*, 9–15.

———. (1948). The Third Summer Seminar in Physical Anthropology. *Yearbook of Physical Anthropology, 3*, 11–24.

———. (1949). The Fourth Summer Seminar in Physical Anthropology. *Yearbook of Physical Anthropology, 4*, 22–39.

———. (1950). New techniques in Physical Anthropology: A Report on the Fifth Summer Seminar in Physical Anthropology. *Yearbook of Physical Anthropology, 5*, 14–33.

———. (1951). The Scope of Physical Anthropology: What Is to Be Taught? A Report of the Sixth Annual Summer Seminar in Physical Anthropology. *Yearbook of Physical Anthropology, 6*, 25–37.

Keys, Ancel, Brožek, Josef, Mickelson, O., & Taylor, H. L. (1950). *The Biology of Human Starvation* (2 volumes). Minneapolis: University of Minnesota Press.

Kroeber, Alfred L. (1952). International Symposium on Anthropology. *Science, 116*, 216.

———. (ed.). 1953. *Anthropology Today: An Encyclopedic Inventory*. Chicago: University of Chicago Press.

Krogman, Wilton M. (1962). *The Human Skeleton in Forensic Medicine*. Springfield, IL: C.C. Thomas.

Kuhn, Thomas S. (1962). *The Structure of Scientific Revolutions*. Chicago: University of Chicago Press.

Lasker, Gabriel W. (1964). Preface. *Yearbook of Physical Anthropology, 9*, iii–v.

———. (1989). Genetics in the Journal Human Biology. *Human Biology, 61*, 615–627.

———. (1999). *Happenings and Hearsay: Experiences of a Biological Anthropologist*. Detroit: Savoyard Books.

Stewart, T. Dale, & Trotter, Mildred. (1955). The Role of Physical Anthropology in the Field of Human Identification. *Science, 122*, 883–884.

Szathmáry, Emőke J.E. (1991). Reflections on Fifty Years of Anthropology and the Role of the Wenner-Gren Foundation: Biological anthropology. In *Report for 1990 and 1991: Fiftieth Anniversary Issue*. New York: Wenner-Gren Foundation for Anthropological Research.

Tappen, Neil C., & Goodale, Jane C. (1954). The Role of Physical Anthropology in Medical and Dental Research. A report of the 1953 Wenner-Gren Foundation Summer Seminar in Physical Anthropology. *Yearbook of Physical Anthropology, 8*, 302–329.

Warren, Katherine B. (ed.). (1951). *Origin and Evolution of Man. Cold Spring Harbor Symposia on Quantitative Biology*, Vol. XV. Cold Spring Harbor, New York: The Biological Laboratory.

Washburn, Sherwood L. (1951). The New Physical Anthropology. *Transactions of the New York Academy of Science, 13*, 298-304.

Wenner-Gren Archives. (1945, 1946). Archives of the Wenner-Gren Foundation for Anthropological Research, Inc. New York: Wenner-Gren Foundation.

Chapter 9

Sherwood L. Washburn and "The New Physical Anthropology"

by

William A. Stini

INTRODUCTION

Sherwood Washburn was one of a cohort of major figures in the history of physical anthropology who studied under Earnest A. Hooton at Harvard. He was a hometown boy, having been born in Cambridge in 1911, the same year that Lord Rutherford first proposed his nuclear theory of the atom. Washburn's formative years at Groton School and as a Harvard undergraduate were eventful ones in the history of science. The series of important discoveries in the physical sciences that had begun in the late–19th century would expand the concepts of atomic theory as originally described by Dalton in the 1840s. Early 20th-century discoveries forced more explicit definitions of Newton's fundamental laws, such as those of the conservation of matter and energy. Both directly and indirectly, developments in the physical sciences set the stage for another succession of breakthroughs that would eventually revolutionize the biological sciences as well. Even a casual examination of a contemporary textbook for an introductory biological anthropology course will illustrate the extent to which this revolution has transformed the subject matter of what was known in the 1930s as "physical anthropology." Although the progression from description to measurement to experiment came later in the morphologically oriented biological sciences, its impact has been profound.

Over the centuries, many scientists and philosophers have offered speculative explanations, sometimes evolutionary in nature, for the range of species diversity. However, the history of evolutionary biology can be traced back to Darwin and Wallace's joint paper in 1858. Many in the scientific community accepted the concept of evolution through natural selection by

173

the beginning of the 20th century. However, application of the scientific method to the testing of evolutionary hypotheses did not occur at once. Such testing had to await the development of techniques to estimate the direction and intensity of natural selection. By applying Mendel's (1866) rules of inheritance, the rediscovery of Mendel's principles in 1900–1901 by Correns (1900), Tschermak-Seysenegg (1900), and DeVries (1900) allowed reinterpretation of the results of August Weissmann's experiments. Weissman (1891–1892) claimed that his results demonstrated a Lamarckian mechanism for evolutionary change. When Mendelian principles were combined with the cytological observations of Morgan (1901), Sutton (1903), Morgan and others (1915), and Bridges (1916), the location of genes on chromosomes and their reassortment during meiosis were demonstrated beyond doubt. Finally, a mechanism by which natural selection could lead to differential reproductive success could become the subject of scientific investigation. Weissmann's (1891–1892) Lamarckian explanation of the mechanism of evolution was one of the first casualties. Nevertheless, the progression from description to measurement to experiment and prediction had produced a body of experimentally verifiable data that would ultimately provide the basis for one of the most dramatic paradigm shifts in the history of biological science.

Research in Mendelian genetics was being conducted between 1903 and 1920 by such investigators as Castle (1903), Pearson (1904), Hardy (1908), and Weinberg (1908). By 1918, most of the differences between those who favored emphasis on the particulate elements of Mendelian traits and those whose interest centered on the measurement of continuous traits were resolved in a landmark paper by R. A. Fisher (1918). In this paper, Fisher argued successfully that all of the results reported by biometricians could be explained by mechanisms of Mendelian inheritance. Subsequently, theoretical work by J. B. S. Haldane (1924, 1932), Fisher (1930), and Wright (1931), showed that natural selection operated through processes of Mendelian inheritance. This work gave rise to what has been called the "synthetic theory of evolution," largely in recognition of Huxley's influential book: *Evolution: The Modern Synthesis* (Huxley, 1942).

One of the early investigators to apply the method and theory of the modern synthesis to field and laboratory research was Theodosius Dobzhansky, who emigrated from the Soviet Union in 1927, and collaborated with a number of geneticists including Sewell Wright. His book, *Genetics and the Origin of Species,* was first published in 1937 (Dobzhansky, 1937). This book was to inspire many investigators throughout the biological sciences, including physical anthropologists, through its many editions up to 1970. Washburn's collaboration with Dobzhansky early in his career at Columbia University was to provide him with access to a major figure in the mainstream of genetic research at a time when population genetics was at the "cutting edge" of biological science.

WASHBURN'S EARLY YEARS

By the time that Washburn was awarded his Harvard AB in 1935, the synthetic theory of evolution was widely accepted, and had inspired a wide range of hypotheses along with the methods and instrumentation to test them. However, his perspective on the biological sciences was strongly influenced by the prevailing emphasis on morphology and taxonomy in general biology and physical anthropology. After graduating from Harvard, Washburn spent the winter semester of 1936 in Ann Arbor where he took a course in anatomy to prepare for a later course in medical anatomy to be given by W. E. Le Gros Clark at Oxford later that year.

He emerged from this period of intensive exposure to the methods and literature of anatomy with a solid grasp of the field as well as its paleontological applications. Accordingly, he was well prepared to begin laboratory research, but his horizons were broadened considerably when an opportunity arose to engage in overseas field work. In 1937, he joined an expedition to collect primates in what were then Borneo and Siam. The Siam (Thailand) work included what was to become one of the most famous studies of primate (gibbon) behavior in the wild by C. Ray Carpenter (1940). Washburn later wrote his thesis on primate anatomy and defended it in 1940.

In 1939, he was appointed instructor of anatomy at the Columbia University Medical School. Here, he worked with the experimental embryologist S. R. Detweiler, who got him interested in the developmental and experimental approach to functional anatomy. In 1943, Washburn and Detweiler (1943) published an article in the *American Journal of Physical Anthropology* entitled "An Experiment Bearing on the Problems of Physical Anthropology." Several of his other early publications dealt with methods and techniques. As was occurring throughout the biological sciences, the shift in emphasis from description and measurement to attempts to develop models and conduct experiments was clearly reflected in Washburn's career trajectory. During that same period, he continued to broaden the scope of his interest in primatology, publishing an article on the genera of Malaysian langurs and on aspects of skeletal maturation in Old World monkeys. Soon, however, he was attracted to a topic that had engaged the attention of physical anthropologists from the earliest days of the profession: human races. In 1944 he published his first paper on race (Washburn, 1944), a topic he would return to on several other occasions during his long career (Washburn 1963c; 1964a; 1964b).

Washburn's continuing interest in applying the experimental approach to anatomical problems led him to apply animal models to assess the effects of environmental factors on the growth process. He published reports on the effects of facial paralysis on the growth of the skull of rats and rabbits (Washburn, 1946a) and on the role of the temporal muscle in determining the form of the cranium and mandible (Washburn, 1947a). During the 1940s, he wrote reports on the facial growth of humans (Washburn, 1947b), sex differences in the pubic bone of Bantu and Bushmen (Washburn, 1949), and on the thoracic viscera of the gorilla (Washburn, 1946b). Another important postwar activity was his establishment of the Viking Fund Summer Seminars in Physical Anthropology, and, along with Gabriel W. Lasker, the foundation of the *Yearbook of Physical Anthropology* (see Little & Kaplan, this volume).

THE 1950 COLD SPRING HARBOR SYMPOSIUM

Probably one of the most significant events during his years at Columbia was the beginning of his collaborative relationship with Theodosius Dobzhansky, who, as mentioned earlier, played such an important role in the application of the methods of population genetics to the testing of evolutionary hypotheses. Although Washburn left Columbia for the University of Chicago in 1947, he and Dobzhansky maintained contact and jointly organized a Cold Spring Harbor Institute symposium in 1950. It was this symposium that launched Washburn's (1951a) career in what was to become the "new physical anthropology." He also contributed a paper on primate evolution to the symposium (Washburn, 1951b).

The 15th Cold Spring Harbor Symposium on Quantitative Biology entitled "The Origin and Evolution of Man" (Warren, 1951) was held from Friday, June 9, to Saturday, June 17, 1950 (nine days, one session/day). The attendance was 129, and of these attendees, 25–30 were anthropologists; others were geneticists, evolutionary biologists, scientists from the Cold Spring Harbor Institute, and a few spouses of the participants. Funding was from the Carnegie Corporation (that funded the Cold Spring Harbor Institute) and the Viking Fund (later the Wenner-Gren Foundation for Anthropological Research). In addition to Dobzhansky and Washburn, the attendees read like a "Who's Who" in biology and anthropology at the midpoint of the century: Ernst Mayr, G. G. Simpson, Leslie Dunn, Richard Lewontin, William C. Boyd, James V. Neel, Bentley Glass, Curt Stern, Marston Bates, Alfred Kroeber, Clyde Kluckhohn, Earnest Hooton, Wilton Krogman, Carleton Coon, Joseph Birdsell, Stanley Garn, Ashley Montagu, Adolph Schultz, T. Dale Stewart, W. W. Howells, J. Lawrence Angel, Gabriel Lasker, James Spuhler, Theodore McCown, and many others.

The principal themes were population rather than typology, evolution of human populations, and race in the context of genetic and population variation. Only five years after the end of WWII and associated Nazi atrocities, Curt Stern's concluding comments were particularly telling in his concerned summary: "The political implications of statements or conclusions regarding the origin and evolution of man have been on our minds again and again. The emotional weighting of such terms as species, race, delinquency, breed, purity, eugenics, selection, and others is heavy." Rather than the symposium defining the "New Physical Anthropology," the Cold Spring Harbor meeting was a culmination of changes that had been underway in physical anthropology since the end of the war—changes to which Washburn had contributed substantially through the Summer Seminars and the *Yearbook of Physical Anthropology*. Although the meeting was successful in some ways, it failed to fully integrate the geneticists and the anthropologists, although such integration continues to the present. Recollections by Rada Dyson-Hudson (then Rada Demerec, the 19-year-old daughter of the Cold Spring Harbor Institute Director and geneticist, Milislav Demerec) were that at the end of each of the sessions (in the late afternoon), the geneticists would sit around and talk more about genetics while the anthropologists headed for the closest bar, presumably to talk more about anthropology (personal communication).

WASHBURN'S DEFINITION OF THE NEW PHYSICAL ANTHROPOLOGY

Washburn's approach to the topic of human origins was the product of a confluence of the several lines of inquiry that he had been pursuing, usually in collaboration with colleagues outside the field of physical anthropology. This approach was an amalgamation of functional anatomy, population genetics, and behavioral biology. It sought to attain greater understanding of human biocultural history as the result of genetic systems evolving through a sequence of increasingly effective behavioral repertoires.

The "New Physical Anthropology" (Washburn, 1951a; 1953) was characterized as the study (1) of the process of primate evolution and (2) human variation. There was to be (3) a return to Darwinism, but with genetics as a unifying perspective, and that (4) races must be studied as populations, not types. Physical anthropologists could (5) contribute to studies of migration, genetic drift, and selection, but not to mutation. And one of the important objectives was to study (6) the adaptation of form to function (linked to Washburn's interests in functional anatomy). He noted that the principal guiding concept is "selection," and he identified four major means for factoring complexes of the body: (1) comparison and evolution, (2) development, (3) variability (in the context of population and away from the traditional "types"), and (4) experiment, emphasizing the application of scientific design.

This description of the new physical anthropology (Washburn, 1951a; 1953) has a contemporary ring to it years later. This is because it is in general agreement with the way that most of us now view the nature of our subject matter. Viewed from our current perspective there is nothing particularly revolutionary about this approach to the study of human biology. However, it was an approach that differed significantly from the prevailing one of that period. The emphasis on functional explanations for anatomical characteristics along with their genetic determinants lent an element of dynamism to the field that is still manifest. The expanded range of research topics now subsumed within the field of physical anthropology has materially enhanced the number of opportunities for productive research open to students in the field. At the same time, it has raised the bar with respect to the level of scientific training needed to compete successfully. While it would be inaccurate to give Sherwood Washburn sole credit for bringing these changes about, there is no doubt that his role in the process was a central one.

It should be kept in mind that Washburn's definition for the "New Physical Anthropology" was published only two years before Watson and Crick (1953) published their letter describing the double helix of DNA in *Nature*. The paradigm shift that occurred in the biological sciences following the identification of DNA as the genetic code continues to define the nature of research over 50 years later. Physical anthropology as it was generally practiced at that time had very little to contribute to the redefinition of the biological sciences. However, the "new physical anthropology" provided a means through which biological anthropologists could join what was to become the mainstream of biological sciences.

Shortly after the 1950 Cold Spring Harbor Institute Symposium, the Wenner-Gren Foundation supported the organization of an International Symposium on Anthropology to be held in June 1952 in celebration of the 10th Anniversary of the Wenner-Gren Foundation. Washburn (1953) was one of the key organizers and contributed one of the 50 papers in the classic volume, edited by Alfred L. Kroeber (1953), which was to be an inventory of anthropology at the midpoint of the 20th century (see Figure 9.1). Washburn (Washburn & Howell, 1960) also contributed to the Darwin Centennial conference in 1959 in the choice of participants at this Chicago celebration (Tax, 1960).

Figure 9.1. Sherwood Washburn (right) discussing illustrations with colleagues at the 1952 Wenner-Gren Conference "International Symposium on Anthropology." (Reprinted by permission of the Wenner-Gren Foundation for Anthropological Research, Inc., New York, New York)

PALEOANTHROPOLOGICAL CONTRIBUTIONS

The fossil evidence for human evolution had been accumulating for a hundred years since the discovery of the first Neanderthal skull. In the spring of 1948, Washburn went to South Africa and Uganda with Paul Fejos. He met with Raymond Dart and Robert Broom and saw many of the specimens of Australopithecines that they had in their collections (Washburn, 1983). Later he visited Alexander Galloway at Makerere Medical School in Kampala, Uganda, where Galloway helped Washburn with his collection of monkeys and found him some working space. These experiences were fundamental in structuring Washburn's ideas and building on his knowledge base of primatology and paleoanthropology.

Discoveries at Olduvai Gorge and at several other sites in South Africa in the early 1950s stimulated his interest in the antiquity of our species (Washburn 1957). Vastly improved dating techniques based upon the use of radioisotopes permitted reliable estimates of the antiquity of early human remains. The stage was set for the synthetic theory of evolution, as developed by population geneticists during the 1920s and 1930s, to be applied to the special case of human evolution. Questions that formerly could only be addressed hypothetically could now be tested experimentally.

BEHAVIORAL STUDIES

Following the Second World War, primate field studies were beginning to develop methodologies that allowed precise description and quantification. Washburn, working with Irvin DeVore, made major contributions to the understanding of the social behavior of baboons in their natural habitat. In their description of baboon behavior, they were careful to take into account the ecological factors that provided opportunities and placed limits on the range of adaptive responses. This work, familiar to everyone who enrolled in an introductory anthropology course during the 1960s and 1970s, was, by Washburn's (1983) own account, inspired by the work of field researchers like C. Ray Carpenter. Carpenter's (1934) descriptions of Howler monkey social behavior had already cast serious doubt on the conclusions of earlier observers that the behavior of non-human primates was driven by sexual activity. Wasburn and Devore, following large troops of baboons through the full range of their behavioral repertoire, found that they acted in response to a complex mix of environmental and social stimuli. Furthermore, the baboons they observed in their natural habitat were quite restrained in the degree of intraspecific aggression expressed. This observation contrasted sharply with that of Zuckerman (1932) who had described a high level of aggression, particularly among males, in a zoo population of baboons.

The work of Washburn and DeVore (1960; Washburn et al., 1960), along with that of other field observers such as Jane Goodall (1962) and George Schaller (1963), soon led to a total reassessment of the behavior of non-human primates under natural conditions. Credit for the enormous increase in the volume and quality of primate behavioral research since that time can be assigned to these investigators. Washburn's role in this important development would, by itself, have earned him a significant place among the major figures in the history of physical anthropology. However, his interests in functional anatomy and human evolutionary history led him to incorporate the insights gained through the observation of primate behavior in the natural habitat into a broader theoretical framework. He was, after all, trained as an anatomist. In addition, his earlier work with Detweiler had sensitized him to the degree to which form and function interact throughout the developmental process. His interest in human variation was strongly influenced by this perspective, as was his understanding of the selective forces that could have shaped human evolution. His work with Dobzhansky had broadened his understanding of those forces and had led him to reject some of the racist interpretations of the fossil evidence that still found their way into the anthropological literature.

Washburn's interest in behavior extended to the role of tool-using and tool-making in human evolution. As he saw it, significant selective advantages were to be enjoyed by an erect bipedal primate whose hands were free to exploit an improved manipulative capacity. These advantages created new opportunities that, in turn, also presented new challenges. The expanding human brain was the chief organ of adaptation to these challenges and Washburn's articles (1959; 1960a; 1960b) argued persuasively for the importance of tool use and manufacture in the evolution of the human brain.

CLASSIFICATION AND HUMAN EVOLUTION

Washburn had long been interested in the process of classification in the interpretation of the fossil evidence. Therefore, his approach to the application of nomenclature to the naming of fossil hominids was cautious and consistent with his interpretations of the evidence of their functional anatomy. He had examined in great detail the muscles and bones of animals that he had also observed in action in their natural habitat. Consequently, his interpretation of the fossil evidence had an added dynamic dimension not always shared by paleontologists. It allowed him to step back and see the "big picture." This he did consistently, and his impact on the field of biological anthropology has been materially enhanced by this ability. He also welcomed the participation of molecular biologists in testing the validity of classification schemes developed through anatomical analyses. Thus, the publication of *Classification and Human Evolution* (Washburn, 1963a; 1963b) provided biological anthropologists with an expanded array of methods to pursue questions about human origins and contemporary relationships. The value of this publication in the motivation of students to acquire laboratory skills hitherto outside the realm of physical anthropology cannot be overestimated. Perusal of the articles now found in the pages of such journals as the *American Journal of Physical Anthropology* reveals just how profound the shift in research methodologies employed by biological anthropologists has been.

If the impact of a scholar is evaluated on the basis of the students he attracted and mentored, Washburn must be considered exceptional. His many students, many of whom have established impressive publication records of their own, are strong testimony to the breadth of his interests. One need only examine Donna Haraway's (1988) brilliant historical treatment of Washburn and a copy of *The New Physical Anthropology, Science, Humanism, and Critical Reflection,* edited by three of his students (Strum et al., 1999) and containing articles by a number of others, to gain an appreciation for the range of interests he encouraged. This volume is also a valuable source of information about Washburn's own thoughts about the directions of his own work and that of his chosen field of research. The bibliographic references contained in this volume are sufficiently comprehensive to make any subsequent listing of his publications redundant, and so will be outside the scope of this brief review.

SYNOPSIS

Washburn was a synthesizer. He was also an effective collaborator. In addition, he was fortunate in that the people with whom he collaborated were themselves innovative and sensitive to the value of "painting outside of lines" in their own area of research. The result was an increased awareness of the potential of physical anthropology to make significant contributions to the biological sciences at a time when a genuine paradigm shift was occurring. Obviously, Sherwood Washburn was not solely responsible for the dramatic changes that have marked the recent history of biological anthropology. However, his long and productive career, spanning over 50 years, is in many respects a history of the maturation and healthy growth of the profession. He can quite properly be viewed as "a man of his time," and the time was one of revolutionary change in our understanding of the history and biology of our species.

REFERENCES

Bridges, Charles. (1916). Non-Disjunction as Proof of the Chromosome Theory of Heredity. *Genetics, 1,* 1–52, 107–163.
Carpenter, C. Ray. (1934). A Field Study of the Behavior and Social Relations of the Howling Monkeys (*Alouatta palliata*). *Comparative Psychology Monographs, 10,* 1–168.
———. (1940). A Field Study in Siam of the Behavior and Social Relations of the Gibbon (*Hylobates lar*). *Comparative Psychology Monographs, 16*(5), 1–212.
Castle, William. (1903). The Laws of Heredity of Galton and Mendel and Some Laws Governing Race Improvement by Selection. *Proceedings of the American Academy of Arts and Sciences, 39,* 233–242.

Correns, Carl G. (1900). Mendel's Regein uber das Verhalten der Nachkommen-schaft der Rassenbastarde. *Berichte der Deutschen Botanischen Gesselschaft, 18,* 158–168.

DeVries, Hugo. (1900). Sur la Loi de Disjonction des Hybrids. *Comptes Rendus de l'Academie des Sciences* (Paris), *130,* 845–847.

Dobzhansky, Theodosius. (1937). *Genetics and the Origin of Species.* New York: Columbia University Press.

Fisher, Ronald. (1918). The Correlation Between Relatives Under the Supposition of Mendelian Inheritance. *Transactions of the Royal Society of Edinburgh, 52,* 399–433.

———. (1930). *The Genetical Theory of Natural Selection.* Oxford: Clarendon.

Goodall, Jane. (1962). Nest-Building Behavior in the Free-Ranging Chimpanzee. *Annals of the New York Academy of Science, 102*(2), 455–467.

Haldane, J.B.S. (1924). A Mathematical Theory of Natural and Artificial Selection. Part I. *Transactions of the Cambridge Philosophical Society,* 23, 19–41.

———. (1932). *The Causes of Evolution.* New York: Harper and Brothers.

Haraway, Donna J. (1988). Remodelling the Human Way of Life: Sherwood Washburn and the New Physical Anthropology, 1950–1980. In *Bones, Bodies, Behavior: Essays on Biological Anthropology,* ed. by G. W. Stocking, 206–259. Madison: University of Wisconsin Press.

Hardy, Godfrey H. (1908). Mendelian Proportions in a Mixed Population. *Science,* 28, 49–50.

Huxley, Julian. (1942). *Evolution: the Modern Synthesis.* London: Allen and Unwin.

Kroeber, Alfred L. (ed.). (1953). *Anthropology Today: An Encyclopedic Inventory.* Chicago: University of Chicago

Mendel, Gregor. (1866). Versuche über Pflantzen-Hybriden. *Verhandlungen des Naturforschenden Vereines* (Brunn), *4,* 3–47.

Morgan, Thomas H. (1901). Sex-Limited Inheritance in Drosophila. *Science, 31,* 201–210.

Morgan, Thomas H., Sturtevant, Arthur, Müller, Hermann, & Bridges, Charles. (1915). *The Mechanism of Mendelian Heredity.* New York: Henry Holt.

Pearson, Karl. (1904). On a Generalized Theory of Alternative Inheritance, With Special References to Mendel's Laws. *Philosophical Transactions of the Royal Society (A), 293,* 53–86.

Schaller, George. (1963). *The Mountain Gorilla: Ecology and Behavior.* Chicago: University of Chicago Press.

Strum, Shirley, Lindburg, Donald, & Hamburg, David (eds.). (1999). *The New Physical Anthropology.* Upper Saddle River, NJ: Prentice-Hall.

Sutton, Walter S. (1903). The Chromosomes in Heredity. *Biological Bulletin, 4,* 213–251.

Tax, Sol, (ed.). (1960). *The Evolution of Man: Mind, Culture, and Society. Volume 2 of Evolution After Darwin,* The University of Chicago Centennial. Chicago: University of Chicago Press.

Tschermak-Seysenegg, Erich. (1900). Historischer Ruckblick auf die Wiederentdeck-ung der Gregor Mendelschen. *Arbeit.Verhandlungen der Zoologische-Botanischer Gesellschaft in Wien, 92,* 25–35.

Warren, Katherine B. (ed.). (1951). *Origin and Evolution of Man. Cold Spring Harbor Symposia on Quantitative Biology,* Vol. XV. Cold Spring Harbor, New York: The Biological Laboratory.

Washburn, Sherwood L. (1940). A Preliminary Metrical Study of the Skeleton of Langurs and Macaques. Ph.D. Dissertation in Anthropology. Cambridge: Harvard University.

———. (1944). Thinking about Race. *Science Education, 28,* 65–76.

———. (1946a). The Effect of Facial Paralysis on the Growth of the Skull in Rat and Rabbit. *The Anatomical Record, 94,* 163–168.

———. (1946b). Thoracic Viscera of the Gorilla. *American Journal of Physical Anthropology, 4,* 262.

———. (1947a). The Effect of the Temporal Muscle on the Form of the Mandibles. *Journal of Dental Research, 26,* 174.

———. (1947b). The Relation of the Temporal Muscle to the Form of the Skull. *The Anatomical Record, 99,* 239–248.

———. (1949). Sex Differences in the Pubic Bone of Bantu and Bushmen. *American Journal of Physical Anthropology* (n.s.), *7,* 263–266.

———. (1951a). The New Physical Anthropology. *Transactions of the New York Academy of Science,* Series II, *13,* 298–304.

———. (1951b). The Analysis of Primate Evolution with Particular Reference to the Origin of Man. In *Origin and Evolution of Man. Cold Spring Harbor Symposia on Quantitative Biology, 15,* 67–78.

———. (1953). The strategy of physical anthropology. In *Anthropology Today: An Encyclopedic Inventory,* ed. by A.L. Kroeber, pp. 714–727. Chicago: University of Chicago Press.

———. (1957). Australopithecines: The Hunters or the Hunted? *American Anthropologist, 59,* 612–614.

———. (1959). Speculations on the Relations of the History of Tools and Biological Evolution. *Human Biology, 31,* 21–31.

———. (1960a). Cultural Determinants of Brain Size. *American Journal of Physical Anthropology, 18,* 349.

———. (1960b). Tools and Human Evolution. *Scientific American, 203,* 63–75.

———. (1963a). Behavior and Human Evolution. In *Classification and Human Evolution,* ed. by S.L. Washburn, pp. 190–203. Viking Fund Publication in Anthropology Number 37, Wenner-Gren Foundation for Anthropological Research. Chicago: Aldine.

———. (ed.). (1963b). *Classification and Human Evolution.* Chicago: Aldine.

———. (1963c). The Origin of Races: Weidenreich's Opinion. *American Anthropologist, 66,* 1165–1167.

———. (1964a). Racial Differences in Skin Color. *American Anthropologist, 66,* 173–174.

———. (1964b). Race, Racism, and Culture. *Princeton University Magazine, 5,* 6–8.

———. (1983). Evolution of a Teacher. *Annual Review of Anthropology, 12,* 1–24.

Washburn, Sherwood L., and Detweiler, E. R. (1943). An Experiment Bearing the Problems of Physical Anthropology. *American Journal of Physical Anthropology,* (ns.) *1,* 171–190.

Washburn, Sherwood L., and Howell, F. Clark. (1960). Human Evolution and Culture. In *Evolution After Darwin, Volume II, The Evolution of Man: Mind, Culture, and Society,* ed. by Sol Tax, pp. 33–56. Chicago: University of Chicago Press.

Washburn, Sherwood L., and DeVore, Irvin. (1960). Baboon Ecology and Human Evolution. In *African Ecology and Human* Evolution, ed. by F.C. Howell and F. Bourlier, pp. 335–367. Viking Fund Publications in Anthropology Number 36. New York: Wenner-Gren Foundation for Anthropological Research.

Washburn, Sherwood L., DeVore, Irvin, & Imanishi, K. (1960). Social Organization of Subhuman Primates in Their Natural Habitat. *Current Anthropology, 1,* 405.

Watson, James, & Crick, Francis. (1953). Molecular Structure of Nucleic Acids. *Nature, 4556,* 737.

Weinberg, W. (1908). Über den Nachweis der Vererbung beim Menschen. *Jahreschefte Verein Naturk,* Wurtemberg, *64,* 368–382.

Weissman, August. (1891–1892). *Essays on Heredity, Volumes 1 and 2.* (Translated by A. E. Shipley, S. Schonland, and others.) Oxford: Oxford University Press.

Wright, Sewall. (1931). Evolution in Mendelian Populations. *Genetics, 16,* 97–159.

Zuckerman, Solly. (1932). *The Social Life of Monkeys and Apes.* London: Routledge and Kegan Paul, Ltd.

Chapter 10

The Two 20th-Century Crises of Racial Anthropology

by

Jonathan Marks

INTRODUCTION

Physical anthropology was introduced in America as a rationalization for slavery. The end of the civil war rendered the field largely superfluous, and it would not be reinvented until the employment of Franz Boas by Columbia University (based on his expertise in measuring schoolchildren and collecting Eskimo skeletons), Aleš Hrdlička by the U.S. National Museum (partly on the recommendation of Boas), and slightly later, Earnest Hooton by Harvard.

Physical anthropology had appropriated to itself the professional voice of the study of human variation. Boas came to emphasize what we might now call its norm of reaction or adaptability; Hrdlička and Hooton came to emphasize its specific forms or expressions. The study of race, as different manifestations of the human form, dominated physical anthropology during the first few decades of the 20th century. The shift of physical anthropology away from race as a central focus was catalyzed by two social and political crises on either side of World War II.

The first came with the accession of the Nazis and their implementation of a state policy based in part on scientific ideas about racial superiority and inferiority. These ideas had been articulated by the French aristocrat Arthur de Gobineau, the British expatriate Houston Stewart Chamberlain, and the American lawyer and naturalist Madison Grant (Barzun, 1937; Poliakov, 1974; Spiro, 2009).

In Germany, the racial ideologies flourished symbiotically with the popularity of Ernst Haeckel's first-generation Darwinism. Haeckel saw Nordicism and militarism as the culmination of human bio-social evolution. His principal antagonist was Rudolf Virchow, pathologist, early anthropologist,

187

and defender of a tolerant humanist-pacifist vision of modern society. To the extent that Haeckel invoked Darwinism in support of his political ideologies, Virchow was obliged to reject it just as strongly—any evidence for human evolution was ostensibly evidence as well for Haeckel's proto-Nazism (Massin, 1996).

Virchow's death in 1902 created a vacuum that was quickly filled by German Haeckelian Darwinians. Virchow's vision of the disjuncture between biological evolution and the nature of the modern political state was taken up in America by his protégé, the physicist turned geographer turned physical anthropologist—Franz Boas.[1] Boas remained cordial for decades with the leading physical anthropologist in Germany, Eugen Fischer, even as Boas's own interests turned more to culture, language, and folklore.

Eugen Fischer, however, was a political opportunist who sought Nazi support for the Kaiser Wilhelm Institute of Anthropology, Genetics, and Eugenics, of which he was director, and was apparently willing to say and do anything to secure that support (Weiss, 2006). By the end of World War II, the expatriate anatomist Franz Weidenreich (1946) was publicly brandishing him a war criminal, a view synoptic with that of the expatriate geneticist Richard Goldschmidt (1942).

It may be worth taking a look at some words published for Eugen Fischer's festschrift in 1934, by his student, the physical anthropologist Otmarr Freiherr von Verschuer:

> We stand upon the threshold of a new era. For the first time in world history, the Führer Adolf Hitler is putting into practice the insights about the biological foundations of the development of peoples—race, heredity, selection. It is no coincidence that Germany is the locus of this event: German science provides the tools for the politician. (Aichel & Verschuer, 1934, vi)

In 1934 it was pretty clear what the Nazis stood for. Racial science and totalitarian politics existed symbiotically in Germany (Müller-Hill, 1988). To a considerable extent American scientists envied the credibility and political clout that their colleagues in Germany seemed to enjoy (Kevles, 1985; Kühl, 1994). Interestingly enough, the two Americans with articles in the collection honoring Fischer were both future presidents of the American Association of Physical Anthropologists, Raymond Pearl of Johns Hopkins and Charles Davenport of Cold Spring Harbor. We obviously cannot hold them responsible for Vershuer's preface, but the presence of their articles behind those words attests to the casual continuity between normative American and German physical anthropology.

By mid-decade, Earnest Hooton was finding it necessary to distinguish publicly between (bad) German physical anthropology and (good) American physical anthropology. "[A] physical anthropologist . . . desires emphatically to dissociate the finding of his science from the acts of human injustice which masquerade as 'racial measures' or 'racial movements' or even 'racial hygiene,' " he wrote in *Science* in 1936.

In retrospect, he was probably largely unsuccessful, given his long-term attraction to Davenport's eugenics, Lombroso's "criminal anthropology" (Rafter, 2004) and Sheldon's "constitutional anthropology" (Rosenbaum, 1995). Nevertheless, we can admire Hooton for at least giving voice to his apprehensions.

Indeed, the politics of American anthropology at the time was so conflicted that when Boas tried to mobilize senior American physical anthropologists to draft and sign a resolution condemning Nazi physical anthropology, only Hooton and Hrdlička would sign (Barkan, 1992). Raymond Pearl, while acknowledging Nazi anthropology as "wholly absurd, unscientific, and in the highest degree mischievous," nevertheless refused Boas's overture, on the grounds that "I am unalterably opposed now and all the time towards an attitude of pontifical authoritarianism under the aegis of science" (Oct. 3, 1935, FBP). One can, of course, wonder whether Pearl expressed himself as stridently to Otmarr Freiherr von Verschuer.

At the time, the United States and Germany were on friendly terms, and many Americans (and American scholars) had no interest in provoking their German counterparts. Unable to get a resolution condemning the Nazis passed at the 1937 meetings of the American Anthropological Association meeting, because it was (correctly) perceived to be initiated by Boas, AAA President Edward Sapir contrived the following year to have the resolution introduced and seconded by two impeccably WASP physical anthropologists: Hooton and Chicago's Fay-Cooper Cole. This time it passed (Barkan, 1992).

The controversial AAA resolution seems banal, almost ridiculously so, today:

Whereas, the prime requisites of science are the honest and unbiased search for truth and the freedom to proclaim such truth when discovered and known, and

Whereas, anthropology in many countries is being conscripted and its data distorted and misinterpreted to serve the cause of an unscientific racialism rather than the cause of truth: Be it resolved, That the American Anthropological Association repudiates such racialism and adheres to the following statement of facts:

1). Race involves the inheritance of similar physical variations by large groups of mankind, but its psychological and cultural connotations, if they exist, have not been ascertained by science.

2). The terms Aryan and Semitic have no racial significance whatsoever. They simply denote linguistic families.

3). Anthropology provides no scientific basis for discrimination against any people on the ground of racial inferiority, religious affiliation or linguistic heritage. (AAA Proceedings, 1938)

This does, however, give us the proper lens for viewing the scientific study of race in the middle third of the century. The appearance of the body, the form of the skull, and its manifestations as mind or culture, were all thought to be intimately, if cryptically, related. And each large group of people had its own peculiarities of all three.

POSTWAR ANTHROPOLOGY

After World War II, the fields of physical anthropology and human genetics lay in tatters and had to be utterly reinvented. The task fell principally to James Neel and Theodosius Dobzhansky in human genetics (the former emphasizing medical genetics, and the latter evolutionary theory) and to Sherwood Washburn in physical anthropology. In 1950 Dobzhansky and Washburn organized a major conference on the evolution of *Homo sapiens,* and began to set forth a radical new agenda, emphasizing evolutionary dynamics over static typology, locally adapted populations over ephemeral and arbitrary clusters of people, and the common themes of being human over the minor differences among peoples—a "new physical anthropology" (Washburn, 1951).

Concurrently, UNESCO President Julian Huxley decided that the time was right for a formal statement about the science of race and convened an international committee of anthropologists and sociologists, along with the head of UNESCO's Social Science Department, the Brazilian anthropologist Arturo Ramos. Upon the sudden death of Ramos, the role of *rapporteur* fell to the Anglo-American Ashley Montagu.

Montagu had been born Israel Ehrenberg, in London's East End, and reinvented himself in college as Montague Francis Ashley Montagu, then emigrated to America. Self-reinvention was actually not an altogether uncommon practice at the time. The social anthropologist A. R. Radcliffe-Brown, the journalist Henry Morton Stanley, the conductor Leopold Stokowski, all concealed their humble or pedestrian origins with name changes. And of course the movies quickly became littered with discarded monikers, usually either too ethnic or too cacophonous, and thus transforming Isidore Demsky into Kirk Douglas and Frances Gumm into Judy Garland.

Montagu had studied social anthropology in England, and had studied physical anthropology largely informally with Sir Arthur Keith, the great British anatomist. After coming to America he managed to land a job teaching dental anatomy, with the help of Aleš Hrdlička. That year he wrote to Hooton,

> I am twenty-six, educated at Cambridge, Oxford, London, Florence, and Columbia. M.A., Ph.D., etc. fifteen anthropological publications. Recommended very generously by Sir Arthur Keith, who has furnished me a too-glowing testimonial which you may see if you wish. Sir Arthur once told me that I can always say that he will speak for me, so I may as well mention this too, for if you hold him in as great respect as I do, this should be impressive. (28 Dec 1931, EAHP)

It is not clear that Montagu had any significant education other than in London, and it is quite clear that he possessed no such advanced degrees when he wrote Hooton. He would, however, earn a doctorate in cultural anthropology from Columbia before the end of the decade. Although Montagu kept up a warm correspondence with Hooton, the latter would include an otherwise positive letter of recommendation for Montagu, "I should advise that his qualifications be inspected very carefully" (Hooton to T. H. Sollman, Feb. 27, 1939, EAHP). You can't really blame him.

By 1950, however, Montagu had distinguished himself as an eloquent critic of the concept of race. Indeed, his criticisms owed a great deal to Julian Huxley himself, whose 1935 book *We Europeans,* co-authored with the Cambridge cultural anthropologist Alfred Cort Haddon, went so far to suggest that the very word "race" be supplanted by "ethnic group." This, in fact, would become a signature crusade of Montagu's. As his friend Dobzhansky would write to him good-naturedly upon returning from the field one year, "The ethnic groups of Australian Drosophilae proved to be most interesting" (Oct. 7, 1960, AMP).

Montagu's hand lay so heavily upon the UNESCO Statement that it was widely assumed to have been written by Montagu alone (Stewart, 1961). In the protracted discussion in the British journal *Man,* it came to be known as "the Ashley Montagu Statement" (Anonymous, 1951). The statement's most obvious feature stemmed from the composition of the group that drafted it: of the committee of seven, only two were physical anthropologists—Juan Comas of Mexico and Montagu himself. This alone served to de-center physical anthropology as the field that pronounced scientifically and authoritatively on race.

To be sure, the statement was sent around and vetted by another panel of experts, including the biologists Edwin G. Conklin, L. C. Dunn, H. J. Muller, Gunnar Dahlberg, and Dobzhansky. Upon receiving the final statement, Dobzhansky wrote to Montagu, "Although I would have changed a few more words, they are excellent and I believe you have done a fine job in pushing them through" (Oct. 15, 1950, AMP).

In some circles, however—which shows just how close to normative the German physical anthropology of World War II had in fact been—the Statement was greeted with hostility, if not outright contempt. Led by right-wing British biologists such as Ronald Fisher and C. D. Darlington, the critics charged that race was a biological problem, and consequently the domination of the UNESCO committee by non-biologists meant that the true nature of race had been improperly represented (Brattain, 2007; Müller-Wille, 2007).

Of particular salience were two passages from the 21-paragraph statement. From paragraph 7, "For all practical social purposes 'race' is not so much a biological phenomenon as a social myth." And from the final paragraph, "[B]iological studies lend support to the ethic of universal brotherhood; for man is born with drives toward co-operation, and unless these drives are satisfied, men and nations alike fall ill" (UNESCO, 1952). The first seemed to de-legitimize biological approaches to human variation altogether; the second to make a far-reaching and eloquent claim with no actual scientific support. In some cases these statements became a wedge that allowed scholars who disagreed with the statement's assertion that innate racial differences in intellect or disposition were negligible ultimately to undermine it.

Thus the primate anatomist W. C. Osman Hill (1951) could voice his distaste for the statement by invoking "the well-known musical attributes of the Negroids and the mathematical ability of some Indian races." He was already on record (1940) with the belief that human races could be considered as taxonomic species.

Under mounting pressure, UNESCO convened a second panel the following year, to be dominated by biologists, of whom the only carryover was Montagu himself. Even Dobzhansky perceived the affair as a political backlash, writing to Montagu, "On the genetical side the group may consist of some people (such as Darlington) who are out and out racists. . . . The British objectors will be present. This may result in a statement which will be pretty sad" (Feb. 24, 1951, AMP).

The (liberal) geneticist L. C. Dunn was chosen as rapporteur, and the Second UNESCO Statement on Race emphasized the indeterminacy of many of the innate differences in intellect and temperament that the first statement had repudiated. The Second Statement walked a fine line between complementing and superseding the Ashley Montagu Statement. A vicious book review by T. Dale Stewart, published in *Science* in 1961, called the statement "so unacceptable that it had to be rewritten." Montagu responded by noting the difference in specialties of the members of the two committees, and emphasized their similarity and complementarity: "The difference is as between Tweedledum and Tweedledee" (Montagu, 1961). Stewart rebutted by rhetorically asking why a textbook by Juan Comas, a member of the first committee, presented only the Second Statement? Why such a catfight would spill over into the pages of the leading science journal in America a decade later is a good question. Clearly the scientific meaning of race had not in fact been adequately resolved.

Nevertheless, the Ashley Montagu Statement was not even as radical as it was made out to be. Emphasizing the equality of races, the statement did not deny that races exist. Thus, paragraph 7 tells us that "most anthropologists agree in classifying the greater part of present-day mankind into three major divisions, as follows:

The Mongoloid Division
The Negroid Division
The Caucasoid Division."

Calling them races, ethnic groups, or divisions, however, does not much matter if the fundamental concept remains the allotment of human beings into a small number of fairly discrete natural categories. The statement's offense lay solely in its aggressive assertion of the fundamentally equal abilities of the members of all races.

Moreover, the Second Statement ("On the nature of race and race differences") generated considerable opposition as well, and from the same quarters. This time, however, UNESCO solicited and collected the criticisms, and published them along with the statement itself.[2] The academic criticisms ran a bizarre gamut, beginning with Fritz Lenz, a former Nazi geneticist, politely disputing the attribution of all human beings to a single species. That position was not completely unique, being espoused by the anatomist W. C. Osman Hill, as noted above, and as well by the geneticist R. R. Ruggles Gates (1944). Many reasonable suggestions to amend certain phrases were made by respected figures such as W. E. Le Gros Clark, William Howells, Stanley Garn, Kirtley Mather, Ernst Mayr, Wilton Krogman, Melville Herskovits, and Joseph Birdsell.[3]

However, when the subject turned to the existence of innate mental characteristics for different groups, the fur began to fly. According to the Second Statement, "It is possible, though not proved, that some types of innate capacity for intellectual and emotional responses are commoner in one human group than in another, but it is certain that, within a single group, innate capacities vary as much as, if not more than, they do between different groups" (UNESCO, 1952). The geneticist and left-wing eugenicist Hermann Muller objected to the statement's downplaying the possibility of a history of differential selection for psychological traits in different races. Other geneticists, especially C. D. Darlington and Ronald Fisher, concurred. The anthropologist Melville Herskovits noted that simply talking about what we know about culture would have been valuable here. Carleton Coon was blunter in insisting that "racial differences in intelligence may or may not occur." Even James Neel felt "that just as there are *relatively minor* physical differences between races, so there may well be *relatively minor* mental differences" (emphasis in original). When it came to denying the influence of genetics upon "cultural achievement" Fritz Lenz again demurred. And on the absence of biologically harmful effects of race-mixture, an old controversy among early 20th-century biologists, Darlington again objected, while another former Nazi anthropologist, Hans Weinert, rhetorically questioned "which of the gentlemen who signed the statement would be prepared to marry his daughter to an Australian aboriginal, for example."

The overall statement, now revised and reconceptualized by a panel of physical anthropologists and geneticists, could still not win unanimous scientific assent. "[C. D.] Darlington, [Ronald] Fisher, [Giuseppe] Genna and [Carleton] Coon are frankly opposed to the Statement."

Indeed, the assertion of racial equality remained a hot-button issue, both in American society and in academic anthropology, even a century after the Civil War. The legal and political machinery at work during the Civil Rights movement would rely to some extent for a scientific grounding upon Boasian anthropology—emphasizing cultural difference and the malleability of human form at the expense of the older essentialist, craniometric, and hereditarian anthropological traditions. Not only would this fulfill Edward Tylor's ambition of seeing anthropology as "a reformer's science," but it would also expose anthropologists especially to vicious political forces at work in American society in the 1950s.

CRISIS II: PHYSICAL ANTHROPOLOGY AND THE CIVIL RIGHTS MOVEMENT

If scientists on the right were swimming against an egalitarian tide, scholars on the left were burdened by the vagaries of history. As Karl Marx had astutely written, "Men make their own history, but they do not make it just as they please . . . [t]he tradition of all the dead generations weighs like a nightmare on the brain of the living."

In the 1930s, as the Nazi menace loomed, many young intellectuals sought to oppose not only their racialized view of history and society, but also the hypocrisy in America that spoke toward equal rights, but in fact concealed institutionalized mechanisms for denying large groups of people those very rights. Further, since the primary enemies of the Nazis were the Communists, not the Americans, it was reasonable to gravitate to the Communists if your primary political issue was to combat racism. The Communists were the ones who most aggressively opposed the Nazis and who seemed to stand most idealistically for the creation of a society without racial prejudice.

This bubble burst with two developments: (1) the non-aggression pact signed by Hitler and Stalin (1939), which seemed to indicate that Communism and Nazism could happily coexist; and (2) the entry of the United States into World War II (1941), which created a new synonymy between being pro-American and being anti-Nazi.

A few years later, the Nazis had been beaten, and the Americans had new enemies: the Communists. Suddenly, anyone with a past that involved having actively worked against racism and Nazism twenty years earlier very likely had an old connection to the American Communist Party. And even if they were never formal members themselves, they had friends who had been.

In the early 1950s the president of Rutgers summarily fired Ashley Montagu, who was an untenured full professor in anthropology. Unable to find another comparable academic post, he became a full-time writer and speaker (Sperling, 2000, 2008).

More notorious, however, was the fate of Columbia's Gene Weltfish (Price, 2004). A respected ethnographer, Weltfish had been teaching at Columbia for many years without tenure. In 1943, at the request of the USO, Weltfish and her senior colleague Ruth Benedict had written a pamphlet called "The Races of Mankind," ostensibly to tell our boys what they were fighting for, and which enjoyed a wide circulation. The chair of the House Military Affairs Committee, Rep. Andrew J. May of Kentucky (D), found its assertions about the equal intellectual abilities of races to be offensive, indeed subversive, and had the pamphlet withdrawn.[4]

Called to testify before a congressional committee investigating Communist infiltration of academia, Weltfish refused to answer the question whether she had ever been a Communist. Columbia University terminated her a few months later, which made the front page of the *New York Times* (Lissner, 1953), but without effect.

Interestingly, Weltfish was the embodiment of a bizarre caricature that would soon be brandished by segregationists attempting to discredit their ideological opponents: the Jewish Communist anthropologist.

While much has been written of late on the admirable role that Boasian cultural anthropologists played in the American Civil Rights movement of the 1950s (Baker, 1998), rather less has been said about physical anthropology. This is probably because there simply isn't much in the history of physical anthropology to connect it to progressive politics. Indeed, far from being the "reformer's science" envisioned by Edward B. Tylor, physical anthropology is burdened by the weight of phrenology, polygenism, racial formalism, eugenics, and sociobiology. One could make the case that from its inception, physical anthropology's role lay in naturalizing difference, while the rest of the field was busy culturalizing it.[5]

The tensions in the field emerged again in the 1950s, shortly after the Cold Spring Harbor Symposium, Washburn's call for a "new physical anthropology," and the two UNESCO statements. One can detect, retrospectively, four strategies for following the political intellectual climate, while still retaining the authority of physical anthropology as the science of human biological variation.

Washburn, for example, simply defined the study of race out of modern physical anthropology, filling the resultant vacuum with primate field studies and evolutionary genetics.

Another strategy was to replace anatomically designated races with genetically designated ones, as attempted by the Boston University serologist William C. Boyd (1950; 1963). Boyd's critique of race was a critique more specifically of race as traditionally defined anatomically, which triggered a controversy in the *American Journal of Physical Anthropology* (Stewart, 1951; Strandskov & Washburn, 1951, Birdsell, 1952). There was, at the very least, something crassly self-serving about geneticists asserting that genetic races were somehow "realer" than anatomical ones. Serological races had been the subject of considerable debate since the 1920s (e.g., Young, 1928), and Boyd's 1963 paper identifying 13 human races—Africans, Asians, American Indians, Indo-Dravidians, Melanesians, Micronesians, Indonesians, Australians, and five from Europe—appears to have killed off the field for good. Boyd does not seem to have appreciated either the arbitrariness or the cultural values implicit in identifying five races of Europeans, but only one race of Africans, for example.

A third strategy was to retain the formalism of races, but to dismiss or downplay any correlated differences in behavior or intellect (e.g., Coon et al., 1950; Garn, 1962). This was the most conservative solution, retaining the traditional methods and foci of physical anthropology. Unfortunately, this also concealed a central paradox: If evolution really did divide the human species into a small number of fairly distinct natural groups physically or genetically, then why not mentally as well?

And a fourth would be to re-conceptualize the fundamental patterns of human biological variation and to emphasize familiar aspects of human biology: local diversity and adaptation, and general overall plasticity or adaptability. Thus, Livingstone's famous epigram from 1962, "There are no races, there are only clines." This approach turned out to be most harmonious with the emergence of "critical race theory" by humanists—relativizing and historicizing the concept of race, to de-legitimize it as a scientific concept and reciprocally to illuminate its fundamentally political nature.

Adherents to the idea that the human species indeed came packaged into a small number of relatively discrete, relatively natural units, which might have different physical and mental abilities, were aging and dwindling in number. Their last stand came in the early 1960s when a convergence of interests brought together a political activist named Carleton Putnam, a psychologist named Henry Garrett, an anatomist named Wesley Critz George, a geneticist named Reginald R. Ruggles Gates, and the physical anthropologist Carleton S. Coon (Jackson, 2005).

A philanthropy called the Pioneer Fund had come into existence in 1937 as an outlet for the racist interests of its founder, Wickliffe Draper. Draper had supported the notorious "Race-Crossing in Jamaica" study by Charles Davenport and Morris Steggerda, which purported to show the physical inferiority of interracial hybrids, but was deemed signally incompetent even by those of a similarly eugenical bent (Castle, 1930; Pearson 1930). In the 1940s, Draper supported studies showing the intellectual inferiority of blacks and in the 1950s was subsidizing the work of segregationists like Henry Garrett, who testified for the State in the landmark *Brown vs. Board of Education* case in 1953 (Winston, 1998; Tucker, 2002; Kenny, 2002).

Ruggles Gates was a Canadian-English plant geneticist, who found a home at Harvard. Rejecting the interbreeding criterion, he argued in the *AJPA* (1944) and in *Human Ancestry* (1948) that human races were so fundamentally different as to be equivalent to species. His 1948 book came with a foreword by Hooton, who politely disavowed it, and would not even recommend it when queried by Robert Yerkes (July 12, 1949, RMYP). In India, the geneticist J. B. S. Haldane refused to host a visit from Ruggles Gates; in New York, the geneticist Theodosius Dobzhansky referred to him privately as "a mutant" (Dobzhansky to Ashley Montagu, July 12, 1947, AMP).

Gates and Garrett served together starting in 1960 as the founding associate editors of *Mankind Quarterly,* funded by Draper. The journal's contents and orientation set off a huge controversy in biological anthropology, loudly denounced by mainstream scholars, notably Juan Comas (1961) and G. A. Harrison (1961). In the journal's first number, Garrett (1961) outlined "the equalitarian dogma"—leveling the accusation that American higher education a generation ago had been hijacked by Jewish Communist anthropologists, led by Franz Boas, promoting the insidious idea of racial equality.

The following year, Carleton Putnam published *Race and Reason,* developing the "scientific" case against school integration, and blaming the influence of those Jewish Communist Boasians once again for the idea of racial equality. The introduction to *Race and Reason* was co-authored by Garrett, Gates, and George (as well as by the editor-in-chief of *Mankind Quarterly,*

Robert Gayre). Moreover, Putnam seemed to have access to some insider's
knowledge about the field of anthropology.

> [A]nthropologists—apart from their position as equalitarian or non-
> equalitarian—may be divided into two classes, social and physical. It is the
> social anthropologists who have led the equalitarian movement although they
> are the least qualified to pass upon racial biology. The physical anthropologists,
> along with the physiologists and anatomists, are the ones who are expert in this
> field. (Putnam, 1961, 51–52)
>   Besides intimidation there has, of course, been a false indoctrination of our
> younger scientists, although some hope on this score may be found in the fol-
> lowing statement in a letter to me from a distinguished scientist younger than I
> am, a scientist not a Southerner, who is a recognized international authority on
> the subject we are considering: "About 25 years ago it seemed to be proved be-
> yond a doubt that man is a cultural animal, solely a creature of the environment,
> and that there is no inheritance of instinct, intelligence or any other capacity.
> Everything had to be learned and the man or race that had the best opportunity
> for learning made the best record. The tide is turning. Heredity is coming back,
> not primarily through anthropologists but through the zoologists. It is the zoolo-
> gists, the animal behavior men, who are doing it, and the anthropologists are
> beginning to learn from them. It will take time, but the pendulum will swing."
> (Putnam, 1961, 50)

Speculation was rife as to who Putnam's source might be. Meanwhile the
American Anthropological Association acted quickly, censuring Putnam's
book at their 1961 meeting. The resolution was introduced by the outgoing
president, archaeologist Gordon Willey, and Putnam was notified of the resolution afterwards by the incoming AAA president. He fumed back: "It is not
sociologists, nor cultural anthropologists, who are best qualified to speak on
this subject, but physical anthropologists and geneticists." He was apparently
unaware that his correspondent, the incoming AAA president, was in fact
a noted physical anthropologist—Sherry Washburn (Putnam to Washburn,
Dec. 12, 1961, WCGP).

Putnam, however, had been corresponding and socializing for a few years
with a senior physical anthropologist, Carleton Coon of the University of
Pennsylvania, the incoming president of the American Association of Physical Anthropologists. In fact, Coon had written to Putnam on June 17, 1960
(CSCP):

> Now about 25 years ago the scientific angle was all against you. It seemed to be
> proved and salted away that man is a cultural animal and there is no inheritance
> of instinct, intelligence, or anything else. Everything had to be learned, and he
> who had the best opportunity for learning came out on top.

The tide is turning. Heredity is coming back into fashion, but not through anthropologists. It is the zoologists, the animal behavior men, who are doing it, and the anthropologists are beginning to learn from them. It will take time, but the pendulum will swing.[6]

A few weeks later (Sept. 1, 1960, CSCP), Putnam negotiated with Coon over rewriting the passage so as to conceal its source.

I must find some way of keeping the quote while disguising the source. There are various ways of doing this. Suppose I cut out the "prize-winning" and the "physical" and the "international reputation" and simply referred to the writer as a "Northern anthropologist," would you let that pass?

Coon agreed. He spent early 1962 finishing up his own magnum opus, *The Origin of Races,* and retrofitting the second edition of his popular book, *The Story of Man,* to accommodate his new theory. In particular, he reduced the number of races from six to five, and changed the order in which they evolved. Coon had written in the first edition, "The Mongoloids are probably not as ancient as the Negroids" (1954, 198), which would no longer do, as he was now trying to associate a ranking of civilizational (i.e., intellectual) capacities with a ranking of racial age, and the Mongoloids would have to become more ancient than the Negroids.

As president of the American Association of Physical Anthropologists, he was the sole dissenter against a motion to condemn Carleton Putnam's book, introduced by Stanley Garn, and he stormed out of the business meeting rather than "preside over such a craven lot" (Coon, 1981, 335; Lasker, 1999, 149).

Coon promptly sent Putnam excerpts from *The Story of Man,* as well as comments on a manuscript by the anatomist Wesley Critz George. By June, Putnam was writing to his correspondents that "the president of the American Association of Physical Anthropologists, a magna cum laude graduate of Harvard and a native of New England, states that recent discoveries indicate the Negro to be 200,000 years behind the White race on the ladder of evolution" (Putnam to James A. Moss, June 4, 1962, CSCP; Putnam to Earnest S. Cox, June 22, 1962, WCGP). Wesley Critz George's manuscript was a pamphlet called "The Biology of the Race Problem," and had been commissioned by the governor of Alabama, and underwritten by Wickliffe Draper. George was a crusader against the races intermingling—in any sense of the term—and his "scientific" study was intended to demonstrate the mental inferiority of the Negro and the left-wing anthropological conspiracy to suppress that knowledge.

At less than 100 pages, the pamphlet was distributed widely in the South. Released on October 3, 1962, the pamphlet also had two curious citations.

One was a summary of Coon's new theory, although directing the reader to the new edition of *The Story of Man*, which had been published the previous May, but did not actually articulate the radical new theory. The other was a footnote which read, "Full documentation of Dr. Coon's position will be found in his *The Origin of Races*, to be published by Alfred Knopf in the autumn of 1962."

On the same day, Carleton Putnam took out a full-page ad in the *New York Times*, in the form of an open letter to President Kennedy, directing him to read George's pamphlet, demonstrating the biologically based inequality of the races. A week later, the *Times* published a letter by the cultural anthropologist Morton Fried, calling attention to the resolutions by both the AAA and AAPA condemning Putnam's scientific racism and case for segregation. On October 24, the *Times* published a response from Henry Garrett and Wesley Critz George, quoting Coon's *The Origin of Races*, which they noted had been published on October 15. But the date on their letter was actually October 14.

In other words, not only were the segregationists invoking Coon's work to support their case, but they had privileged access to it prior to publication.

The actual publication of *The Origin of Races* was therefore eagerly anticipated. Coon was deluged by queries about what he really meant. The first, and most obvious, response to the segregationists' invocation of Coon is that they were somehow misrepresenting or misinterpreting him (Price & Sanders, 1962), a position Coon himself never adopted. Coon adopted, rather, an apparently naïve (if transparently self-interested) position of apolitical scientific detachment. In a response he wrote, but ultimately declined to send to the *New York Times* (CSCP), he articulated this position:

> I submit that I have neither finally proved nor the anthropological communities utterly disproved the superiority or inferiority of any group of people, which are matters presently beyond all of us. . . . Meanwhile let those of us who call ourselves scientists stick to our work, and let our books be read by everyone interested in what we have to say, without prejudice of any kind, remembering that for us who call ourselves scientists to enter into political disputes only breaks down the communication between us, and will hinder the progress of science in the end.

But people on both sides of the political spectrum saw the political value of Coon's work. On the left, most anthropologists deferred politely to Coon's scientific stature, while decrying the segregationists' apparent abuse of his scholarly work. Theodosius Dobzhansky, the great evolutionary geneticist, was the one who ultimately called the question on Coon: either Coon didn't mind being misrepresented by the segregationists (which would be so non-normative as to be remarkable), or he wasn't actually being misrepresented by them at all (which would suggest that his book really was intended to provide some kind of naturalistic justification for racist practices).

Dobzhansky, it emerged, was an ideal person to go after Coon. As a fruit fly geneticist, a member of the Russian Orthodox church, and an émigré from the Soviet Union, he was especially immune to the charges of being a participant in the Jewish-Communist-anthropologist cabal. (Putnam later numbered him incorrectly as among the students of Boas.)

Asked to review *The Origin of Races* for the *Saturday Review,* Dobzhansky wrote the review, submitted it, and mailed a copy as a professional courtesy to Coon himself. Coon had actually written him rather obsequiously a few months earlier, upon reading Dobzhansky's *Mankind Evolving:*

> I have made an astonishing discovery. What you say is almost identical to what I am saying in my book, The Origin of Races . . .
> We have obviously drawn on the same sources and come up with the same results. This makes me very happy, because now I have much more confidence that I am right. (Coon to Dobzhansky, May 26, 1962, TDP)

Dobzhansky, however, did not find their ideas all that similar, and was politely critical of the degree of parallel evolution that would be necessary to change five subspecies of *Homo erectus* separately into five subspecies of *Homo sapiens,* as Coon's theory held. But more bluntly, he held Coon at least partly responsible for the hay the segregationists were making from his work.

> It is most unfortunate that some semantic mischief in Coon's work has made it usable as grist for racist mills. A scientist should not and cannot eschew studies on the racial differentiation of mankind, or examine all possible hypotheses about it, for fear that his work will be misused. But neither can he disclaim all responsibility for such misuses. . . . There are absolutely no findings in Coon's book that even suggest that some human races are superior or inferior to others in their capacity for culture or civilization. There are, however, some unfortunate misstatements that are susceptible to such misinterpretation. (Dobzhansky, 1963)

Coon, however, would have none of it, and not only prevailed upon the editor to pull Dobzhansky's review (later published in both *Scientific American* and *Current Anthropology*), but threatened the geneticist with a lawsuit as well:

> You accused me of "mischievously" altering my style so as to provide easy quotes for political people. That is libel. (Coon to Dobzhansky, Oct. 29 1962, CSCP)

And Dobzhansky wrote him right back:

> If you "mischievously altered" your "style so as to provide easy quotes for
> political peoples," I was unaware of that. No such allegation is contained in
> my review. Should I then offer you apologies for what I did not write? What
> I did write is that you got yourself "into semantic mischief," and this makes
> your "book usable as grist for racist mills." (Dobzhansky to Coon, Oct. 29,
> 1962, CSCP)

Coon would ultimately even complain to Detlev Bronk, president of
Rockefeller University, Dobzhansky's home at the time, and in the pages of
Science. And yet he would not repudiate the segregationists' apparent abuse
of his work (Jackson, 2001). The reason, of course, is that the segregationists
were not abusing it at all; they were citing it in the way the author intended for
it to be cited. There was nothing to repudiate. Coon hoped to say anything he
pleased as a scientific authority, without assuming responsibility or bearing
consequences for his words and ideas.

With the publication of *The Origin of Races,* and Coon's help with Putnam's *Race and Reason* and George's *The Biology of the Race Problem,*
the segregationists had good reason to number him as an ally. Coon was
quickly invited to join the editorial board of the *Mankind Quarterly* on
Ruggles Gates's death (he declined the honor, while expressing sympathy
with the cause). The connection between Coon and Gates was not terribly
obscure, either: Coon's racial taxonomy (which split subSaharan Africans,
and lumped Americans into Asians) was identical to the one presented by
Gates in *Human Ancestry,* but at a lower taxonomic level; and Gates had
acknowledged Coon's assistance in reading and commenting on his 1948
book (see Eckhardt, 2000).

Ultimately, Coon was unable to evade the responsibility and consequences of his work. Sherry Washburn, in his 1962 Presidential Address to
the American Anthropological Association, consigned Coon's work to the
trash bin of history (as he had been doing for about a decade). A tradition
emerged among Coon's friends that Washburn had personally attacked
Coon in the address (Shipman, 1994). This seems unlikely, given that
Washburn's principal argument was to sideline Coon's work, by defining
it as anachronistic (Washburn, 1963)—an intellectual survival, perhaps
analogous to that of the horseshoe crab. In any event, standing against the
evils of scientific racism and whatever support it may have enjoyed within
the ranks of the scholarly community, this was arguably American physical anthropology's finest moment.

CONCLUSION

The aftermath of the Nazi crisis in the 1930s and the segregationist crisis of the 1960s is that physical anthropology largely abandoned the study of race, to the population geneticists on one side, and to the cultural anthropologists on the other. Two influential texts of the 1970s, for example, Frank Johnston's *Microevolution of Human Populations* (1973) and Jane Underwood's *Human Variation and Human Microevolution* (1979), could get by without even mentioning "race" in the index.

The problem with that generation's approach to race is that it effectively undermines what is really biological anthropology's major contribution to the study of race—mediating the cultural and natural realms. It is not that the problem of race is reducible to natural patterns of allele frequencies (on the one hand) or to political violence (on the other), but rather that race is itself the result of a constant negotiation between objective patterns of difference (i.e., biology) and subjective perceptions of otherness (i.e., culture).

Biological anthropology has always been uniquely situated to speak authoritatively on race, as a result of partaking of both anthropology and biology. The 20th century was the century in which the domains of the cultural and the natural were set apart and analytically fenced off from one another, which was itself one of the major (and largely unheralded) advances in modern scientific thought. The 21st century will be the one in which the fences come down and we look once again at the ways in which our reality is a co-construction of what is "out there"—the naturalistic product of human microevolution—and what is "in here"—the culturalistic product of local social and political history. As scholars such as Bruno Latour and Donna Haraway have been articulating it, we study not so much the boundary of discrete nature and culture, but an organically integrated "nature culture" (Goodman et al., 2003).

ARCHIVAL SOURCES

FBP: Franz Boas Papers, American Philosophical Society.
AMP: Ashley Montagu Papers, American Philosophical Society.
TDP: Theodosius Dobzhansky Papers, American Philosophical Society.
EAHP: Earnest A. Hooton Papers, Peabody Museum, Harvard.
RMYP: Robert Mearns Yerkes Papers, Sterling Library, Yale.
CSCP: Carleton S. Coon Papers, National Anthropological Archives, Smithsonian.
WCGP: Wesley Critz George Papers, University of North Carolina.

ENDNOTES

1. It should be noted that Boas's liberal humanism and work against the stability of racial form, and his stance against racism, are all continuous with the work of his mentor Virchow, and are not necessarily related at all to his Jewish origins (*contra* Sarich & Miele, 2004).
2. All quotations are from UNESCO, 1952.
3. Conspicuous among the non-respondents was Earnest Hooton.
4. May himself, ironically enough, was pardoned by President Truman in 1950 after being convicted of accepting bribes, which he apparently did not consider subversive or unAmerican.
5. Although eugenics was in many ways a progressive movement, it was also elitist, totalitarian, and in most versions, racist.
6. Coon's perspicacity here is worth noting, given the publication of E. O. Wilson's *Sociobiology* fifteen years later, and its attendant controversy.

REFERENCES

Aichel, O., & Verschuer, O. von. (1934). Vorwort. *Zeitschrift für Morphologie und Anthropologie, 34,* v–vi.

Anonymous. (1951). Note. *Man, 51,* 17–18.

Baker, L. D. (1998). Unraveling the Boasian Discourse: The Racial Politics of "Culture" in School Desegregation, 1944–1954. *Transforming Anthropology, 7*(1), 15–32.

Barkan, Elazar. (1992). *The Retreat of Scientific Racism.* New York: Cambridge University Press.

Barzun, Jacques. (1937). *Race: A Study in Superstition.* New York: Harcourt, Brace, and Co.

Birdsell, Joseph B. (1952). On Various Levels of Objectivity in Genetical Anthropology. *American Journal of Physical Anthropology, 10,* 355–362.

Boyd, William C. (1950). *Genetics and the Races of Man.* Boston: Little, Brown.

———. (1963). Genetics and the Human Race. *Science, 140,* 1057–1065.

Brattain, M. (2007). Race, Racism, and Antiracism: UNESCO and the Politics of Presenting Science to the Postwar Public," *American Historical Review, 112,* 1386–1413.

Castle, W. E. (1930). Race Mixture and Physical Disharmonies. *Science, 71,* 603–606.

Comas, Juan. (1961). "Scientific" Racism Again? *Current Anthropology, 2,* 303–340.

Coon, Carleton S. (1954). 1962. *The Story of Man.* New York: Knopf.

———. (1962). *The Origin of Races.* New York: Knopf.

———. (1981). *Adventures and Discoveries: The Autobiography of Carleton S. Coon.* Englewood Cliffs, NJ: Prentice-Hall.

Coon, Carleton S., Stanley M.Garn, and Joseph B. Birdsell. (1950). *Races: A Study of the Problems of Race Formation in Man .* Springfield, IL: Charles C. Thomas.

Dobzhansky, Theodosius. (1963). Probability That *Homo sapiens* Evolved Independently 5 Times Is Vanishingly Small. *Current Anthropology, 4*(4), 360, 364–366.

Eckhardt, Robert B. (2000). The Dangers in Editing Past Human History to Fit Present Methodological Constraints. *Kroeber Anthropological Papers, 84,* 45–58.

Garn, Stanley M. (1962). *Human Races.* Springfield, IL: Charles C. Thomas.

Garrett, Henry E. (1961). The Equalitarian Dogma. *Mankind Quarterly, 1,* 253–257.

Gates, R. Ruggles. (1944). Phylogeny and Classification of Hominids and Anthropoids. *American Journal of Physical Anthropology* (n.s.), *2,* 279–292.

———. (1948). *Human Ancestry: From A Genetical Point of View.* Cambridge, MA: Harvard University Press.

Goldschmidt, Richard. (1942). Anthropological Determinism of "Aryanism." *Journal of Heredity, 33,* 215–216.

Goodman, Alan H., Heath, Deborah, & Lindee, M. Susan (eds.). (2003). *Genetic Nature/Culture: Anthropology and Science Beyond the Two-Culture Divide.* Berkeley, CA: University of California Press.

Harrison, G. Ainsworth. (1961). The Mankind Quarterly. *Man, 61,* 163–164.

Hooton, Earnest A. (1936). Plain Statements About Race. *Science, 83,* 511–513.

Jackson, John P. Jr. (2001). "In Ways Unacademical": The reception of Carleton S. Coon's *The Origin of Races. Journal of the History of Biology, 34,* 247–285.

Jackson, John P. Jr. (2005). *Science for Segregation.* New York: NYU Press.

Johnston, Francis E. (1973). *Microevolution of Human Populations.* Englewood Cliffs, NJ: Prentice-Hall.

Kenny, M. G. (2002). Toward a Racial Abyss: Eugenics, Wickliffe Draper, and the Origins of the Pioneer Fund. *Journal of the History of the Behavioral Sciences, 38,* 259–283.

Kevles, D. J. (1985). *In the Name of Eugenics.* Berkeley: University of California Press.

Kühl, S. (1994). *The Nazi Connection.* New York: Oxford University Press.

Lasker, Gabriel W. (1999). *Happenings and Hearsay: Reflections of a Biological Anthropologist.* Detroit, MI: Savoyard Books.

Lissner, W. (1953) Columbia Is Dropping Dr. Weltfish, Leftist. *New York Times,* April 1.

Livingstone, Frank B. (1962). On the Non-Existence of Human Races. *Current Anthropology, 3,* 279–281.

Massin, Benoit. (1996). From Virchow to Fischer: Physical Anthropology and "Modern Race Theories" in Wilhelmine Germany. In *Volksgeist as Method and Ethic: Essays on Boasian Ethnography and the German Anthropological Tradition,* ed. by G. Stocking, pp. 79–154. Madison: University of Wisconsin Press.

Montagu, Ashley. (1961). UNESCO Statements on Race. *Science, 133,* 1632–1633.

Müller-Hill, Benno. (1988). *Murderous Science.* New York: Oxford University Press.

Müller-Wille, S. (2007). Race et Appartenance Ethnique: La Diversité Humaine et l'UNESCO Déclarations sur la Race (1950 et 1951). In *60 Ans d'Histoire de l'UNESCO. Actes du Colloque International, Paris, 16–18 Novembre 2005.* Paris: UNESCO, pp. 211–220.

Osman Hill, W. C. (1940). Classification of Hominidae. *Nature, 146,* 402–403.

———. (1951). UNESCO on Race. *Man, 51,* 16–17.

Pearson, Karl. (1930). Race Crossing in Jamaica. *Nature, 126,* 427–429.

Poliakov, L. (1974). *The Aryan Myth.* New York: Basic Books.

Price, B. J., & Sanders, E. R. (1962). Origin of Races: Misrepresentation of Dr. Coon's Book Charged in Thesis on Evolution. *New York Times,* October 30.

Price, David H. (2004). *Threatening Anthropology.* Durham, NC: Duke University Press.

Putnam, Carlton. (1961). Race and Reason. Washington, DC: Public Affairs Press.

———. (1967). *Race and Reality.* Washington, DC: Public Affairs Press.

Rafter, Nicole Hahn. (2004). Earnest A. Hooton and the Biological Tradition in American Criminology. *Criminology, 42*(3), 735–771.

Rosenbaum, R. (1995). The Great Ivy League Nude Posture Photo Scandal. *New York Times Sunday Magazine* January 15: 27–31, 40, 46, 55–56.

Sarich, Vincent, & Miele, F. (2004). *Race: The Reality of Human Differences.* New York: Westview.

Shipman, P. (1994). *The Evolution of Racism.* New York: Simon and Schuster.

Sperling, Susan. (2000). Ashley Montagu, 1905–1999. *American Anthropologist, 102*(3), 583–588.

———. (2008). Ashley's Ghost: McCarthyism, Science, and Human Nature. In *Anthropology at the Dawn of the Cold War,* ed. by D. M. Wax. London: Pluto Press, pp. 3–24.

Spiro, J. P. (2009). *Defending the Master Race: Conservation, Eugenics, and the Legacy of Madison Grant.* Burlington, VT: University of Vermont Press.

Strandskov, H. H., & Washburn, Sherwood L. (1951). Genetics and Physical Anthropology. *American Journal of Physical Anthropology, 9,* 261–263.

Stewart, T. Dale. (1951). Objectivity in Racial Classifications. *American Journal of Physical Anthropology, 9,* 470–472.

———. (1961). Book review. *Science, 133,* 873.

Tucker, William H. (2002). *The Funding of Scientific Racism: Wickliffe Draper and the Pioneer Fund.* Urbana, IL: University of Illinois Press.

Underwood, Jane H. (1979). *Human Variation and Human Microevolution.* Englewood Cliffs, NJ: Prentice-Hall.

UNESCO. (1952). The Race Concept: Results of an Inquiry. In *The Race Question in Modern Science.* Paris: UNESCO.

Washburn, Sherwood L. (1951). The New Physical Anthropology. *Transactions of the New York Academy of Sciences, Series II, 13,* 298–304.

———. (1963). The Study of Race. *American Anthropologist, 65,* 521–531.

Weidenreich, Franz. (1946). On Eugen Fischer. *Science, 104,* 399.

Weiss, Sheila Faith. (2006). Human Genetics and Politics as Mutually Beneficial Resources: The Case of the Kaiser Wilhelm Institute for Anthropology, Human Heredity and Eugenics during the Third Reich. *Journal of the History of Biology, 39,* 41–88.

Winston, Andrew S. (1998). Science in the Service of the Far Right: Henry E. Garrett, the IAAEE, and the Liberty Lobby. *Journal of Social Issues, 54,* 179–210.

Young, M. (1928). The Problem of the Racial Significance of the Blood Groups. *Man, 28,* 153–159, 171–176.

Chapter 11

Race and the Conflicts within the Profession of Physical Anthropology During the 1950s and 1960s

by

John H. Relethford

INTRODUCTION

As is often the case, changes in academic disciplines parallel those in social life. The 1950s and 1960s were a time of great social change in American history, including the escalation of the Cold War, the civil rights movement, the Vietnam war, and the space race, to name but a few. The profession of physical anthropology also went through a period of tumultuous change during these two decades, particularly the relationship of the discipline to changing scientific and cultural views regarding the reality of biological race and its relative importance in research and teaching.

The purpose of this chapter is to review in chronological order some of what I perceive as the major changes in the profession during the 1950s and 1960s in the treatment of race. I must preface this review by noting that it is based entirely on my reading of other histories and of the papers written during that time. Though I lived through the 1950s and 1960s, I was born after Washburn's famous call for a "new physical anthropology" and first heard about anthropology only after arriving in college in the early 1970s. By the time that I entered graduate school in the mid-1970s, the changes outlined in this paper had already occurred and set the stage for even further developments in the discipline. With retrospect, however, it is clear how the players in the 1950s and 1960s shaped the future direction of physical anthropology.

WASHBURN AND THE "NEW PHYSICAL ANTHROPOLOGY"

Without a doubt, the most influential event of the early 1950s in American physical anthropology was a brief, but groundbreaking, paper entitled "The New Physical Anthropology" written by Sherwood Washburn in 1951 in the *Transactions of the New York Academy of Sciences*. In this paper, Washburn noted "evolutionary studies have been revitalized and revolutionized by an infusion of genetics into paleontology and systematics" (1951, 298), and argued that a similar transformation would be appropriate for physical anthropology. In particular, Washburn advocated a change in emphasis in physical anthropology away from classification to a more evolutionary approach. He noted that "There has been almost no development of theory in physical anthropology itself, but the dominant attitude may be described as static, with an emphasis on classification on types" (1951, 298).

According to Washburn, an infusion of population genetics theory was an essential part in moving away from old-style racial typologies. In his view,

> If a new physical anthropology is to differ effectively from the old, it must be more than the adoption of a little genetic terminology. It must change its ways of doing things to conform with the implications of modern evolutionary theory. For example, race must be based on the study of populations. There is no way to justify the division of a breeding population into a series of racial types. It is not enough to state that races should be based on genetic traits; races which cannot be reconciled with genetics should be removed from consideration. (Washburn, 1951, 299)

It is somewhat ironic that he argued somewhat both for and against the use of race (Weiss & Fullerton, 2005). He was clearly not advocating removing race as a concept in physical anthropology (that would come later from other anthropologists), but instead was arguing for a different view on race. Here, Washburn's views on typology, race, and populations was very much at odds with the views of his mentor, Earnest A. Hooton, who was perhaps the leading figure in establishing the rise of academic physical anthropology in the United States in the first half of the 20th century (Spencer, 1981). Hooton's typological approaches to human variation and history continued through the posthumous publication of *The Physical Anthropology of Ireland* (Hooton et al., 1955), a work I personally find interesting because of my own continuing research on the exact same body of data, but from a microevolutionary rather than racial perspective (e.g., Relethford & Crawford, 1995). I find the Hooton et al. volume particularly interesting because it shows both new and old approaches to human variation. Part of the monograph consists of geographic-based analyses (often clinal in nature) that made insightful conclusions regarding the relationship between anthropometric variation and population history, while other parts of the book dwelt on attempts to enumerate the relative contributions of different morphological types (e.g., Nordic, Celtic, Dinaric, and the like). This latter approach was criticized by Edward E. Hunt Jr. (1959), another Hooton student, providing yet another example of a generational change occurring in physical anthropology in the 1950s as some of Hooton's students were breaking away in new directions.

It is clear that looking back on the 1950s from many years later that the "new physical anthropology" is now the only game in town. Washburn drew attention to changes that were happening in evolutionary biology (Hunt, 1981) and had a major influence on the next generation of students (Strum & Lindburg, 1999). At the time, however, change was still very much underway, and an emphasis on racial thinking persisted among a number of physical anthropologists, leading to a split between the old guard and the new, as described by Lasker (1999).

CARLETON COON AND *THE ORIGIN OF RACES*

Although developments in genetics and evolutionary biology certainly contributed to shifting views on race within physical anthropology, it is also clear that the scientific study of race was bound up with socio-cultural considerations of race and racism brought about by reaction to the horrors of the Holocaust and Nazi pseudo-science, as well as growing concern over racism and civil rights in the United States (Caspari, 2003). It is not unexpected that the scientific study of human variation is often interlinked with social and cultural attitudes (Marks, 1995). By the 1960s, a number of Hooton's students were following Washburn's lead and rejecting typological notions of race. Certainly, some of this reaction came from consideration of social change (Caspari, 2003). Scientific positions on race became difficult to sort out from social positions.

Thus, there were changes both social and scientific affecting the direction of physical anthropology. Resistance to new ideas, compounded by growing social and political implications, led to increasingly heated debate that appears to have reached a peak following the publication of *The Origin of Races* by Carleton Coon in 1962. Much of the history concerning Coon, publication of his book, and the reaction has been discussed in depth elsewhere (e.g., Shipman, 1994; Marks, 1995; Jackson, 2001; Caspari, 2003; Brace, 2005; among others). Here, I will focus only on the main history.

In *The Origin of Races,* Coon argued for the existence of five major living human races, and then considered the fossil evidence for the evolution of these races. Coon's five races, which he treated as biologically equivalent to subspecies, were Australoid, Mongoloid, Caucasoid, Congoid, and Capoid. To Coon, the evolution from *Homo erectus* to *Homo sapiens* took place through anagenesis resulting from the spread of favorable mutations through gene flow. He further noted that because it takes time for a mutation to spread geographically, then

> we will see that related populations, which in our case are subspecies, passed from species A, which is *Homo erectus,* to species B, *Homo sapiens,* at different times, and the time at which each one crossed the line depended on who got the new trait first, who lived next to whom, and the rates of gene flow between neighboring populations. (Coon, 1962, 30)

It is possible that had Coon discussed his ideas about gene flow and anagenesis in a population-genetics framework his book might not have generated the reaction that it did. However, his units of analysis were races, which he took as equivalent to subspecies, an idea that had been losing ground scientifically when applied to humans, and which was politically charged. He further summarized his views in suggestive and potentially inflammatory language:

> My thesis is, in essence, that at the beginning of our record, over half a million years ago, man was a single species, *Homo erectus,* perhaps already divided into five geographic races or subspecies. *Homo erectus* then gradually evolved into *Homo sapiens* at different times, as each subspecies, living in its own territory, passed a critical threshold from a more brutal to a more *sapient* state, by one genetic process or another. (Coon, 1962, 658)

According to Coon's analysis of the fossil record then available, it was the African races that lagged behind Asians and Europeans in their biological and cultural evolution. By this time, anthropologists had been convinced that Darwin and Dart were correct, and that the beginning of the human line (considered *Australopithecus* by the 1960s) arose in Africa. Coon agreed with this assessment, and also agreed that the genus *Homo* began in Africa, but that subsequent evolution varied by geographic region:

> Wherever *Homo* arose, and Africa is at present the likeliest continent, he soon dispersed, in a very primitive form, throughout the warm regions of the Old World. Three of the five human subspecies crossed the *sapiens* line elsewhere. If Africa was the cradle of mankind, it was only an indifferent kindergarten. Europe and Asia were our primary schools. (Coon, 1962, 656)

REACTION TO *THE ORIGIN OF RACES*

Reaction to Coon's book was mixed. The eminent biologist Ernst Mayr gave the book a very positive review, citing it as "a milestone in the history of anthropology" (1962, 420). Other reviewers, such as Frederick Hulse, praised the book's presentation of data while disagreeing with the underlying conclusions:

> A good many of the conclusions are highly speculative in nature, and leave me quite unconvinced. The evidence is, however, presented with a wealth of detail. As a review of the fossil remains of our ancestors, *The Origin of Races* is really comprehensive and thoroughly up to date. No better text for a course in Fossil Man has yet been published. (Hulse, 1963, 685)

Reviews by both Theodosius Dobzhansky (1963) and Ashley Montagu (1963) took Coon to task for his proposed evolutionary mechanism and argued the unlikelihood of five subspecies all independently evolving into *Homo sapiens*. Although Coon had pointed out the potential influence of gene flow for spreading favorable mutations among populations (1962, 29), such a caveat was at odds with a general tone of parallel racial evolution throughout the book (note: the reviews of Dobzhansky and Montagu, along with replies by Coon, and further comments by Dobzhansky and Montagu all appeared in the October 1963 issue of the journal *Current Anthropology*).

From a purely scientific assessment, it appears that most reviewers felt that Coon has done an outstanding job of summarizing the then-available fossil evidence, but there was debate over the inferences and conclusions regarding Coon's model of racial anagenesis. The framing of human evolution in terms of races (i.e., subspecies) was out of touch with the changing nature of physical anthropology. In my own reading of *The Origin of Races*, I found the book to be data-intensive but with his evolutionary model briefly and poorly stated, and difficult to reconcile with the book's overarching typological flavor. In my view, the book is an unsuccessful attempt to marry population genetics and evolutionary biology to racial classification and typologies, just the kind of problem that Washburn had warned about in his 1951 paper.

Apart from consideration of Coon's evolutionary models, the implications of Coon's work, particularly his implication of racial differences in cultural evolution, was what generated the most vociferous reaction, particularly as evidenced in Dobzhansky and Montagu's reviews. Both were concerned that Coon's approach to human evolution and variation could be misread and/or misused by those with a racist social and political agenda. For example, Dobzhansky commented that "Professor Coon states some of his conclusions in a way that makes his work susceptible to misuse by racists, white supremacists and other special pleaders" (1963, 360). In a scathing review, Montagu expressed the same general sentiments, suggesting that Coon's interpretations "are likely to be misunderstood by the unwary, or rather understood for what they are not, and misused by racists and others for their own nefarious purposes" (1963, 362).

We must keep in mind that at the time of the publication of *The Origin of Races* there was already considerable activity within the anthropological community to counter the racist claims of Carleton Putnam, a prosegregationist who blamed the evils of the world on Boasian anthropologists (Jackson, 2001). Putnam and other segregationists took Coon's work as clear "proof" that American blacks were less evolved than whites. Thus, part of the controversy surrounding the publication of *The Origin of Races* concerned scientific methodology and the continuing rejection of a typological, rather than evolutionary, approach to human variation, while another part concerned the social dimensions and implications of Coon's work, particularly some of the wording and presentation.

One of the most controversial remarks concerning Coon's work appeared in Dobzhansky's *Current Anthropology* review (which had originally appeared in the February 1963 issue of *Scientific American*). Dobzhansky wrote that

> it is most unfortunate that some semantic mischief in Coon's work has made it usable as grist for racist mills. A scientist should not and cannot eschew studies on the racial differentiation of mankind, or examine all hypotheses about it, for fear that his work will be misused. But neither can he disclaim all responsibilities for such misuses. Scientists living in ivory towers are quaint relics of a bygone age. (1963, 366)

Dobzhansky was not advocating censorship, but rather caution in how material is presented and potentially misused, and further stated that "there are absolutely no findings in Coon's book that even suggest that some human races are superior or inferior to others in their capacity for culture or civilization. There are, however, some unfortunate misstatements that are susceptible to such misinterpretation" (1963, 366).

Dobzhansky's comments and Coon's reactions continued through the 1960s, including an essay by Dobzhansky and a letter by Coon in the *Journal of Heredity* in 1968 concerning their opposing views on the appropriate responsibility of a scientist whose work is being misused (Shipman, 1994; Marks, 1995). I suggest that the debate over the social responsibility of a scientist is far from over, and that both Dobzhansky and Coon would find supporters for their views on the social responsibilities of the scientist.

Different accounts of the publication of, and reaction to, *The Origin of Races* have painted somewhat different pictures of Coon. These accounts have ranged from someone trying to maintain scientific objectivity while caught up in political machination, to a naive man that did not understand the potential harm of his writings, to a racist (see, for example, discussions in Shipman, 1994; Marks, 1995; Wolpoff & Caspari, 1997; as well as Coon's [1981] autobiography). One of the more recent and detailed treatments is Jackson's (2001) analysis of correspondence between Coon and Putnam, which argues that even while Coon publicly maintained a case for his scientific objectivity, he had long worked with Putnam, and helped Putnam hone his arguments against Boasian anthropology (and anthropologists) and thus aided in the segregationist cause.

CHANGING VIEWS ON RACE IN THE 1960s

As noted earlier, many scholars view the publication of *The Origin of Races* and the reaction to it as key events in transforming the nature of physical anthropology and the study of race (e.g., Marks, 1995; Caspari, 2003). The shift is apparent in several key publications that appeared during the mid-1960s. One is Washburn's written version of his presidential address "The Study of Race" delivered to the American Anthropological Association in 1962 (Washburn, 1963). This paper continued Washburn's arguments against typological approaches to human variation, noted the arbitrary nature of race (used more in the sense of geographic races rather than biological subspecies) and focused on the interaction of human culture and evolutionary forces, specifically selection, gene flow, and genetic drift. His address also continued a long tradition in anthropology of a Boasian separation of race, culture, and biology. Coon's work is mentioned only in passing in the published version, although those actually present have commented that the actual address contained more mention and direct criticism of Coon's book (Wolpoff & Caspari, 1997).

Another landmark publication in the 1960s was Ashley Montagu's (1964) edited volume *The Concept of Race*. This highly influential volume contained both old and new material, including Washburn's presidential address and a revised version of Montagu's *Current Anthropology* review of Coon's book. In my view, two of the other chapters in *The Concept of Race* have been particularly influential in setting the stage for future generations of physical anthropology students (which, almost a decade after its publication included me). One chapter was Loring Brace's (1964) chapter "A Nonracial Approach towards the Understanding of Human Diversity" and the other was Frank Livingstone's (1964) chapter "On the Nonexistence of Human Races."

Livingstone's chapter was an expanded version of a paper he had previously written for *Current Anthropology* (Livingstone, 1962a). Instead of updating and revising the race concept in light of population genetics as Washburn and Dobzhansky had suggested, Livingstone advocated what he termed "a rather unorthodox position among anthropologists" (1962a, 279), arguing for abandoning the concept of race as applied to humans. Noting that racial classification was arbitrary and that human genetic variation was discordant (such that a racial classification based on one trait might not match that of any other trait), Livingstone argued that the most appropriate method of analyzing human variation was clinal analysis, thus showing the actual geographic distribution of a trait without imposing any classification scheme upon observed variation. Livingstone's contribution was important not only for its critique of biological race, but also for proposing an alternative mode of analysis.

Interestingly, Livingstone's original short article in *Current Anthropology* was commented on in the same issue by Dobzhansky, who argued for the continued use of biological race. Further, Dobzhansky and Livingstone had their own small battle over the public perception of race and human variation, with Dobzhansky stating that

the multiplication of racial or subspecific names has gone beyond the limits of convenience in the human and in some animal species. This was bound to pro- voke a reaction, and up to a point this was salutary. But if the reaction goes too far in its protest it breeds confusion. To say that mankind has no races plays into the hands of race bigots, and this is least of all desirable when the "scientific" racism attempts to rear its ugly head. (1962, 280)

Livingstone disagreed with this judgment and shot back that Dobzhansky's criticism was

incompetent, irrelevant, and immaterial. The fact that some crank may make political hay of a biological fact, concept, or theory is no criterion of the valid- ity of any of these in biological science. I also fail to comprehend how a posi- tion which denies the validity of a concept supports anyone using that concept. (1962b, 280)

Their exchanges indicate that even while typological concepts of race were fading away in many scientists' approaches to human variation and evolution, there remained debates over the utility of a revised biological race concept, as well as debate over the social responsibility of scientific writings. As noted earlier, I think these questions will remain with us.

The chapter in *The Concept of Race* authored by C. Loring Brace (1964) is a masterful review of global patterns of human morphological variation with particular emphasis on those traits that had most often been used in racial classification: skin color, hair form, and color, tooth size, nasal shape, and body build. In each case, Brace examined the clinal distribution of these traits and related them to past evolutionary history, primarily natural selection and changing patterns of cultural adaptation. The beauty of Brace's chapter is that he clearly showed that traditional schemes of racial classification did not work well for describing the actual patterns of human variation, often obscuring them. Furthermore, like Livingstone, his clinical analysis showed an alternative to racial typology, thus setting, I believe, the stage for future generations to approach the study of human variation.

Two lessons can be learned from the work in the early 1960s of Livingstone, Brace, and others. First, not only does the race concept break down in many cases, but by focusing on description, it never actually provides much of an *explanation* for the causes of human biological variation. Second, a productive analysis of the causes of human biological variation can be made *without* invoking the race concept at all. Geographic origin can be described just that simply, without need for arguments about the number and defining characteristics of racial categories.

WHERE HAVE WE BEEN AND WHERE ARE WE NOW?

It would be a mistake to characterize the history of physical/biological anthropology in the 1950s and 1960s as being solely about debates over the race concept. There were many developments in the field and in allied disciplines that continue to shape the nature of the profession today. A partial list of developments in the 1950s and 1960s includes the acceptance of *Australopithecus* as a human ancestor, the first use of newer dating methods (such as potassium-argon dating), the discovery of important fossil finds in East Africa, reevaluation of the taxonomy of Miocene apes, field studies of monkeys and apes, experiments in ape language acquisition, the spread in use of multivariate statistics, the availability of "canned" computer programs for statistical analysis, increased discovery of genetic polymorphisms, the birth of human adaptability studies, and the development in the field of molecular anthropology, to name only a few. Yet, it is also important that we not underestimate the importance of the changes in how biological race was viewed, because the change from a static and typological view of human variation and evolution allowed all of these other developments to happen, or at least to make sense. In sum, the change in the biological race concept was nothing short of a major paradigm shift in the science of physical/biological anthropology.

Although these changes cannot be denied, the extent to which the biological race concept was *abandoned,* rather than *changed,* is less clear. Even during the 1960s, a number of the proponents of new approaches on human variation still adhered to the race concept (e.g., Dobzhansky, 1962; Washburn, 1963), while others argued to abandon it (e.g., Livingstone, 1962a; 1962b; 1964; Brace, 1964). There are continuing arguments today over the biological race concept, with some arguing against it (e.g., Brace, 2005) and some arguing for it (e.g., Sarich & Miele, 2004). There are also disagreements over the extent to which the use of the race concept has changed over time, as reflected in its use or lack thereof in journal articles over time (e.g., Cartmill, 1998; Lieberman et al., 2003; Cartmill & Brown, 2003).

   Some of this disagreement may be semantic, and depend in large part on how someone defines "race" in a biological sense (Weiss & Fullerton, 2005). However, my own reading of the literature suggests that, apart from a rare exception (e.g., Rushton, 1995), there has been a shift away from treating races as independent evolutionary units. Nor does anyone deny the existence of human variation. In my view, the arguments really concern *how* human genetic variation is structured and the extent to which "race" is a suitable unit of analysis. At the risk of oversimplifying studies of human variation, I can identify two major findings about global patterns of genetic diversity. First, human genetic variation is geographically structured, where populations closer to one another geographically are generally more similar genetically to each other than those further away (e.g., Imaizumi et al., 1973; Cavalli-Sforza et al., 1994; Eller, 1999; Relethford, 2004). Second, when one considers major geographic regions (such as Europe, subSaharan Africa, and so forth) as units of analysis, akin to what some would call "geographic races," there is clearly more genetic variation that exists *within* these groupings than *between* them, a finding that consistently applies to genetic variation whether measured by blood group polymorphisms, DNA markers, craniometrics, or dental metrics (e.g., Barbujani et al., 1997; Relethford, 1994; 2002; Hanihara & Ishida, 2005). This pattern runs counter to an idea of typological race that emphasizes among-group variation over within-group variation (Templeton, 1998). Exceptions to this trend, such as skin color (Relethford, 2002) or the Duffy blood group system (Cavalli-Sforza et al., 1994) represent the clear impact of natural selection across diverse environments leading to increased among-group variation. Even here, the actual geographic distribution does not clearly fit a typological model; skin color varies by latitude, even within geographic regions such as Europe or sub-Saharan Africa, such that defining discrete groupings based on skin color remains subjective.

   The fact that actual patterns of genetic diversity reject the old typological notion of races does not mean that the concept has been altogether rejected by everyone. Some still argue that race serves as a convenient label for describing human variation. Does this then mean that the races are "real"? Or does our assigning a label mean that race is culturally determined, and if so, then is it *completely* culturally determined? Consider the statistical distribution of human height as an analogy. Height is a continuous measure, yet we frequently use crude and imprecise labels to describe height—"short," "medium," and "tall." Are these three categories "real?" We can answer this question "yes," in the sense that some people are shorter or taller than others, and "no" in the sense that there are clearly not just three *types* of height in the world. Also, it is obvious that any grouping of height classes is arbitrary in terms of their numbers (e.g., should we add "medium-tall") and cut-off points (e.g., is 5 feet, 10 inches "medium" or "tall"?).

In any event, I expect that these discussions about race will continue, even though, as pointed out by Weiss and Fullerton (2005), we are often running in circles. Still, I like to be an optimist and think that we have made some progress by moving the study of human variation away from static typologies and independent evolutionary lineages, a shift started by Washburn and apparent throughout the 1950s and 1960s.

REFERENCES

Barbujani, Guido, Magagni, Arianna, Minch, Eric, & Cavalli-Sforza, L. Luca. (1997). An Apportionment of Human DNA Diversity. *Proceedings of the National Academy of Sciences, 94,* 4516–4519.

Brace, C. Loring. (1964). A Nonracial Approach Towards the Uunderstanding of Human Diversity. In *The Concept of Race,* ed. by Ashley Montagu, pp. 103–152. New York: Collier Books.

——. (2005). *"Race" Is a Four-Letter Word: The Genesis of the Concept.* New York: Oxford University Press.

Cartmill, Matt. (1998). The Status of the Race Concept in Physical Anthropology. *American Anthropologist, 100,* 651–660.

Cartmill, Matt, & Brown, Kaye. (2003). Surveying the Race Concept: A Reply to Lieberman, Kirk, and Littlefield. *American Anthropologist, 105,* 114–115.

Caspari, Rachel. (2003). From Types to Populations: A Century of Race, Physical Anthropology, and the American Anthropological Association. *American Anthropologist, 105,* 65–76.

Cavalli-Sforza, L. Luca, Menozzi, Paolo, & Piazza, Alberto. (1994). *The History and Geography of Human Genes.* Princeton: Princeton University Press.

Coon, Carleton S. (1962). *The Origin of Races.* New York: Alfred A. Knopf.

——. (1981). *Adventures and Discoveries: The Autobiography of Carleton S. Coon.* Englewood Cliffs, NJ: Prentice-Hall.

Dobzhansky, Theodosius. (1962). Comment on "On the Non-Existence of Human Races." *Current Anthropology, 3,* 279–280.

——. (1963). Possibility that *Homo sapiens* Evolved Independently 5 Times Is Vanishingly Small. *Current Anthropology, 4,* 360, 364–366.

Eller, Elise. (1999). Population Substructure and Isolation by Distance in Three Continental Regions. *American Journal of Physical Anthropology, 108,* 147–159.

Hanihara, Tsunehiko, & Ishida, Hajime. (2005). Metric Dental Variation of Major Human Populations. *American Journal of Physical Anthropology, 128,* 287–298.

Hooton, Earnest A., Dupertuis, C. Wesley, & Dawson, Helen. (1955). The Physical Anthropology of Ireland. *Papers of the Peabody Museum of Archaeology and Ethnology,* Harvard University Vol. 30, Nos. 1–2. Cambridge, MA: Peabody Museum.

Hulse, Frederick S. (1963). Review of *The Origin of Races. American Anthropologist, 65,* 685–687.

Hunt, Edward E., Jr. (1959). Anthropometry, Genetics and Racial History. *American Anthropologist, 61,* 64–87.

———. (1981). The Old Physical Anthropology. *American Journal of Physical Anthropology, 56,* 339–346.

Imaizumi, Yoko, Morton, Newton E., & Lalouel, Jean Marc. (1973). Kinship and Race. In *Genetic Structure of Populations,* ed. by Newton E. Morton, pp. 228–233. Honolulu: University of Hawaii Press.

Jackson, John P., Jr. (2001). "In Ways Unacademical": The Reception of Carleton S. Coon's *The Origin of Races. Journal of the History of Biology, 34,* 247–285.

Lasker, Gabriel W. (1999). *Happenings and Hearsay: Experiences of a Biological Anthropologist.* Detroit: Savoyard Books.

Lieberman, Leonard, Kirk, Rodney C., & Littlefield, Alice. (2003). Perishing Paradigm: Race — 1931–99. *American Anthropologist, 105,* 110–113.

Livingstone, Frank B. (1962a). On the Non-Existence of Human Races. *Current Anthropology, 3,* 279.

———. (1962b). Reply to Dobzhansky. *Current Anthropology, 3,* 280–281.

———. (1964). On the Nonexistence of Human Races. In *The Concept of Race,* ed. by Ashley Montagu, pp. 46–60. New York: Collier Books.

Marks, Jonathan. (1995). *Human Biodiversity: Genes, Races, and History.* New York: Aldine de Gruyter.

Mayr, Ernst. (1962). Origin of the Human Races. *Science, 138,* 420–422.

Montagu, Ashley. (1963). What Is Remarkable about Varieties of Man Is Likenesses, Not Differences. *Current Anthropology, 4,* 361–363.

———. (1964). *The Concept of Race.* New York: Collier Books.

Relethford, John H. (1994). Craniometric Variation Among Modern Human Populations. *American Journal of Physical Anthropology, 95,* 53–62.

———. (2002). Apportionment of Global Human Genetic Diversity Based on Craniometrics and Skin Color. *American Journal of Physical Anthropology, 118,* 393–398.

———. (2004). Global Patterns of Isolation by Distance Based on Genetic and Morphological Data. *Human Biology, 76,* 499–513.

Relethford, John H., & Crawford, Michael H. (1995). Anthropometric Variation and the Population History of Ireland. *American Journal of Physical Anthropology, 96,* 25–38.

Rushton, J. Phillipe. (1995). *Race, Evolution, and Behavior: A Life History Perspective.* New Brunswick, NJ: Transaction Publishers.

Sarich, Vincent, & Miele, Frank. (2004). *Race: The Reality of Human Differences.* Boulder, CO: Westview Press.

Shipman, Pat. (1994). *The Evolution of Racism: Human Differences and the Use and Abuse of Science.* New York: Simon & Schuster.

Spencer, Frank. (1981). The Rise of Academic Physical Anthropology in the United States (1880–1980): A Historical Overview. *American Journal of Physical Anthropology, 56,* 353–364.

Strum, Shirley C. & Lindburg, Donald G. (1999). Preface. In *The New Physical Anthropology: Science, Humanism, and Critical Reflection,* ed. by Shirley C. Strum, Donald G. Lindburg, and David Hamburg, pp. vii–viii. Upper Saddle River, NJ: Prentice Hall.

Templeton Alan R. (1998). Human Races: A Genetic and Evolutionary Perspective. *American Anthropologist, 100,* 632–650.

Washburn, Sherwood L. (1951). The New Physical Anthropology. *Transactions of the New York Academy of Sciences, 13,* 298–304.

———. (1963). The Study of Race. *American Anthropologist, 65,* 521–531.

Weiss, Kenneth M., & Fullerton, Stephanie M. (2005). Racing Around, Getting Nowhere. *Evolutionary Anthropology, 14,* 165–169.

Wolpoff, Milford, & Caspari, Rachel. (1997). *Race and Human Evolution.* New York: Simon & Schuster.

Chapter 12

75 Years of the Annual Meetings of the American Association of Physical Anthropologists, 1930–2004

by

Kaye Brown and Matt Cartmill

INTRODUCTION

Throughout its history, the American Association of Physical Anthropologists has performed two principal services for its membership: It has overseen the publication of the *American Journal of Physical Anthropology,* and it has held annual meetings where physical anthropologists can meet, listen to, and argue with each other. The annual meetings are where the AAPA has its life as a social institution. Perhaps the most valuable thing about them has been their democratic intellectual traditions, under which young and old scientists engage each other as peers. This sort of interaction on an equal footing is not always characteristic of professional associations. Yet despite the all too human prejudice, folly, and egotism of physical anthropologists as individuals, our meetings have somehow contrived to remain faithful to the egalitarian ideals of science, as a system of inquiry in which no authorities are recognized and all disputes are settled by an appeal to replicable experience.

THE INAUGURAL MEETING IN HISTORICAL CONTEXT

The first AAPA meeting, held at the University of Virginia in 1930, adopted a constitution that recognized two classes of members (AAPA proceedings 1930, 325). So-called *active* members had to do physical anthropology research, be nominated by two other active members, and be approved at the annual business meeting. Anyone who simply wanted to join could be enrolled as an Associate

Member by a vote of the Executive Committee. Subscription to the *AJPA* was not yet part of the deal, and so dues were low, even for 1930: $2.00 per year for voting members. There would be no increase in these basic dues for 38 years.

A list of aims for the association, originally written by Aleš Hrdlička, was included in the new constitution. Some of these aims still seem worthwhile: promotion of contacts with other branches of anthropology, promotion of research and publication in physical anthropology, and popular dissemination of physical anthropological research. Some of the other stated goals of the new association had a distinct 1930s flavor, betraying Hrdlička's preoccupation with anthropometry. They included standardization of anthropometric instruments and methods, the establishment of a national center of anthropometric instruction, and the extension of anthropometry into all American colleges, schools, armed forces, and "institutions for special classes of defectives and abnormals." The constitution called for the furtherance of these aims in all other countries.

Some of the assumptions that lay behind these goals, and the varieties of scientific interests of physical anthropologists in the early 1930s, can be discerned in the paper titles from that first meeting. Many of the papers were on topics that would fit right into an AAPA meeting today—for example, papers by Gregory and others on human and primate comparative anatomy and evolution, by Hrdlička and others on the tempo and metrics of growth, and on a variety of human anatomical topics, some of them with a clinical slant. Other titles from the first meeting reflect preoccupations that seem quaint to us today, dealing with the classification of races, some primordial manifestations of somatotyping, and the refinement of those anthropometric methods that the AAPA had sworn to carry into every corner of American society.

Table 12.1 presents a classification by topic of the papers from the first two published proceedings of the AAPA meetings, organized under seven headings commonly used for podium and poster sessions since the 1990s: paleoanthropology (including primate evolution), human biology and variation (including anthropometry), skeletal biology, primate biology, genetics, dental anthropology, and paleopathology (including forensics). These are compared with similar percentages, based on session subfield headings, for the 10 years (1994–2003) preceding the 75th meeting. These session tallies approximate the distribution of topics covered at each meeting.

This topical comparison reveals both changes and continuities. Paleoanthropology and paleopathology receive a great deal more attention in today's AAPA meetings than they did in the early days. Sessions dealing with skeletal biology and primates are the most variable from year to year, but recent percentages for sessions in these subfields do not differ systematically from the early ones. The most striking difference between the early and recent tallies is the decline in presentations dealing with modern human biological

Table 12.1. Percentage representation of subfields of physical anthropology in the programs of AAPA meetings Nos. 1, 6, and 63–74. Tallies represent topics of either papers or sessions, as indicated.

TOPIC	PAPERS (%)		SESSIONS (%)									
	1930	1935	1994	1995	1996	1997	1998	1999	2000	2001	2002	2003
Paleoanthropology	7	4	21	27	24	19	24	22	21	28	31	26
Human Biol. Variation	53	43	31	24	25	20	18	13	21	19	21	9
Skeletal Biology	23	18	8	19	8	20	15	9	14	11	14	11
Primates	13	18	17	14	22	23	18	21	13	22	21	25
Genetics	0	0	8	5	8	8	9	12	13	9	4	9
Dental	3	14	8	5	8	5	5	6	5	2	2	9
Paleopath/Forensics	0	4	6	5	5	6	11	17	14	9	7	9
TOTALS:	99	101	99	99	100	101	100	100	101	100	100	98

variation, which have fallen from a majority (53%) of the papers in 1930 to an average of around 20% over the period 1994–2003.

It might be conjectured that this drop is due to the siphoning off of such papers by one or more of the ancillary societies that now meet annually in conjunction with the AAPA. We are inclined to reject this interpretation, for three reasons. First, if the presence of ancillary society meetings in the same venue as the AAPA affected the number of related sessions offered at the AAPA meetings, then there should be a conspicuous biennial fluctuation in the percentage of paleoanthropology sessions, since the Paleoanthropology Society meets with the AAPA only in odd-numbered years. There is no such fluctuation: the average number of paleoanthropology sessions per meeting is the same for odd- and even-numbered years. Second, some other subfields that are associated with narrowly focused ancillary societies (e.g., primatology and paleopathology) have shown no decline. Third, a decline in human-variation sessions is discernible even in the recent numbers. We believe that the difference in this regard between the 1930s and the 1990s reflects the mid-century decay of the ideas of racial classification and hierarchy that provided the driving force behind many of the early studies.

Purged of this ideological baggage, research into modern human variation continues to be a vital and important part of the agenda of the annual meetings. It accounts for a larger percentage of the sessions held during the period 1994–2003 than any other subfield except paleoanthropology. Although some once-popular topics have disappeared from the AAPA's annual meetings, none of the large subfields has declined below viability, and no one specialty or area of interest has come to dominate the meeting agenda.

At the first AAPA meeting, most of the presentations were given by senior researchers. However, student papers were on the program from the beginning. Hrdlička's protégé, T. Dale Stewart, then still a student at Johns Hopkins, gave his first paper ever at that 1930 meeting. Afterwards, Hrdlička took him to task for reading a prepared text instead of speaking off the cuff. Having learned his lesson, Stewart tried to ad lib all his speeches in public for the rest of his life (Trotter, 1956).

Hrdlička put a lot of effort into mentoring the young professionals in the science he had worked so hard to bring into being in America. Unfortunately, his influence was not always benign. Like Earnest Hooton's abhorrence of the word "population" (Mayr, 1982), Hrdlička's fear and loathing of statistics may have retarded the progress of early physical anthropology. Harry Shapiro recalled that at one early AAPA meeting, Hrdlička "took me to one side and warned me in a very fatherly and benign way to eschew statistics like the plague." At the third AAPA meeting, held at the Smithsonian in 1932 (Comas,

1969), Edith Boyd gave a paper in which she talked about the "probable errors of the means"—the term back then for the standard error. Hrdlička turned to Harold Cummins and said, "That illustrates . . . what I have been . . . saying about the uselessness of statistics. Even Dr. Boyd admits that there are probable errors in her work" (Trotter, 1956).

MEETING PATTERNS OVER THE YEARS

In all, 30 papers were presented at that first meeting. Nobody will be surprised to hear that the number of papers given at each meeting has grown since then. But the growth curve has not followed the exponential pattern that we might expect to see if it simply reflected the intellectual reproductive rates of the professors. Rather, it can be divided into two distinct phases (Fig. 12.1). In the first phase, lasting from 1930 to 1965, the size of the meeting program grew from 30 papers to only 50 papers—a glacial growth rate of one additional paper every two years. In the second phase, from 1966 on, the

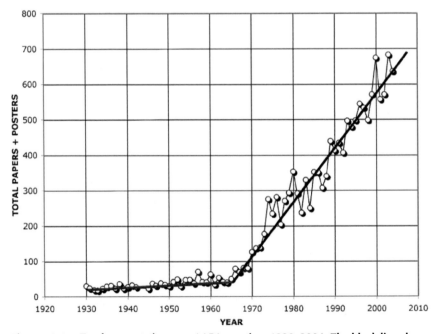

Figure 12.1. Total presentations per AAPA meeting, 1930–2004. The black line shows the abrupt change in growth rate of the meetings in the mid-1960s. Data for this and the following figures are taken from Comas (1969) and the meeting schedules and proceedings published in the *American Journal of Physical Anthropology*.

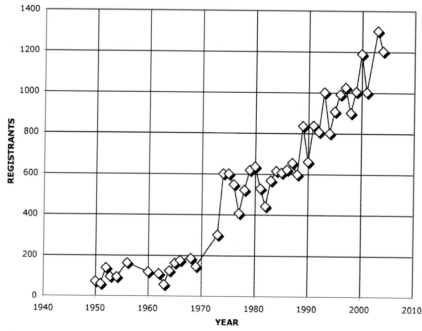

Figure 12.2. Numbers of registrants at the AAPA meetings, 1930–2004.

annual meeting program grew in an erratic but linear fashion, from 79 in 1966 to an average of 624 for the past four years—an overall growth rate 25 times as great as that seen during the first 35 years of the association's history.

What explains this sharp inflection in the curve? It is unlikely to be some simple change in the policies of the program chair, because similar but less distinct inflections appear in the late 1960s in the curve traced by the numbers of registrants at the annual meetings (Fig. 12.2), and also in the growth of AAPA membership (Fig. 12.3). We suspect that unique social factors of the 1960s contributed heavily to these upward trends. One such factor was demography. Children born during the postwar baby boom began entering graduate schools around 1967, and continued to do so throughout the 1970s. Graduate training programs increased in number and size during this period, a trend driven partly by the boom in science education that followed the launching of Sputnik in 1957.

No matter what the cause of the dramatic increase in the attraction of physical anthropology in the late 1960s may have been, it does not account for the sustained growth seen ever since. The baby boom or cohort effect may have been the proximate cause of this trend, but it cannot be invoked to explain its persistence for the last forty years.

Our meetings gradually changed to accommodate the new growth rates. At the business meeting in Berkeley in 1966, there were complaints about the still-novel scheduling of two simultaneous sessions, which had made it impossible to hear all the podium presentations. But these changes were no longer reversible. The number of concurrent sessions rose to three in 1972, and to five and even six just three years later. Yet although the AAPA has continued to grow arithmetically, our scientific meetings still last only three days and have no more than four concurrent podium sessions. This limitation was made possible by the introduction of poster sessions.

In 1980, the number of podium presentations was 353, just seven short of the "doomsday number" of 360 (Fig. 12.4). This is the maximum number of 15-minute talks that can be given in three days with only four simultaneous podium sessions lasting four hours each with a 15-minute break. The Executive Committee and the business meeting have steadfastly held podium talks to this limit in order to minimize conflicts between concurrent sessions with overlapping topics.

Yet despite this limitation, the scientific program at the annual meeting had to grow, because giving a paper at least once a year has become a marker of

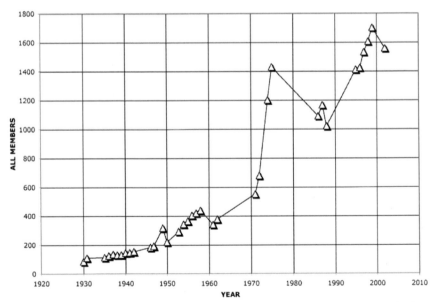

Figure 12.3. Membership in the American Association of Physical Anthropologists, 1930–2004.

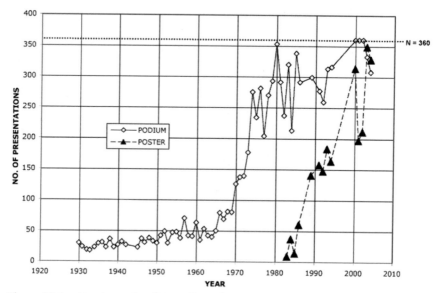

Figure 12.4. Numbers of podium talks and posters presented at the AAPA meetings, 1930–2004.

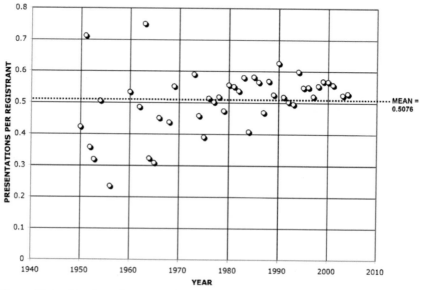

Figure 12.5. Number of presentations per registrant at the AAPA annual meetings, 1950–2004.

active professional engagement. Since the mid-1960's, over half of all registrants at our annual meeting come to deliver reports on their research (Fig. 12.5). This is intellectually healthy; the people who attend AAPA meetings are not a passive audience coming to absorb wisdom from the authorities. And it is also a matter of economics; university support for meeting attendance is usually contingent on the presentation of a paper. For the membership to grow, the program therefore has to grow. The only way to manage this without increasing the number of meeting days or concurrent sessions is to introduce increasing numbers of posters. The challenge is to overcome the inherent status inequalities of these venues.

In many other professional societies, the podium is reserved for the professionals, and posters are viewed as a kind of practice arena for students. But at the AAPA meetings in 2004, students appeared to be first authors of roughly half the podium papers, whereas senior researchers are first authors of about one-third of the poster presentations. These proportions reflect association policies. Since 1999, the AAPA has followed Mark Teaford's policy of allowing no more than nine podium symposia per year, to prevent senior researchers (who dominate these invited sessions) from hogging the microphones and turning poster sessions into a student ghetto.

The beneficial effects of this policy are discernible in recent preregistration figures. Because those who submit abstracts for the scientific sessions are required to preregister for the AAPA meetings, preregistration numbers reflect the number of principal authors of podium presentations and posters. Unlike the final overall attendance figures, preregistration figures (when reported) distinguish student preregistrants from regular members and nonmembers. Preregistrations for the annual meetings have not been consistently tallied, and we can reconstruct them only for the years 1994–2000. But during those years, a consistent upward trend in the percentage of student preregistrants is evident (Fig. 12.6). That trend corroborates our surmise, based on the abstracts, that students throughout the 1990s attained virtual parity with regular members in gaining access to a professional audience to hear and discuss their ideas. We consider this a fundamental reason why our society and our discipline continue to grow and flourish.

The AAPA's policy of limiting the number of simultaneous sessions has also helped to prevent it from fragmenting into dozens of interest groups, as some of the leading professional societies in the social sciences have done. Like our charter members 75 years ago, we continue to cleave to the ideal of a shared universe of discourse in which we try to understand one another. Our annual meetings with our sister societies remind us that there is such a thing in academia as being so specialized that you face difficulty growing

Figure 12.6. Students as a percentage of total preregistrants for the annual AAPA meetings, 1994–2000.

as a discipline. We suspect that this phenomenon afflicted the AAPA during its first three decades, and that the difference in membership growth rates before and after the mid-1960s reflects the penetration of neo-Darwinian evolutionary theory into biological anthropology, which released the study of human biology and evolution from the antiquated theoretical matrix in which it had originally formed.

THE FUTURE OF THE AAPA: ITS STUDENTS

Perhaps the most significant policies underlying the growth of our society and its meetings are those dealing with students. Student awards began with a single, unnamed prize to a student named Henry McHenry in 1968. We now give five. Dozens of AAPA members participate in judging these awards, and many recipients go on to become luminaries in our science. The program selection committees do not discriminate against student first authors in assigning access to the podium. Students are not identified as such on the program or marked by special badges as they are in many other professional societies. By creating equality among meeting attendees, these policies further our greater goal of socializing young researchers to the standards for professional conduct within our discipline.

There will always be social forces at play that reward senior researchers with the trappings of power and privilege. But we have tempered the inequalities these forces create by reminding ourselves continually that our job is to train the young to take over from us. To our credit, we have done this in ways that are transparent and professional. Our students are encouraged to speak for themselves, and they usually do. Unlike their peers in some other professional societies, they do not have to rely on their mentors to plead their cases in brokered conversations in hotel lobbies. And unlike the meetings of many comparable societies, our annual meetings provide students with far more than a timeworn binder listing job vacancies. At our meetings, anyone with a vacancy to fill can usually hear a research report from an interested job applicant. Most of us create our short lists for any departmental vacancy while we attend the annual meetings. These practices are made possible by the AAPA's policy of encouraging students to participate on an equal footing in the scientific program.

We all benefit from a policy of training the young to take over from us rather than to serve us. We have adopted a course, perhaps unwittingly several times in our society's history, of continually renewing ourselves as a professional society by allowing everyone in who can do the job. This course was set in the constitution adopted at our first meeting, which resolved to create and maintain an eclectic society consisting of scientists of any sex, American or from other countries, as well as anyone else with a professional interest in physical anthropology. We rededicate ourselves in earnest to this resolution every year at our annual meetings. Judging by the continued growth in our membership, we seem to be successful.

ACKNOWLEDGMENTS

We are grateful to Michael Little for inviting us to contribute to this book and to the symposium at the 2004 meetings on which it is based, and for providing us with an invaluable English translation by Marta Alfonso of Juan Comas's history of the AAPA (Comas, 1969; Alfonso & Little, 2005).

REFERENCES

AAPA Proceedings. (1930). Meeting of the American Association of Physical Anthropologists, University of Virginia, Charlottesville, Virginia. *American Journal of Physical Anthropology, 14*(2), 321–329.

Alfonso, Marta P., & Little, Michael A. (tran. and ed.). (2005). Juan Comas's Summary History of the American Association of Physical Anthropologists (1928–1968). *Yearbook of Physical Anthropology, 48,* 163–195.

Comas, Juan. (1969). *Historia Sumaria de la Asociación Americana de Antropólogos Físicos, (1928–1968).* Departamento de Investigaciones Antropológicas, Publication 22. Mexico: Instituto Nacional de Antropología e Historia.

Mayr, Ernst. (1982). Reflections on Human Paleontology. In *A History of American Physical Anthropology, 1930–1980,* ed. by F. Spencer, 231–237. New York: Academic Press.

Trotter, Mildred. (1956). Notes on the History of the AAPA. *American Journal of Physical Anthropology, 14,* 350–364.

Chapter 13

Description, Hypothesis Testing, and Conceptual Advances in Physical Anthropology: Have We Moved On?

by

Clark Spencer Larsen

INTRODUCTION

Rarely do we get the chance to reflect back and take a look at the progress we've made in our discipline over the last several decades, at least since the American Association of Physical Anthropologists gathered for its last big anniversary—the 50th—in 1981. This is not to say that we haven't thought about current directions and past history, but certainly the occasion of the 75th anniversary of the founding of our association, the world's largest devoted to the discipline of physical anthropology, provides us with an opportunity to assess our science and what has worked and what hasn't. At the 50th anniversary meetings in Detroit, Michigan, I recall my own excitement in seeing the leaders in the field—T. Dale Stewart, Harry Shapiro, Montague Cobb, Wilton Krogman, Mildred Trotter, Sherwood Washburn, Phyllis Eveleth, George Armelagos, and others—talk about the first 50 years of the association and the growth of physical anthropology. At the time, I had recently been awarded my PhD from the University of Michigan and was in my first job at a small school in Massachusetts. I was eager to hear what these men and women had to say, on topics ranging from biographies of early leaders to changing views on primate and human evolution, human genetics, and primate behavior.

Most of the papers were laudatory about the discipline, its research, and its practitioners. There was an air of celebration, highlighting the crowning achievements in a half century. I shared the excitement of our intellectual leaders about physical anthropology. However, several rather critical papers presented in a day-long symposium had an especially profound impact on me. These more critical papers and their follow-up publication in the *AJPA* (Boaz & Spencer, 1982) and in the volume on the history of American physical anthropology edited by Frank Spencer (1982) strongly influenced the way that I thought about the field, carried with me to the present day. In the banter at the 1981 meetings following the presentation of these critical papers, some among us expressed irritation; others expressed outrage that such a critical tone was taken. After all, our association had just reached 50, and wonderful progress had been made in our science since 1930 when Aleš Hrdlička and his colleagues held the first AAPA meeting in Charlottesville, Virginia.

The especially critical papers focused largely on anthropological skeletal biology, but had implications for the wider discipline and its research practices and goals. In particular, the collective of George Armelagos and three of his former students, Owen Lovejoy, Dennis Van Gerven, and David Carlson, reviewed the themes and literature of skeletal biology, including a decade-by-decade assessment from the first 50 years of the flagship journal of the discipline and the association, the *American Journal of Physical Anthropology*, founded by Aleš Hrdlička in 1918 (Armelagos et al., 1982; Lovejoy et al., 1982). Their assessment presented a bleak picture in the following way. They argued that this area of physical anthropology had not reached the analytical or theoretical successes of other sciences, especially in regard to what they thought was missing from the published literature—namely, articles published in the journal lack inference, lack theory, lack problem, and over-emphasize description. They concluded that inference building and theoretical application was a minor part of the subarea—skeletal biology was a descriptive enterprise and not a maturing science. As stated by Armelagos et al. (1982, 305), "Theoretical perspectives have failed to keep pace with the development of new techniques. Reliance on a descriptive-historical model utilizing racial typologies has proved a major deterrent to other theoretical approaches." In the companion paper by Lovejoy et al., they state, based on their content analysis of the *AJPA*, "Essentially, skeletal biology has remained primarily a descriptive science during the 50-year history [of the *AJPA*]" (1982, 335). One trend observed was an increasing sophistication of analysis, from simple metric description to complex multivariate morphometrics. But in the end, they said, it was still descriptive and focused on "identification and sorting." They concluded that rather than the *problem* directing the study of bones and teeth, the *data* are directing the study of skeletons.

Frankly, Armelagos and group were puzzled by the situation. General theoretical issues were certainly not lacking: What are the environmental factors that determine skeletal form, cranial and postcranial? What are the effects of health on major demographic transitions? What behavioral shifts had occurred in conjunction with major adaptive changes in human history, such as from foraging to farming? In other words, *where* are the hypotheses and problems that drive the science? Despite the presence of these theoretically motivated questions and issues, the science of skeletal biology was descriptive. In their view, it had remained mired in a descriptive morass with nothing inferential or predictive to hold it together. Answers without questions do not move the science forward. Questions are not driving the research, data are driving the research. They concluded, "It is clearly the time for the analysis and construction of general theory to begin" (Lovejoy et al., 1982, 336).

I was profoundly affected by their critique of my chosen profession. Not so much because the critique said anything new. But I recall being surprised with my response as I heard the papers: these guys are right and the state-of-the-art of anthropological skeletal biology was rather ho-hum. It had not the message of the New Physical Anthropology, articulated so eloquently by Sherwood Washburn in the 1950s (Washburn, 1951, 1953). My colleagues in other areas, such as in paleoanthropology and primatology, were talking about significant and provocative questions about human origins and human behavior. Their studies were strongly inferential and theoretically motivated. Yet, much of my corner of the discipline was still talking typology and classification, in the absence of inference and theory. To be sure, the multivariate statistics then being applied to the investigation of skeletal data sets were impressive. Armelagos, Lovejoy, Van Gerven, and Carlson had it right— what do we have beyond just another disease diagnosed, another tooth typed, or another cranium classified?

The important question for now—25 years later—is the following: Have we heeded the advice given in 1981 and begun to develop hypothesis-driven research that allows inference about wider issues relating our findings to the human condition? Has our science matured, keeping pace with other sciences, even in comparison with other subareas of our discipline?

THE MEASURE OF MATURITY: THE RECORD OF THE *AMERICAN JOURNAL OF PHYSICAL ANTHROPOLOGY*

I offer in this chapter some observations based on my own experience in the field, but especially as it is revealed in the pages of the *American Journal of Physical Anthropology,* the journal with which I have grown to become quite familiar in my role as its editor from 2001 to 2007. My assessment is largely qualitative, informed by opinions drawn by me over the last couple of decades and by my own experience with the *AJPA* over the last half decade. Others, including former and future editors of the journal, could very well develop their own analysis of the record—the record is readily available for anyone to analyze and draw conclusions about the state of the field.

Theory is of course built on hypotheses, preliminary answers to questions. Thus, the guts of science—any science—are those hypotheses that frame the questions we ask about the natural world around us. It is the question or the hypothesis that promotes inference and building a larger understanding of human evolution and variation, the crux of physical anthropology and those who study it. In a science, we would expect to see the elements of hypothesis—either actual hypotheses addressed or questions and problems that are motivated by hypotheses.

In light of this, I went back over a four-year period (July 2001 issue to November 2005) of the *AJPA*—53 issues of the journal, to be precise—and re-read each of the 242 skeletal biology papers. I defined the area of skeletal biology more broadly than Armelagos and group 25 years ago. I included just about anything dealing with primate and human skeletal, dead or alive. Each article was identified as to one of the following four groups: (1) a hypothesis was addressed; (2) a question was raised; (3) a problem was considered; or (4) a description was made as the primary focus. The first three have in common some kind of analytical approach. As anyone who has ever attempted this kind of simple literature analysis will say—some might refer to as "meta-analysis"—the categories can be vague. For example, what is largely a descriptive article, sometimes (rarely) ends with a question—the purpose of this study is to describe an anatomical variant on a bone. The variant is described. The question is then asked: What does it mean? Moreover, most questions asked or problems considered are couched within the context of a hypothesis currently being discussed in the discipline—the hypothesis is implied. In fact, for the most part, it was straightforward identifying the type of paper for the purposes of this analysis. I looked for key sentences in the introductions to all articles, such as from the following examples:

1. *Hypothesis:* The purpose of this study is "to test the hypothesis that mobility decreased significantly in Europe during the Upper Paleolithic" (Holt, 2003, 220).
2. *Question:* "Did the Neolithic revolution in the Levant reduce labor costs and decrease workload (and) is there any evidence for a division of labor?" (Eshed et al., 2004, 304).
3. *Problem:* "The examination of sex-related differences within modern (primate) taxa provides a crucial empirical background for the evaluation of variation (of joint size dimorphism in the elbow) within fossil assemblages" (Lague, 2003, 278).

4. *Description:* "The purpose of this paper is to present the results of recent research on pathological lesions in a large western Pacific Island skeletal sample . . . (and to) . . . quantify the degree and type of skeletal responses to pathological processes" (Buckley & Tayles, 2003, 303).

The articles fall into one of the four categories—24%, hypothesis; 11%, question; 31%, problem; 35%, description. Far more commonly than not, the categorization is made possible by the fact that authors included a clear purpose statement in the introductions to their articles.

There are some clear patterns in what areas of research fall into which of the four categories. Typically, an area that explicitly addresses hypotheses includes functional morphology, whereas descriptive papers include disease diagnosis and forensic applications, such as sex determination, taphonomy, or dental development.

Here, I address the hypothesis that anthropological skeletal biology has shifted from description and classification and identification and sorting (Lovejoy et al., 1982) to hypothesis testing, inference building, and problem solving—the elements of modern science. Has the stagnation identified by Armelagos and group in the early 1980s passed? Has skeletal biology caught up and shifted the focus from description to processually based explanation? The Lovejoy et al. data set presented in their 1982 paper reveals a decade-by-decade decline in descriptive-oriented articles to articles that are analytical. It reveals the highly descriptive nature of physical anthropology as represented by the *AJPA* from approaching 90% descriptive in the 1930s to 56% descriptive in the 1970s.

Taking my data set and collapsing the first three groups—hypothesis, question, problem—into an "analytical" category and comparing with a description category, the composition of the journal has clearly changed in regard to number of papers in the last four years compared to the Lovejoy et al. analysis (see Figure 13.1). In this regard, Lovejoy et al. estimate that some 56% of articles in the *AJPA* were descriptive in the 1970s. My assessment of the four years of the *AJPA* for 2001–2005 in the bar on the far right of the graph reveals a continuation of the downward trend in frequency of descriptive articles they observed—37% are descriptive, down considerably since the Lovejoy et al. analysis.

The conclusion that I draw from this simple analysis is that anthropological skeletal biology has caught up—it is now largely motivated by testing hypotheses and addressing important questions and problems with newly emerging and well-informed analytical approaches. I believe we have moved on. Why we moved on is unknown; it was probably due in no small measure to colleagues like Armelagos, Lovejoy, Van Gerven, and Carlson cajoling the skeletal

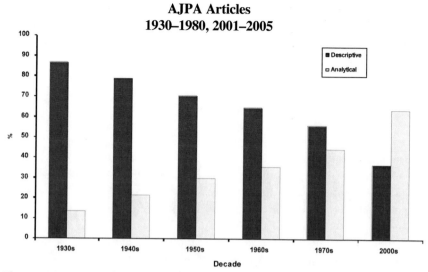

**AJPA Articles
1930–1980, 2001–2005**

Figure 13.1. Comparison of frequency of descriptive relative to analytical articles published in the *American Journal of Physical Anthropology* for the 1930s (n = 96), 1940s (n = 95), 1950s (n = 145), 1960s (n = 212), 1970s (n = 447), and partial 2000s (n = 196). Data for 1930s to 1970s from Lovejoy et al., 1982.

biologists to join the wave of modern science. It took the insight of Armelagos and his collaborators to give us the necessary kick to mature as a science.

OTHER ASSESSMENTS

There are at least two other published opinions about the progress (or not) of physical anthropology as a science-based enterprise. In 2003, Armelagos and Van Gerven revisited the question regarding the development of skeletal biology. They, like me, asked the question: Has the science shifted from description to one "characterized by hypothesis testing and heightened concern for causality" and process? Their assessment showed optimism on the one hand. For example, the development of functional analyses of cranial and postcranial remains and the biocultural approach to disease in past societies shows the strong presence of function and process. They note—and I am the first to agree—that the development of bioarchaeology, a field developing since the late 1970s and linking archaeological and skeletal analysis, has fostered a dialog in the wider community, resulting in meaningful answers to questions about adaptation in past societies. As they point out, bioarchaeology, in their words, "shifted the focus away from simple description toward analytical questions of biocultural adaptation and *in situ* evolution." Clearly, these areas have developed and matured.

In light of these advancements, what place has old-hat description taken on in the field? They found from their reading of the record of articles in the *AJPA* for the early 1980s and late 1990s that the picture was still dominated by descriptive articles—57% for both periods. In other words, they see *no change* from the 1970s. Narrowly defined in this way, that may be the case. My analysis does not include the 1980s or the 1990s, so I won't comment on their analysis. I suspect that their analysis of the first half of the present decade may not be as optimistic as my analysis. While they regard the field more descriptive than ever, is that the most important question that we should be asking? Is there a role to play for description in our science? Is the 37% I report here too much for a respectable science? Why might description be important? My reading of the record shows a fundamental shift in the journal. I think hypothesis testing and analytical approaches have become fundamental to our science. I also see an important role for the presence of description. These descriptions may provide important data for testing hypotheses. For example, it is crucial that accurate characterizations of pathological conditions in archaeological skeletons be provided. These descriptions can have the important role of providing published, descriptive context, laying the foundation for future analytical research.

Stojanowski and Buikstra (2005) have looked at the two intervals of 1980–1984 and 1996–2000. They found that the percentages of analytical to descriptive articles have leveled off, equivalent to what the data show for the 1970s by Lovejoy et al. (1982). For the 1980s, they found 39% were analytical and 61% descriptive, and for the 1990s the values were 43% analytical and 57% descriptive. This contrasts with the values generated in my analysis of the record. However, my analysis likely defines analytical and descriptive in a different way than Stojanowski and Buikstra. My record of descriptive includes those articles that contain no analysis, and I suspect that Stojanowski and Buikstra did not limit their "descriptive" category in this manner. But like my observations, and unlike Armelegos and Van Gerven's assessment, there was not an increase in descriptive relative to analytical articles. Moreover, Stojanowski and Buikstra's comparison of citation rates for analytical and descriptive articles reveals a higher citation rate for the former than the latter. I regard this as indicative of relative value—analytical articles have more intellectual, scientific impact, at least as it is measured by citation rate. On the other hand, description plays an important role in any science, including skeletal biology, and for the reasons outlined above.

The question remains, then, has anthropological skeletal biology developed beyond the minimal presence of problem-oriented research that characterized the discipline prior to the 1980s? I think it has. My reading of the record shows that researchers using skeletal biology as a focus of study are keenly aware of the issues in the discipline and how their data contribute to new understanding. The successes illustrating the science's growing maturity are all around us, providing new and important understanding of the biological world as it involves humankind.

ACKNOWLEDGMENTS

I thank Michael Little and Kenneth Kennedy for inviting me to contribute to this book. I am especially grateful to Christopher Stojanowski for his comments on an earlier draft of the chapter.

REFERENCES

Armelagos, George J., & Van Gerven, Dennis P. (2003). A Century of Skeletal Biology and Paleopathology: Contrasts, Contradictions, and Conflicts. *American Anthropologist, 105,* 53–64.

Armelagos, George J., Carlson, David S. & Van Gerven, Dennis P. (1982). The Theoretical Foundations and Development of Skeletal Biology. In *A History of American Physical Anthropology: 1930–1980,* ed. by F. Spencer, 305–328. New York: Academic Press.

Boaz, Noel T., & Spencer, Frank. (1982). 1930–1980 Jubilee Issue. *American Journal of Physical Anthropology, 56*(4): 327–557.

Buckley, H. R., & Tayles, Nancy. (2003). Skeletal Pathology in a Prehistoric Pacific Island Sample: Issues in Lesion Recording, Quantification, and Interpretation. *American Journal of Physical Anthropology, 122,* 303–324.

Eshed, Vered, Gopher, Avi, Galili, Ehud, & Hershkovitz, Israel. (2004). Musculoskeletal Stress Markers in Natufian Hunter-Gatherers and Neolithic Farmers in the Levant: The Upper Limb. *American Journal of Physical Anthropology, 123,* 303–315.

Holt, Brigette M. (2003). Mobility in Upper Paleolithic and Mesolithic Europe: Evidence from the Lower Limb. *American Journal of Physical Anthropology, 122,* 200–215.

Lague, Michael R. (2003). Patterns of Joint Size Dimorphism in the Elbow and Knee of Catarrhine Primates. *American Journal of Physical Anthropology, 120,* 278–297.

Lovejoy, C. Owen, Mensforth, Robert P., & Armelagos, George J. (1982). Five Decades of Skeletal Biology as Reflected in the *American Journal of Physical*

Anthropology. In *A History of American Physical Anthropology: 1930–*1980, ed. by F. Spencer, 329–336. New York: Academic Press.

Spencer, Frank (ed.). (1982). *A History of American Physical Anthropology, 1930–1980*. New York: Academic Press.

Stojanowski, Christopher M., & Buikstra, Jane E. (2005). Research Trends in Human Osteology: A Content Analysis of Papers Published in the *American Journal of Physical Anthropology*. *American Journal of Physical Anthropology, 128*, 98–109.

Washburn, Sherwood L. (1951). The New Physical Anthropology. *Transactions of the New York Academy of Science, 213*, 298–304.

———. (1953). The New Physical Anthropology. *Yearbook of Physical Anthropology, 7*, 124–130.

Appendix

Development of Physical/Biological Anthropology: Historical Timeline

Date	Biological Anthropology	Biology	Sociopolitical Events
1850	At the midpoint of the nineteenth century, racial typology and European superiority dominate thinking. Biology, heredity, behavior, morals, and temperament are thought to be integrated and fixed in the races. Slavery still in place in the U.S. Evolutionary ideas in the air, but no clear theoretical framework. Human genetics, paleontology, primatology not yet established. Human health sciences not well advanced, with the exception of anatomy and rudimentary physiology.		
1851	Death of Samuel G. Morton (craniologist)		Great Exhibition of the Works of Industry of All Nations (Crystal Palace, Hyde Park)
1856	Discovery of the first Neanderthal remains	Louis Pasteur demonstrates that germs cause infection	
1859	Paul Broca founds Société d'Anthropologie de Paris	*Origin of Species* published (Charles Darwin)	
1861–1865		Gregor Mendel publishes experiments	U.S. Civil War (Emancipation Proclamation—1862)
1871		*Descent of Man* published (Charles Darwin)	
1875–1876	Broca's Ecole d'Anthropologie founded		
1883		Claude Bernard's work on physiology	Death of Karl Marx

243

Date	Biological Anthropology	Biology	Sociopolitical Events
1891	Boas's longitudinal growth study		
1894	Boas's first Nat'l growth standards		
1896	Aleš Hrdlička spends 3 months in Paris with Léonce Manouvreir		
1898			
			Spanish-American War (U.S. acquired Philippines, Cuba, Puerto Rico)

1900 At the beginning of the twentieth century, Gregor Mendel's laws of genetics were rediscovered by Correns (Germany), von Tschermak (Austria), and de Vries (Holland). Also, ABO blood groups were discovered by Landsteiner, so this might be identified as the beginning of the era of genetics. Although "race" was still the common conceptualization of human biological variation, Boas had already begun to formulate ideas about genetic plasticity. Human variation was largely "typological." There was continued interest in craniology and skeletal anatomy.

Date	Biological Anthropology	Biology	Sociopolitical Events
1908		Hardy-Weinberg Principle	
1911	Boas's migrant study published		
1913	E. A. Hooton at Harvard		
1914– 1919		Walter Cannon's first work on "flight or fight" principle	World War I, Russian Revolution
1918	Founding of *American Journal of Physical Anthropology* by Aleš Hrdlička	World Influenza Pandemic	
1924	*Australopithecus* found in South Africa		
1929	Founding of journal *Human Biology* by Raymond Pearl		
1930	Founding of Amer Assoc of Physical Anthropologists		
1930s	Australopithecines & *Sinanthropus* found T. W. Todd at Western Reserve Univ/Brush Foundation	Evolutionary syntheses of Fisher, Haldane, Wright, and Dobzhansky	Worldwide economic depression
1937	Primate expedition to Siam, C. R. Carpenter's study of gibbon behavior		Japanese invade SE Asia

1938	Cayo Santiago rhesis monkey colony established by C. R. Carpenter Death of T. Wingate Todd	
1939–1945	Sheldon's "somatology"	World War II Nazi racism/ atrocities
1940	Death of Raymond Pearl	
1940s		Evolutionary syntheses of Mayr, Simpson, Dobzhansky, and J. Huxley
1941	Viking Fund formed (Wenner-Gren Foundation)	Bombing of Pearl Harbor
1946	Viking Fund Summer Seminars began and the *Yearbook of Physical Anthropology* founded	
1947	Krogman to Penn from Chicago & Washburn to Chicago	
1950	At the midpoint of the twentieth century, there were a number of significant events based on knowledge accumulated during the first half of the century. First, there were two publications that indicated shifts from the typological approach to race (Coon, Garn, and Birdsell's book on race and adaptation & Boyd's book on genetics and race). Second, the Cold Spring Harbor Conference brought together the old and the new concepts on human races, evolution, and human population biology. Third, the 1st UNESCO statement on race was formulated. Fourth, Anthony Allison demonstrated the association between hemoglobin variants (sickle-cell trait) and selection to afford protection from malaria. In the late 1950s, primate behavior studies were revived.	
1950–1953	Army Quartermaster Corps Climate Studies	Korean War, Cold War McCarthyism in U.S.
1951	Washburn's "New physical anthropology" published	
1953	Piltdown recognized as fraud by Joseph S. Weiner and Kenneth Oakley	Watson/Crick DNA Model discovered
1954	Hooton dies & W. W. Howells moves to Harvard	Beginning of the U.S. Civil Rights Movement
1955–1956	Washburn's & DeVore's Kenya Baboon studies	

(Continued)

Date	Biological Anthropology	Biology	Sociopolitical Events
1956		Hans Selye published *Stress of Life* (first work published in 1936)	
1957	Gadjusek & Zigas discover Kuru in New Guinea P. T. Baker to Penn State		Soviet *Sputnik* launched
1958	Washburn goes to Berkeley		
1959	Beginning of Olduvai discoveries	Darwin Centennial in Chicago (Sol Tax edited)	
1960s	Ecological anthropology in vogue in both sociocultural and biological anthropology		
1961	Goodall's chimpanzee work begins		
1962	Publication of Coon's book on *Origin of Races* M. Goodman shows ape/human relationships with serum albumins	Rise of molecular studies (Molecular clock) International Biological Programme (IBP) begins	
1964	*Human Biology* text published International Association of Human Biologists founded		
1964– 1972	!Kung Bushman, Andean Altitude, Circumpolar (Eskimo/Aleut) and Yanomama studies (HA)		Vietnamese War
1966		G. C. Williams published *Adaptation and Selection*	
1967	Wilson & Sarich estimate divergence of ape/human by molecular clock		
1969			First human walks on the moon
1974	"Lucy" discovered at Hadar by Johanson *Annals of Human Biology* began Founding of the Human Biology Council (now Association)	UNESCO Man and the Biosphere (MaB) Programme begins	

1975   Publication of E. O. Wilson's
                             Sociobiology

1976   D. Carleton Gajdusek and Baruch
        Blumberg win Nobel Prize

1980s   Beginning of world HIV pandemic

1987   Mitochondrial Eve

1989   *American Journal of*   Beginning of the Human   End of the "Cold War"
        Human   Genome Project
        Biology began

1990   Death of W. Montague Cobb

1991   Beginning of the   Gulf War
                             Diversitas
                             Programme (IUBS/ICSU)—
                             Beginning
                             awareness of loss of
                             biodiversity &
                             climate change

2000   Human variation focuses on molecular characteristics. Genetics has moved
        from gene markers inferred from phenotypes to DNA sequences. Some
        biology departments are split into molecular/biochemical vs. evolutionary/
        ecological/organismal, while several anthropology departments have
        biological anthropology splitting off into a separate unit (e.g., Duke,
        Stanford). American Anthropological Association attempts to move back
        into a more scientific mode. Funding in NIH is increasingly molecular,
        while NSF moves to embrace multiyear, multidisciplinary,
        and integrated research funding.

Index